A SHORT GUIDE TO
Writing about Literature

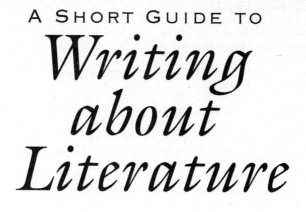

SIXTH EDITION

Sylvan Barnet
Tufts University

HarperCollins*Publishers*

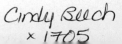

Sponsoring Editor: Lisa Moore
Development Editor: Judith Leet
Project Coordination, Text and Cover Design: PC&F, Inc.
Cover Illustration: PC&F, Inc.
Production Manager: Michael Weinstein
Compositor: PC&F, Inc.
Printer and Binder: R.R. Donnelley & Sons Company
Cover Printer: The Lehigh Press, Inc.

HarperCollins has made available an impressive array of video and audiotape productions of literary works to enrich students' experience of literature. For more information contact your local HarperCollins representative or the Marketing Manager for Literature, College Division, HarperCollins Publishers, 10 East 53rd Street, New York, NY 10022.

For permission to use copyrighted material, grateful acknowledgment is made to the copyright holders on page xiv, which is hereby made part of this copyright page.

A Short Guide to Writing about Literature, Sixth Edition
Copyright © 1992 by Sylvan Barnet

Library of Congress Cataloging-in-Publication Data

Barnet, Sylvan.
    A short guide to writing about literature / Sylvan Barnet. — — 6th
ed.
        p.   cm.
    Includes index.
    ISBN 0—673—52127—3
    1. English language — — Rhetoric.   2. Criticism — — Authorship.
3. Exposition (Rhetoric)   4. Report writing.   I. Title.
PE1479.C7B3   1991
808'.0668 — — dc20   91-17392
                                                              CIP

        93 94   9 8 7 6 5 4 3 2

Contents

PART TWO

Preface

Favorable response to the fifth edition has allowed me to revise the book again. Many changes have been made throughout, but the most obvious is the greatly increased amount of writing by students—annotations, preliminary notes, entries in journals, drafts, as well as six new essays by students. Less obvious but also important are new lists of questions that writers can ask themselves in order to generate ideas for essays.

Part One (three chapters emphasizing the close connection between reading and writing) assumes that we can't write well unless we can read well. If nothing else, we must be able to read *our own* prose thoughtfully. Reading, after all, is a way of getting ideas for writing. These early chapters emphasize the importance in the writing process of such activities as annotating a text, brainstorming, keeping a journal, and (especially) asking oneself questions in order to generate ideas. (Oddly, these activities are often called "pre-writing," but in fact they are part of the process of writing.)

Part Two, on writing about essays, fiction, poetry, drama, and film, introduces the reader to the elements of each genre, but looks back to Part One and provides some drafts and essays by students on representative works. In accordance with the assumption in Part One that asking oneself questions is an invaluable way of getting ideas, each chapter on writing about a genre ends with a list of questions that readers may ask themselves as they read, reread, and think about a work.

Part Three contains three chapters. The first of these, "Style and Format," is a fairly short and direct approach to the elements of clear writing. It treats such matters as denotation, connotation, subordination, paragraphs, and so forth, and it provides numerous examples of effective writing. The latter part of the chapter, devoted to manuscript form, is concerned chiefly with mechanical matters, ranging from the form of the title of an essay to advice about how to introduce quotations. The second chapter in this section, "Research Papers," includes material on settling on a topic and thesis, on finding material, and on the MLA system of documentation. The third chapter briefly discusses essay examinations.

Two appendixes conclude the book: The first includes two stories ("Young Goodman Brown" and "The Lottery") that are the subjects of student essays, and the second provides a glossary of literary terms.

I hope that the preceding remarks tell readers all they want to know about the scope of the book, but some further words must be added. Dr. Johnson said, "There is not so poor a book in the world that would not be a prodigious effort were it wrought out entirely by a single mind, without the aid of previous investigators." I cannot name all the previous investigators who have helped shape my ideas about literature, about writing about literature, and about teaching writing, but I must acknowledge my indebtedness to Morton Berman, William Burto, and Marcia Stubbs, who never tire of improving my pages, and (at HarperCollins) to Judith Leet and Lisa Moore. Others who have offered valuable suggestions include Rebecca Argall, James Blake, Randall Brune, David Cavitch, Warren Chelline, Charles Christensen, William Evans, Shearle Furnish, Bruce Golden, Okey Goode, Patricia Graves, Dean Hall, James Heldman, Deena Linnett, William T. Liston, Janet Madden, Gratia Murphy, J. M. Pair, Diane Quantic, Virginia Shale, Beverly Shields, Isabel Bonnyman Stanley, and Tom Zaniello. My thanks, too, to the PC&F staff, who turned a messy manuscript into a handsome book.

Sylvan Barnet

A Key to Types
of Writing
Assignments

The index is the best guide if you want to draw together all references to a given topic, such as references to "character" or "theme," but the following key may be useful if you want to locate material—especially a sample essay—that will be of assistance in writing a particular kind of essay. Because the topics are not mutually exclusive, most of the sample essays are listed more than once.

Analysis (*for specific topics, see all other headings*)
Defined 38–44
Sample analytic essays 24, 36, 63, 71, 157

Annotations
Examples 7, 20, 34, 61

Atmosphere (*see* Setting)

Character
In fiction 69–71, 102
In drama 132–134, 140
In poetry 142–144

Comparison and Contrast
Sample patterns of organization 41–42
In essay examinations 255
Student essay, "A Japanese *Macbeth*" 192–197

Documented Paper (*see* Research Paper)

Evaluation (*see also* Review)
Implicit versus explicit 51–52

Examinations
Sample kinds 254–255

Explication
Defined and compared with paraphrase 32, 162–163, 254

TEXT CREDITS

Part One

1
The Writer as Reader: Reading and Responding

Learning to write is in large measure learning to read. The text you must read most carefully is the one you produce, an essay you will ask someone else to read. It may start as a jotting in the margin of a book you are reading or as a brief note in a journal, and it will go through several drafts before it becomes an essay. To produce something that another person will find worth reading, you yourself must read each draft with care, trying to imagine the effect your words are likely to have on your reader. In writing about literature, you will apply some of the same critical skills to your reading; that is, you will examine your responses to what you are reading and will try to account for them.

Let's begin by looking at a very short story by Kate Chopin (1851–1904). (The name is pronounced in the French way, something like "show pan.") Kate O'Flaherty, born into a prosperous family in St. Louis, in 1870 married Oscar Chopin, a French-Creole businessman from Louisiana. They lived in New Orleans, where they had six children. Oscar died of malaria in 1882, and in 1884 Kate returned to St. Louis, where, living with her mother and children, she began to write fiction.

Ripe Figs
Kate Chopin

Maman-Nainaine said that when the figs were ripe Babette might go to visit her cousins down on the Bayou-Lafourche where the sugar cane grows. Not that the ripening of figs had the least thing to do with it, but that is the way Maman-Nainaine was.

It seemed to Babette a very long time to wait; for the leaves upon the trees were tender yet, and the figs were like little hard, green marbles.

But warm rains came along and plenty of strong sunshine, and though Maman-Nainaine was as patient as the statue of la Madone, and Babette as restless as a humming-bird, the first thing they both knew it was hot summer-time. Every day Babette danced out to where the fig-trees were in a long line against the fence. She walked slowly beneath them, carefully peering between the gnarled, spreading branches. But each time she came disconsolate away again. What she saw there finally was something that made her sing and dance the whole long day.

When Maman-Nainaine sat down in her stately way to breakfast, the following morning, her muslin cap standing like an aureole about her white, placid face, Babette approached. She bore a dainty porcelain platter, which she set down before her godmother. It contained a dozen purple figs, fringed around with their rich, green leaves.

"Ah," said Maman-Nainaine arching her eyebrows, "how early the figs have ripened this year!"

"Oh," said Babette. "I think they have ripened very late."

"Babette," continued Maman-Nainaine, as she peeled the very plumpest figs with her pointed silver fruit-knife, "you will carry my love to them all down on Bayou-Lafourche. And tell your Tante Frosine I shall look for her at Toussaint—when the chrysanthemums are in bloom."

READING AS RE-CREATION

If we had been Chopin's contemporaries, we might have read this sketch in *Vogue* in 1893 or in an early collection of her works, *A Night in Acadie* (1897). But we are not Chopin's original readers, and, since we live in the late twentieth century, we inevitably read "Ripe Figs" in a somewhat different way. This difference gets us to an important point about writing and reading. A writer writes, sets forth his or her meaning, and attempts to guide the reader's responses, as we all do when we write a letter home saying that we are thinking of dropping a course or asking for news or money or whatever. To this extent, the writer creates the written work and puts a meaning in it.

The reader, whether reading as an assignment or for recreation, *re*-creates it according to his or her experience and understanding. For instance, if the letter writer's appeal for money is indirect, the reader may miss it entirely or may sense it but feel that the need is not urgent. If, on the other hand, the appeal is direct or demanding, the reader may feel irritated or imposed on, even assaulted. "Oh, but I didn't mean it that way," the writer later protests. Still, that's the way the reader took it. The letter is "out there," between the writer and the reader, but the *meaning* is something the reader, as well as the writer, makes.

Since all readers bring themselves to a written work, they bring something individual. For instance, although many of Chopin's original readers knew that she wrote chiefly about the people of Louisiana, especially Creoles (descendants of the early French and Spanish settlers), Cajuns (descendants of the French whom the British had expelled from Canada in the eighteenth century), blacks, and mulattoes, they must have varied in their attitudes about such people. Many of today's readers do not (before they read a work by Chopin) know anything about her subject. Some readers may know where Bayou-Lafourche is, and they may have notions about what it looks like, but other readers will not; indeed, many readers will not know that a bayou is a sluggish, marshy inlet or outlet of a river or lake. Moreover, even if a present-day reader in Chicago, Seattle, or Juneau knows what a bayou is, he or she may assume that "Ripe Figs" depicts a way of life still current; a reader from Louisiana may see in the work a depiction of a lost way of life, a depiction of the good old days (or perhaps of the bad old days, depending on the reader's point of view). Much depends, we can say, on the reader's storehouse of experience.

To repeat: Our reading is a *re*-creation; the author has tried to guide our responses, but inevitably our own experiences, including our ethnic background and our education, contribute to our responses.

MAKING REASONABLE INFERENCES

Does this re-creation mean, then, that there is no use talking (or writing) about literature since all of us perceive it in our relatively private ways, rather like the seven blind men in the fable? One man, you will recall, touched the elephant's tail (or was it his trunk?) and said that the elephant is like a snake; another touched the elephant's side and said the elephant is like a wall; a third touched the elephant's leg and said the elephant is like a tree, and so on. Notice that each of the blind men *did* perceive an aspect of the elephant— an elephant is massive, like a wall or a tree, and an elephant is (in its way) remarkably supple, as you know if you have given peanuts to one.

As readers we can and should make an effort to understand what the author seems to be getting at; that is, we should make an effort to understand the words in their context. Perhaps we shouldn't look up every word we don't know, at least on the first reading, but if certain unfamiliar words are repeated and thus seem especially important, we will probably want to look them up. It happens that in "Ripe Figs" a French word appears: "*Tante* Frosine" means "*Aunt* Frosine." Fortunately, the word is not crucial, and the context probably makes it clear that Frosine is an adult, which is all that we really need to know about her. The point is this: The writer is pitching, and she expects the reader to catch. A reader who does not know that chrysanthemums bloom in the late summer or early autumn, for instance, will miss part of Chopin's meaning.

Although writers tell us a good deal, they cannot tell us everything. We know that Maman-Nainaine is Babette's godmother, but we don't know exactly how old Maman-Nainaine and Babette are. Further, Chopin tells us nothing of Babette's parents. It rather *sounds* as though Babette and her godmother live alone, but readers may differ. One reader may argue that Babette's parents must be dead or ill; another may say that the status of her parents is irrelevant and that what counts is that Babette is supervised by only one person, a mature woman. In short, a text includes **indeterminacies** (passages that careful readers agree are open to various interpretations) and **gaps** (things left unsaid in the story, such as why a godmother rather than a mother takes care of Babette). As we work our way through a text, we keep reevaluating what we have read, pulling the details together to make sense of them in a process called **consistency building.**

Whatever the gaps, careful readers are able to draw many reasonable inferences about Maman-Nainaine. We can list some of them:

> She is older than Babette.
>
> She has a "stately way," and she is "patient as the statue of la Madone."
>
> She has an odd way (is it exasperating or engaging or a little of each?) of connecting actions with the seasons.
>
> Given this last point, she seems to act slowly, to be very patient.
>
> She apparently is used to being obeyed.

You may at this point want to go back and reread "Ripe Figs" to see what else you can say about Maman-Nainaine.

And now, what of Babette?

> She is young.
>
> She is active and impatient ("restless as a hummingbird").
>
> She is obedient.

And at this point too you may want to add to the list.

READING WITH A PEN IN HAND

Perhaps the best way to read attentively is to mark the text, underlining or highlighting passages that seem especially interesting, and to jot notes or queries in the margins. Here is the work once more, this time with the marks that a student added after a second reading.

Ripe Figs
Kate Chopin

(marginal note: odd)

(marginal note: ?)

Maman-Nainaine said that when the (figs) were ripe Babette might go to visit her cousins down on the <u>Bayou-Lafourche</u> where the sugar cane grows. Not that the ripening of figs had the least thing to do with it, but that is the way Maman-Nainaine was.

It seemed to Babette a very long time to wait; for the leaves upon the <u>trees</u> were tender yet, and the figs were like little hard, (green marbles.)

(marginal note: Contrast between M-N and B)

But warm rains came along and plenty of strong sunshine, and though Maman-Nainaine was as <u>patient as the statue</u> of la Madone, and Babette as <u>restless as a hummingbird</u>, the first thing they both knew it was hot summer-time. Every day Babette <u>danced out</u> to where the fig-trees were in a long line against the fence. She walked slowly beneath them, carefully peering between the gnarled, spreading branches. But each time she came disconsolate away again. What she saw there finally was something that made her sing and (dance) <u>the whole long day.</u>

(marginal note: another contrast)

(marginal note: Check this ?)

When Maman-Nainaine (sat) down in her stately way to breakfast, <u>the following morning,</u> her muslin cap standing like an (aureole) about her white, placid face, Babette approached. <u>She bore a dainty porcelain platter,</u> which she set down before her godmother. It contained a dozen (purple figs,) fringed around with their rich, green leaves.

(marginal note: ceremonious?)

(marginal note: nice echo; contrast; like a song)

"Ah," said Maman-Nainaine arching her eyebrows, "how (early the figs have ripened this year!"

"Oh," said Babette. "I think they have ripened very (late.")

(marginal note: time passes fast for M-N, slowly for B)

(marginal note: B entrusted with a message of love)

"Babette," continued (Maman-Nainaine,) as she peeled the <u>very plumpest figs</u> with her pointed silver fruit-knife, "<u>you will carry my love</u> to them all down on Bayou-Lafourche. And tell your <u>Tante Frosine</u> I shall look for her at Toussaint—when the (chrysanthemums) are in <u>bloom.</u>"

(marginal note: is M-N herself like a plump fig?)

(marginal note: opens with figs; ends with chrys. (autumn))

(marginal note: fulfillment? Equivalent to figs ripening?)

RECORDING YOUR FIRST RESPONSES

After you annotate your text, another useful way of getting at meanings is to write down your initial responses to the story, jotting down your impressions as they come to you in any order—almost as though you are talking to yourself. Since no one else is going to read your notes, you can be entirely free and at ease. You can write in sentences or not; it's up to you. Write whatever comes into your mind, whatever the story triggers in your own imagination, whatever rings true or reminds you of your own experiences.

Here is the response of the student who annotated the text.

> I like the way the "green marbles" turn into "purple figs." And I like the way Babette and M-N are sort of opposite. B sings and dances and is restless. On the other hand, M-N is "patient" and like a statue and she sits "in a stately way." A young girl and a mature woman. But, come to think of it, B can also be dignified -- she serves M-N the figs in a fancy dish. I feel I can see these people, I almost know them. And I'd like to see Aunt Frosine in the fall, in chrysanthemum time. She's probably a mature woman, like M-N, with lots of dignity.

Here is another student's first response to "Ripe Figs."

> This is a very short story. I didn't know stories were this short, but I like it because you can get it all quickly and it's no trouble to reread it carefully. The shortness, though, leaves a lot of gaps for the reader to fill in. So much is <u>not</u> said. Your imagination is put to work.
>
> But I can see Maman-N sitting at her table -- pleasantly powerful -- no one you would want to argue with. She's formal and distant -- and definitely has quirks. She wants to postpone Babette's trip, but we don't know why. And you can sense B's frustration. But maybe she's <u>teaching</u> her that something really good is worth waiting for and that anticipation is as much fun as the trip. Maybe I can develop this idea.
>
> Another thing. I can tell they are not poor -- from two things. The pointed silver fruit knife and the porcelain platter, and the fact that Maman sits down to breakfast in a "stately" way. They are the leisure class. But I don't know enough about life on the bayous to go into this. Their life is different from mine; no one I know has that kind of peaceful rural life.

AUDIENCE AND PURPOSE

Suppose you are beginning the process of writing about "Ripe Figs" for someone else, not for yourself. The first question to ask yourself is: For whom am I writing? In other words, Who is my *audience*? (Of course, you probably are writing because an instructor has asked you to do so, but you still must imagine an audience. Your instructor may tell you, for instance, to write for your classmates or for the readers of the college newspaper.) If you are writing for people who are familiar with some of Chopin's work, you will not have to say much about the author. If you are writing for an audience that perhaps has never heard of Chopin, you may want to include a brief biographical note of the sort given in this book. If you are writing for an audience that (you have reason to believe) has read several works by Chopin, you may want to make some comparisons, explaining how "Ripe Figs" resembles or differs from Chopin's other work.

In a sense, the audience is your collaborator; it helps you decide what you will say. You are helped also by your sense of *purpose:* If your aim is to introduce readers to Chopin, you will make certain points; if your aim is to tell people what you think "Ripe Figs" means about human relationships or about time, you will say some different things; if your aim is to have a little fun and to entertain an audience that is familiar with "Ripe Figs," you may write a parody (a humorous imitation).

A WRITING ASSIGNMENT ON "RIPE FIGS"

The Assignment

Let's assume that you are trying to describe "Ripe Figs" to someone who has not read it. You probably will briefly summarize the action, such as it is, will mention where it takes place and who the characters are (including their relationship), and what, if anything, happens to them. Beyond that, you will probably try to explain as honestly as you can what makes "Ripe Figs" appealing or interesting or trifling or boring or whatever.

Here is an essay that a student, Marilyn Brown, wrote for this assignment.

A Sample Essay

Ripening

Kate Chopin's "Ripe Figs" describes a growing season in a young girl's life. Maman-Nainaine agrees to allow young Babette to visit relatives away from home, but Babette must delay her trip until the figs ripen. Babette watches the signs of the natural world, impatiently observing, straining to have time pass at her own speed. At last, Babette finds that the figs have ripened and she presents them to her godmother, Maman-Nainaine, who gives Babette her leave to go on the journey to Bayou-Lafourche.

Chopin sets the action within the context of the natural world. Babette, young and tender as the fig leaves, can't wait to "ripen." Her visit to Bayou-Lafourche is no mere pleasure trip but represents Babette's coming into her own season of maturity. Babette's desire to rush this process is tempered by a condition that Maman-Nainaine sets: Babette must wait until the figs ripen, since everything comes in its own season. Maman recognizes in the patterns of the natural world the rhythms of life. By asking Babette to await the ripening, the young girl is made to pay attention to these patterns as well.

In this work, Chopin asks her readers to see the relationship of human time to nature's seasons. Try as we may to push the process of maturity, growth or ripening happens in its own time. If we pay attention and wait with patience, the fruits of our own growth will be sweet, plump, and bountiful. Chopin uses natural imagery effectively, interweaving the young girl's growth with the rhythms of the seasons. In this way, the reader is connected with both processes in a very intimate and inviting way.

Other Possibilities for Writing

Of course, one might write a paper of a very different sort. Consider the following possibilities:

1. Write a sequel, moving from fall to spring.
2. Write a letter from Babette, at Bayou-Lafourche, to Maman-Nainaine.
3. Imagine that Babette is now an old woman, writing her memoirs. What does she say about Maman-Nainaine?
4. Write a narrative based on your own experience of learning a lesson in patience.

2

The Reader as Writer: Drafting and Writing

PRE-WRITING: GETTING IDEAS

"All there is to writing," Robert Frost said, "is having ideas. To learn to write is to learn to have ideas." How does one "learn to have ideas"? Among the methods are the following: reading with a pen or pencil in hand so that (as we have already seen) one can annotate the text; keeping a journal in which one jots down reflections about one's reading; and talking with others about the reading. Let's take another look at the first method, annotating.

Annotating a Text

In reading, if you own the book don't hesitate to mark it up, indicating (by highlighting or underlining, or by marginal notes) what puzzles you, what pleases or interests you, and what displeases or bores you. Of course, later you'll want to think further about these responses, asking yourself if, on rereading, you still feel this way, and if not, why not, but these first responses will get you started.

Annotations of the sort given on page 7, which chiefly call attention to contrasts, indicate that the student is thinking about writing some sort of analysis of the story, an essay in which the parts are examined to see how they relate to each other or in which a part is examined to see how it relates to the whole.

More About Getting Ideas: A Second Story by Kate Chopin, "The Story of an Hour"

Let's look at a story that is a little longer than "Ripe Figs," and then we'll discuss how, in addition to annotating, one might get ideas for writing about it.

The Story of an Hour

Kate Chopin

Knowing that Mrs. Mallard was afflicted with a heart trouble, great care was taken to break to her as gently as possible the news of her husband's death.

It was her sister Josephine who told her, in broken sentences, veiled hints that revealed in half concealing. Her husband's friend Richards was there, too, near her. It was he who had been in the newspaper office when intelligence of the railroad disaster was received, with Brently Mallard's name leading the list of "killed." He had only taken the time to assure himself of its truth by a second telegram, and had hastened to forestall any less careful, less tender friend in bearing the sad message.

She did not hear the story as many women have heard the same, with a paralyzed inability to accept its significance. She wept at once with sudden, wild abandonment, in her sister's arms. When the storm of grief had spent itself she went away to her room alone. She would have no one follow her.

There stood, facing the open window, a comfortable, roomy armchair. Into this she sank, pressed down by a physical exhaustion that haunted her body and seemed to reach into her soul.

She could see in the open square before her house the tops of trees that were all aquiver with the new spring life. The delicious breath of rain was in the air. In the street below a peddler was crying his wares. The notes of a distant song which some one was singing reached her faintly, and countless sparrows were twittering in the eaves.

There were patches of blue sky showing here and there through the clouds that had met and piled above the other in the west facing her window.

She sat with her head thrown back upon the cushion of the chair quite motionless, except when a sob came up into her throat and shook her, as a child who has cried itself to sleep continues to sob in its dreams.

She was young, with a fair, calm face, whose lines bespoke repression and even a certain strength. But now there was a dull stare in her eyes, whose gaze was fixed away off yonder on one of those patches of blue sky. It was not a glance of reflection, but rather indicated a suspension of intelligent thought.

There was something coming to her and she was waiting for it, fearfully. What was it? She did not know; it was too subtle and elusive to name. But she felt it creeping out of the sky, reaching toward her through the sounds, the scents, the color that filled the air.

Now her bosom rose and fell tumultuously. She was beginning to recognize this thing that was approaching to possess her, and she was striving to beat it back with her will—as powerless as her two white slender hands would have been.

When she abandoned herself a little whispered word escaped her slightly parted lips. She said it over and over under her breath: "Free, free, free!" The vacant stare and the look of terror that had followed it went from her eyes. They stayed keen and bright. Her pulses beat fast, and the coursing blood warmed and relaxed every inch of her body.

She did not stop to ask if it were not a monstrous joy that held her. A clear and exalted perception enabled her to dismiss the suggestion as trivial.

She knew that she would weep again when she saw the kind, tender hands folded in death; the face that had never looked save with love upon her, fixed and gray and dead. But she saw beyond that bitter moment a long procession of years to come that would belong to her absolutely. And she opened and spread her arms out to them in welcome.

There would be no one to live for her during those coming years; she would live for herself. There would be no powerful will bending her in the blind persistence with which men and women believe they have a right to impose a private will upon a fellow creature. A kind intention or a cruel intention made the act seem no less a crime as she looked upon it in that brief moment of illumination.

And yet she had loved him—sometimes. Often she had not. What did it matter! What could love, the unsolved mystery, count for in face of this possession of self-assertion which she suddenly recognized as the strongest impulse of her being.

"Free! Body and soul free!" she kept whispering.

Josephine was kneeling before the closed door with her lips to the keyhole, imploring for admission. "Louise, open the door! I beg; open the door—you will make yourself ill. What are you doing, Louise? For heaven's sake open the door."

"Go away. I am not making myself ill." No; she was drinking in the very elixir of life through that open window.

Her fancy was running riot along those days ahead of her. Spring days, and summer days, and all sorts of days that would be her own. She breathed a quick prayer that life might be long. It was only yesterday she had thought with a shudder that life might be long.

She arose at length and opened the door to her sister's importunities. There was a feverish triumph in her eyes, and she carried herself unwittingly like a goddess of Victory. She clasped her sister's waist and together they descended the stairs. Richards stood waiting for them at the bottom.

Some one was opening the front door with a latchkey. It was Brently Mallard who entered, a little travel-stained, composedly carrying his grip-sack and umbrella. He had been far from the scene of accident, and did not even know there had been one. He stood amazed at Josephine's piercing cry; at Richards' quick motion to screen him from the view of his wife.

But Richards was too late.

When the doctors came they said she had died of heart disease—of joy that kills.

Brainstorming for Ideas for Writing

Unlike annotating, which consists of making brief notes and small marks on the printed page, "brainstorming"—the free jotting down of ideas—requires that you jot down whatever comes to mind, without inhibition. Don't worry about spelling, about writing complete sentences, or about unifying your thoughts; just let one thought lead to another. Later, you will review your jottings, deleting some, connecting with arrows others that are related, amplifying still others. For now, you want to get going, and so there is no reason to look back. Thus, you might jot down something about the title:

```
Title speaks of an hour, and story covers an hour, but maybe
takes five minutes to read
```

And then, perhaps prompted by "an hour," you might happen to add something to this effect:

```
Doubt that a woman who got news of the death of her husband
could move from grief to joy within an hour.
```

Your next jotting might have little or nothing to do with this issue; it might simply say:

```
Enjoyed "Hour" more than "Ripe Figs" partly because "Hour"
is so shocking
```

And then you might ask yourself:

```
By shocking, do I mean "improbable," or what? come to think
of it, maybe it's not so improbable. A lot depends on what
the marriage was like.
```

Focused Free Writing

Focused free writing, or directed free writing, is a related method that some writers use to uncover ideas they want to write about. Concentrating on one issue, such as a question that strikes them as worth puzzling over (What kind of person is Mrs. Mallard?), they write at length, nonstop, for perhaps 5 or 10 minutes.

Writers who find free writing helpful put down everything that has bearing on the one issue or question they are examining. They do not stop at this stage to evaluate the results, and they do not worry about niceties of sentence structure or of spelling. They just explore ideas in a steady stream of writing, using whatever associations come to mind. If they pause in their writing, it is only to refer to the text, to search for more detail—perhaps a quotation—that will help them answer their question.

After the free-writing session, these writers usually go back and reread what they have written, highlighting or underlining what seems to be of value. Of course, they find much that is of little or no use, but they also usually find that some strong ideas have surfaced and have received some development. At this point the writers are often able to make a scratch outline and then begin a draft.

Here is an example of one student's focused free writing:

> What do I know about Mrs. Mallard? Let me put everything down here I know about her or can figure out from what Kate Chopin tells me. When she finds herself alone after the death of her husband, she says, "Free. Body and soul free" and before that she said "free, free, free." Three times. So she has suddenly perceived that she has not been free; she has been under the influence of a "powerful will." In this case it has been her husband, but she says no one, man nor woman, should impose their will on anyone else. So it's not a feminist issue -- it's a power issue. No one should push anyone else around is what I guess Chopin means, force someone to do what the other person wants. I used to have a friend that did that to me all the time; he had to run everything. They say that fathers -- before the women's movement -- used to run things, with the father in charge of all the decisions, so maybe this is an honest reaction to having been pushed around by a husband. I think Mrs. Mallard is a believable character, even if the plot is not all that believable -- all those things happening in such quick succession.

Listing

In your preliminary thinking you may find it useful to make lists. In the previous chapter we saw that listing the traits of characters was helpful in thinking about Chopin's "Ripe Figs":

Maman-Nainaine

> older than Babette
>
> "stately way"
>
> "patient as the statue of la Madone"
>
> expects to be obeyed

```
    connects actions with seasons
Babette
    young
    active
    obedient
```

For "The Story of an Hour" you might list Mrs. Mallard's traits, or you might list the stages in her development. (Such a list is not the same as a summary of the plot. The list helps the writer see the sequence of psychological changes.)

```
weeps (when she gets the news)
goes to room, alone
"pressed down by a physical exhaustion"
"dull stare"
"something coming to her"
strives to beat back "this thing"
"Free, free, free!" The "vacant stare went from her eyes"
"A clear and exalted perception"
Rejects Josephine
"She was drinking in the very elixir of life"
Gets up, opens door, "A feverish triumph in her eyes"
Sees B, and dies
```

Of course, unlike brainstorming and annotating, which let you go in all directions, listing requires that you first make a decision about what you will be listing—traits of character, images, puns, or whatever. Once you make the decision you can then construct the list, and, with a list in front of you, you will probably see patterns that you were not earlier fully conscious of.

Asking Questions

If you feel stuck, ask yourself questions. (You'll recall that the assignment on "Ripe Figs" in effect asked you to ask yourself questions about the work—for instance, a question about the relationship between the characters—and about your responses to it: "You will probably try to explain as honestly as you can what makes 'Ripe Figs' appealing or interesting or trifling or boring or whatever.")

If you are thinking about a work of fiction, ask yourself questions about the plot and the characters: Are they believable? Are they interesting? What does it all add up to? What does the story mean *to you*? (The chapters on the essay, fiction, drama, poetry, and film include questions on each form.) One student found it helpful to jot down the following questions:

```
Plot
    Ending false? Unconvincing? Or prepared for?
Character
    Mrs. M. unfeeling? Immoral?
    Mrs. M. unbelievable character?
    What might her marriage have been like? Many gaps.
    (Can we tell what her husband was like?)
    "And yet she loved him -- sometimes." Fickle? Realistic?
    What is "this thing that was approaching to possess her?"
Symbolism
    Set on spring day = symbolic of new life?
```

You don't have to be as tidy as this student. You may begin by jotting down notes and queries about what you like or dislike and about what puzzles or amuses you. What follows are the jottings of another student. They are, obviously, in no particular order—the student is "brainstorming," putting down whatever occurs to her—though it is equally obvious that one note sometimes led to the next:

```
Title nothing special. What might be a better title?
Could a woman who loved her husband be so heartless?
Is she heartless? Did she love him?
What are (were) Louise's feelings about her husband?
Did she want too much? What did she want?
Could this story happen today? Feminist interpretation?
Sister (Josephine) -- a busybody?
Tricky ending -- but maybe it could be true
"And yet she had loved him -- sometimes. Often she had not."
    Why does one love someone "sometimes"?
Irony: plot has reversal. Are characters ironic too?
```

These jottings will help the reader-writer think about the story, find a special point of interest, and develop a thoughtful argument about it.

Keeping a Journal

A journal is not a diary, a record of what the writer did during the day ("today I read Chopin's 'Hour'"). Rather, a journal is a place to store some of the thoughts you may have inscribed on a scrap of paper or in the margin of the text, such as your initial response to the title of a work or to the ending. It is also a place to jot down further reflections, such as thoughts about what the work means to you, and what was said in the classroom about writing in general or about specific works. You may, for instance, want to reflect on why your opinion is so different from that of another student, or you may want to apply a concept such as "character" or "irony" or "plausibility" to a story that later you may write about in an essay. You might even make an entry in the form of a letter to the author or from one character to another. You might write a dialogue between characters in two works or between two authors, or you might record an experience of your own that is comparable to something in the work.

A student who wrote about "The Story of an Hour" began with the following entry in his journal. In reading this entry, notice that one idea stimulates another. The student was, quite rightly, concerned with getting and exploring ideas, not with writing a unified paragraph.

> Apparently a "well-made" story, but seems clever rather than moving or real. Doesn't seem plausible. Mrs. M's change comes out of the blue -- maybe <u>some</u> women might respond like this, but probably not most.
>
> Does literature deal with unusual people, or with usual (typical?) people? Shouldn't it deal with typical? Maybe not. (Anyway, how can I know?) Is "typical" same as "plausible"? Come to think of it, prob. not.
>
> Anyway, whether Mrs. M is typical or not, is her change plausible, believable? Think more about this.
>
> Why did she change? Her husband dominated her life and controlled her actions; he did "impose a private will upon a fellow creature." She calls this a crime, even if well-intentioned? Is it a crime?

Arriving at a Thesis

Having raised some questions—having set oneself thinking—a reader goes back to the work, hoping to read it now with increased awareness. Some jottings will prove to be dead ends, but some will lead to further ideas. The thesis of the essay is still in doubt at this stage of the process, but there is no doubt about one thing: A good essay will have a thesis, a point, an argument that can be stated in a *thesis sentence.*

Consider these candidates as possible thesis sentences:

1. Mrs. Mallard dies soon after hearing that her husband has died.

True, but scarcely a point that can be argued or even developed. About the most the essayist can do with this sentence is amplify it by summarizing the plot of the story, a task not worth doing unless the plot is unusually obscure. An essay may include a sentence or two of summary to give readers their bearings, but a summary is not an essay.

2. The story is a libel on women.

In contrast to the first statement, this one can be developed into an argument. Probably the writer will try to demonstrate that Mrs. Mallard's behavior is despicable. Whether this point can be convincingly argued is another matter; the thesis may be untenable, but it is a thesis. A second problem, however, is this: Even if the writer demonstrates that Mrs. Mallard's behavior is despicable, he or she will have to go on to demonstrate that the presentation of one despicable woman constitutes a libel on women in general. That's a pretty big order.

3. The story is clever but superficial because it is based on an unreal character.

Here, too, is a thesis, a point of view that can be argued. Whether this thesis is true is another matter. The writer's job will be to support it by presenting evidence. Probably the writer will have no difficulty in finding evidence that the story is "clever"; the difficulty probably will be in establishing a case that the characterization of Mrs. Mallard is "unreal." The writer will have to set forth some ideas about what makes a character real and then will have to show that Mrs. Mallard is an "unreal" (unbelievable) figure.

4. The irony of the ending is believable partly because it is consistent with earlier ironies in the story.

It happens that the student who wrote the essay printed on page 24 began by drafting an essay based on the third of these thesis topics, but as she worked on a draft she found that she could not support her assertion that the character was unconvincing. In fact, she came to believe that although Mrs. Mallard's joy was the reverse of what a reader might expect, several early reversals in the story helped make Mrs. Mallard's shift from grief to joy acceptable.

Remember: It's not likely that you will quickly find a thesis. Annotating, making entries in a journal, and writing a first draft are *ways of finding* a thesis.

WRITING A DRAFT

After jotting down notes, and further notes stimulated by rereading and further thinking, you probably will be able to formulate a tentative thesis. At this point most writers find it useful to clear the air by glancing over their preliminary notes and by jotting down the thesis and a few especially promising notes—brief statements of what they think their key points may be, such as key quotations that may help support the thesis.

Here are the notes (not the original brainstorming notes, but a later selection from them, with additions) and a draft (page 20) that makes use of them. The final version of the essay—the product produced by the process—is given on page 24.

```
title? Ironies in an Hour (?) An Hour of Irony (?) Kate
   Chopin's Irony (?)
thesis: irony at end is prepared for by earlier ironies
chief irony: Mrs. M. dies just as she is beginning to enjoy
   life
smaller ironies: 1. "sad message" brings her joy
                 2. Richards is "too late" at end;
                 3. Richards is too early at start
```

A Sample Draft: "Ironies in an Hour"

Now for the student's draft—not the first version, but a revised draft with some of the irrelevancies of the first draft omitted and some evidence added.

The digits within the parentheses refer to the page numbers from which the quotations are drawn, though with so short a work as "The Story of an Hour," page references are hardly necessary. Check with your instructor to find out if you must always give citations. (Detailed information about how to document a paper is given on pages 233–245.)

```
                    Ironies in an Hour

   After we know how the story turns out, if we reread it we
find irony at the very start, as is true of many other sto-
ries. Mrs. Mallard's friends assume, mistakenly, that Mrs.
Mallard was deeply in love with her husband, Brently
Mallard. They take great care to tell her gently of his
death. The friends mean well, and in fact they do well. They
bring her an hour of life, an hour of freedom. They think
their news is sad. Mrs. Mallard at first expresses grief
when she hears the news, but soon she finds joy in it. So
Richards's "sad message" (12) though sad in Richards's eyes,
is in fact a happy message.
   Among the ironic details is the statement that when Mal-
lard entered the house, Richards tried to conceal him from
Mrs. Mallard, but "Richards was too late" (13). This is
```

ironic because earlier Richards "hastened" (12) to bring his
sad message; if he had at the start been "too late" (13),
Brently Mallard would have arrived at home first, and Mrs.
Mallard's life would not have ended an hour later but would
simply have gone on as it had been. Yet another irony at the
end of the story is the diagnosis of the doctors. The doctors say she died of "heart disease -- of joy that kills"
(14). In one sense the doctors are right: Mrs. Mallard has
experienced a great joy. But of course the doctors totally
misunderstand the joy that kills her.

    The central irony resides not in the well-intentioned but
ironic actions of Richards, or in the unconsciously ironic
words of the doctors, but in her own life. In a way she has
been dead. She "sometimes" (13) loved her husband, but in a
way she has been dead. Now, his apparent death brings her
new life. This new life comes to her at the season of the
year when "the tops of trees...were all aquiver with the
new spring life" (12). But, ironically, her new life will
last only an hour. She looks forward to "summer days" (13)
but she will not see even the end of this spring day. Her
years of marriage were ironic. They brought her a sort of
living death instead of joy. Her new life is ironic too. It
grows out of her moment of grief for her supposedly dead
husband, and her vision of a new life is cut short.

Work Cited

Chopin, Kate. "The Story of an Hour." <u>Literature for Compo-
    sition.</u> 3rd ed. Ed. Sylvan Barnet et al. New York: Harp-
    er, 1992. 12-13.

Revising a Draft

The draft, though excellent, is not yet a finished essay. The student went
on to improve it in many small but important ways.

First, the draft needs a good paragraph that will let readers know where the writer will be taking them. (Chapter 9 discusses introductory paragraphs.) Doubtless you know, from your own experience as a reader, that readers can follow an argument more easily and with more pleasure if early in the discussion the writer alerts them to the gist of the argument. (The title, too, can strongly suggest the thesis.) Second, some of the paragraphs could be clearer.

In revising paragraphs—or, for that matter, in revising an entire draft—writers unify, organize, clarify, and polish.

1. **Unity** is achieved partly by eliminating irrelevancies. Notice that in the final version, printed on page 24, the writer has deleted "as is true of many other stories."
2. **Organization** is largely a matter of arranging material into a sequence that will help the reader grasp the point.
3. **Clarity** is achieved largely by providing concrete details and quotations to support generalizations and by providing helpful transitions ("for instance," "furthermore," "on the other hand," "however").
4. **Polish** is small-scale revision. For instance, one deletes unnecessary repetitions. (In the second paragraph of the draft the phrase "the doctors" appears three times, but it appears only once in the final version of the paragraph.) Similarly, in polishing, a writer combines choppy sentences into longer sentences and breaks overly long sentences into shorter sentences.

Later, after producing a draft that seems close to a finished essay, writers engage in yet another activity. They edit.

5. **Editing** is concerned with such matters as checking the accuracy of quotations by comparing them with the original, checking a dictionary for the spelling of doubtful words, and checking a handbook for doubtful punctuation—for instance, whether a comma or a semicolon is needed in a particular sentence.

Peer Review

Your instructor may encourage (or even require) you to discuss your draft with another student or with a small group of students; that is, you may be asked to get a review from your peers. Such a procedure is helpful in several ways. First, it gives the writer a real audience, readers who can point to what pleases or puzzles them, who make suggestions, who may disagree (with the writer or with each other), and who frequently, though not intentionally, *misread*. Though writers don't necessarily like everything they hear (they seldom hear "This is perfect. Don't change a word!"), reading and discussing their work with others almost always gives them a fresh perspective on their work, and a fresh perspective may stimulate thoughtful revision. (Having your intentions *misread* because your writing isn't clear enough can be particularly stimulating.)

The writer whose work is being reviewed is not the sole beneficiary. When students regularly serve as readers for each other, they become better readers of their own work and consequently better revisers. As was said in Chapter 1, learning to write is in large measure learning to read.

If peer review is a part of the writing process in your course, the instructor may distribute a sheet with some suggestions and questions. Here is an example of such a sheet.

QUESTIONS FOR PEER REVIEW   ENGLISH 125a

Read each draft once, quickly. Then read it again, with the following questions in mind.

1. What is the essay's topic? Is it one of the assigned topics, or a variation from it? Does the draft show promise of fulfilling the assignment?

2. Look at the essay as a whole. What thesis (main idea) is stated or implied? If implied, try to state it in your own words.

3. Look at each paragraph separately:
   a. What is the basic point?
   b. How does the paragraph relate to the essay's main idea or to the previous paragraph?
   c. Should some paragraphs be deleted? Be divided into two or more paragraphs? Be combined? Be put elsewhere? (If you outline the essay by jotting down the gist of each paragraph, you will get help in answering these questions.)
   d. Is each sentence clearly related to the sentence that precedes and to the sentence that follows?
   e. Is each paragraph adequately developed? Are there sufficient details, perhaps brief supporting quotations from the text?

4. What are the paper's chief strengths?

5. Make at least two specific suggestions that you think will help the author improve the paper.

THE FINAL VERSION

Here is the final version of the student's essay. The essay that was submitted to the instructor was typed, but here, so that you can easily see how the draft has been revised, we print the draft with the final changes written in, by hand.

Ironies of Life in Kate Chopin's "The Story of an Hour"

~~Ironies in an Hour~~

Kate Chopin's "The Story of an Hour" — which takes only a few minutes to read — turns out to have an ironic ending, but on rereading it one sees that the irony is not concentrated ~~only~~ in the outcome of the plot — Mrs. Mallard dies just when she is beginning to live — but is also present in many details.

After we know how the story turns out, if we reread it we find irony at the very start/ ~~as is true of many other stories.~~ *Because* Mrs. Mallard's friends *and her sister* assume, mistakenly, that ~~Mrs. Mallard~~ *she* was deeply in love with her husband, Brently Mallard/, ^They take great care to tell her gently of his death. ~~The friends~~ *They* mean well, and in fact they *do* well, ~~They~~ bring^ing her an hour of life, an hour of^ freedom/, *joyous* *but it is ironic that* ^They think their news is sad. *True,* Mrs. Mallard at first expresses grief when she hears the news, but soon^ *(unknown to her friends)* she finds ~~joy~~ joy in it. So Richards's "sad message" (12) though sad in Richards's eyes, is in fact a happy message.

Among the^ *small but significant* ironic details is the statement^ *near the end of the story* that when Mallard entered the house, Richards tried to conceal him from Mrs. Mallard, but "Richards was too late" (13). This is *almost at the start of the story, in the second paragraph* ironic because ~~earlier~~ ^ Richards "hastened" (12) to bring his sad message; if he had at the start been "too late" (13), Brently Mallard would have arrived at home first, and Mrs. Mallard's life would not have ended an hour later but would simply have gone on as it had been. Yet another irony at the

end of the story is the diagnosis of the doctors. ~~The doc-~~ They
~~tors~~ say she died of "heart disease -- of joy that kills"

(14). In one sense ~~the doctors~~ they are right: Mrs. Mallard has for the last hour
experienced a great joy. But of course the doctors totally

misunderstand the joy that kills her. It is not joy at seeing her husband alive, but her realization that the great joy she experienced during the last hour is over.

All of these ironic details add richness to the story, but The central irony resides not in the well-intentioned but

ironic actions of Richards, or in the unconsciously ironic Mrs. Mallard's
words of the doctors, but in ~~her~~ own life. ~~In a way she has~~

~~been dead.~~ She "sometimes" (13) loved her husband, but in a a body subjected to her husband's will.
way she has been dead. Now, his apparent death brings her
appropriately, new life. This new life comes to her at the season of the

year when "the tops of trees ... were all aquiver with the

new spring life" (12). But, ironically, her new life will She is "Free, free, free" — but only until her husband walks through
last only an hour. She looks forward to "summer days" (13) the doorway.
bringing
but she will not see even the end of this spring day. Her
years of marriage were ironic, ~~They brought~~ her a sort of not only because
living death instead of joy, Her new life is ironic too, It

grows out of her moment of grief for her supposedly dead but also because her vision of "a long progression of years."
husband, ~~and her vision of a new life~~ is cut short within an hour on a spring day.

Work Cited

Chopin, Kate. "The Story of an Hour." <u>Literature for Composition.</u> 3rd ed. Ed. Sylvan Barnet et al. New York: Harper, 1992. 12-13.

A Brief Overview of the Final Version

Finally, as a quick review, let's look at several principles illustrated by this essay.

1. The **title of the essay** is not merely the title of the work discussed; rather, it gives the reader a clue, a small idea of the essayist's topic.
2. The **opening or introductory paragraph** does not begin by saying

"In this story ...." Rather, by naming the author and the title it lets the reader know exactly what story is being discussed. It also develops the writer's thesis a bit so that readers know where they will be going.

3. The **organization** is effective. The smaller ironies are discussed in the second and third paragraphs, the central (chief) irony in the last paragraph; that is, the essay does not dwindle or become anticlimactic—rather, it builds up.

4. Some **brief quotations** are used, both to provide evidence and to let the reader hear—even if only fleetingly—Kate Chopin's writing.

5. The essay is chiefly **devoted to analysis, not to summary.** The writer, properly assuming that the reader has read the work, does not tell the plot in great detail. But, aware that the reader has not memorized the story, the writer gives helpful reminders.

6. The **present tense** is used in narrating the action: "Mrs. Mallard dies"; "Mrs. Mallard's friends and relatives all assume."

7. Although a **concluding paragraph** is often useful—if it does more than merely summarize what has already been clearly said—it is not essential in a short analysis. In this essay, the last sentence explains the chief irony and, therefore, makes an acceptable ending.

8. **Documentation** is given according to the form set forth in Chapter 10.

3

Writing about Literature: An Overview

THE NATURE OF CRITICAL WRITING

In everyday talk the commonest meaning of **criticism** is something like "finding fault." And to be critical is to be censorious. But a critic can see excellences as well as faults. Because we turn to criticism with the hope that the critic has seen something we have missed, the most valuable criticism is not that which shakes its finger at faults but that which calls our attention to interesting things going on in the work of art. Here are two statements, the first by John Dryden (1631–1700), the second by W. H. Auden (1907–1973), suggesting that criticism is most useful when it calls our attention to things worth attending to:

> They wholly mistake the nature of criticism who think its business is principally to find fault. Criticism, as it was first instituted by Aristotle, was meant a standard of judging well; the chiefest part of which is, to observe those excellencies which should delight a reasonable reader.
>
> *Essays,* ed. W. P. Ker (Oxford, 1926), I, p. 179

Now Auden:

> What is the function of a critic? So far as I am concerned, he can do me one or more of the following services:
>
> 1. Introduce me to authors or works of which I was hitherto unaware.
> 2. Convince me that I have undervalued an author or a work because I had not read them carefully enough.
> 3. Show me relations between works of different ages and cultures which I could never have seen for myself because I do not know enough and never shall.

4. Give a "reading" of a work which increases my understanding of it.
5. Throw light upon the process of artistic "Making."
6. Throw light upon the relation of art to life, science, economics, ethics, religion, etc.

The Dyer's Hand (New York, 1963), pp. 8–9

Dryden is chiefly concerned with literature as a means of delight, and his criticism aims at increasing the delight we can get from literature; Auden does not neglect this delight, but he extends (especially in his sixth point) the range of criticism to include topics beyond the literary work itself. But in both Dryden and Auden the emphasis on observing, showing, and illuminating suggests that the function of critical writing is not very different from the commonest view of the function of imaginative writing.

SOME KINDS OF ESSAYS

Historical, Biographical, Psychological, Feminist, and Formalist Criticism

Useful discussions of literature are not all of one kind. Let's look briefly at a few kinds. **Historical scholarship** studies a work in its historical context. Thus, a student of *Julius Caesar, Hamlet,* or *Macbeth*—plays in which ghosts appear—may try to find out about Elizabethan attitudes toward ghosts. We may find, for instance, that the Elizabethans did not take ghosts seriously, or perhaps we will find that ghosts were regarded as shapes taken by the devil in order to mislead the virtuous. In any case, research may help us understand the play, or at least part of it. Similarly, a historical critic studying *The Taming of the Shrew* may want to examine Elizabethan attitudes toward marriage, especially the degree to which the Elizabethans subscribed to the view expressed by Paul in the New Testament: "Wives, submit yourselves to your own husbands, as unto the Lord; for the husband is the head of the wife, even as Christ is the head of the church" (Ephesians 6:22–23). Historical critics argue, and one can hardly dispute the point, that works of art, however individualistic, arise in a particular social context and that an understanding of the context may help us understand the work.

One kind of historical research is the study of **biography.** What experiences, for example, did Mark Twain undergo? Are some of the apparently sensational aspects of *Huckleberry Finn* close to events that Twain experienced? If so, is he a "realist"? If not, is he writing in the tradition of the "tall tale"? Biographical study may illuminate even the work of a living author. If you are writing about the poetry of Adrienne Rich, for instance, you may want to consider what she has told us in many essays about her life, especially about her relations with her father and her husband.

One form that biographical study may take is **psychological** or **psychoanalytic criticism,** which usually examines the author and the author's work in the framework of Freudian psychology. A central Freudian doctrine is the Oedipus complex, the view that all males (Freud seems not to have made his mind up about females) wish to displace their fathers and to sleep with their mothers. According to Freud, hatred for the father and love of the mother, normally repressed, may appear disguised in dreams. Works of art, like dreams, are disguised versions of repressed wishes.

Consider, for instance, Edgar Allan Poe. An orphan before he was three years old, he was brought up in the family of John Allan, though he was never formally adopted. His relations with Allan were stormy, though he seems to have had better relations with Allan's wife, and still better relations with an aunt, whose daughter he married. In the Freudian view, Poe's marriage to his cousin (the daughter of a mother figure) was a way of sleeping with his mother. If we move from Poe's life to his work, we see, it is alleged, this hatred for his father and love for his mother. Thus, the murderer in "The Cask of Amontillado" is said to voice Poe's hostility to his father, and the wine vault in which much of the story is set (an encompassing structure associated with fluids) is interpreted as symbolizing Poe's desire to return to his mother's womb. In Poe's other works the longing for death is similarly taken to embody his desire to return to the womb. In like fashion, efforts have been made to interpret Willa Cather's work as that of a suppressed lesbian. Thus, studies have been made of the female friendships in her writing and of her depiction of males estranged from society. These isolated males are sometimes interpreted as disguised versions of Cather's own sense of isolation. Skeptics, it should be pointed out, have denied that Cather's sexuality influenced her writing.

One additional example—and it is the most famous—of a psychoanalytic study of a work of literature may be useful. In *Hamlet and Oedipus,* Ernest Jones, amplifying some comments by Freud, argued that Hamlet delays killing Claudius because Claudius (who has killed Hamlet's father and married Hamlet's mother) has done exactly what Hamlet himself wanted to do. For Hamlet to kill Claudius, then, would be to kill himself. (If this approach to literature interests you, take a look at Norman N. Holland's *Psychoanalysis and Shakespeare;* for applications to authors other than Shakespeare, look at Simon O. Lesser's *Fiction and the Unconscious* or at an anthology of criticism, *Literature and Psychoanalysis,* edited by Edith Kurzweil and William Phillips.)

Psychological criticism can also turn from the author and the work to the reader, seeking to explain why we as readers respond in certain ways. Why, for example, is *Hamlet* so widely popular? The Freudian answer is that it is universal because it deals with a universal (Oedipal) impulse. One can, however, ask why it appeals as strongly to women as to men (again, Freud was unsure about the Oedipus complex in women). Or, more generally, one can ask if males and females read in the same way.

This last question brings us to **feminist criticism,** an approach that grew out of the women's movement of the 1960s. Where the women's movement insisted (at least at first) that women are the same as men and therefore should be treated equally, much feminist criticism has tended to emphasize the difference between women and men. Because the experiences of the sexes are different, the argument goes, the values and sensibilities are different, and their responses to literature are different. Further, literature written by women is different from literature written by men. (If you have read Charlotte Perkins Gilman's "The Yellow Wallpaper" or Susan Glaspell's "Trifles" or Glaspell's "A Jury of Her Peers," you'll recall that these literary works themselves are largely concerned about the differing ways that males and females perceive the world.) Of course, not all women are feminist critics, and not all feminist critics are women. Further, feminist critics do not agree in all details, but for a good example of a feminist approach, see Elaine Showalter's *A Literature of Their Own* or Showalter's "Towards a Feminist Perspective" in *Women Writing and Writing about Women,* edited by Mary Jacobus.

Feminist critics rightly point out that men have established the conventions of literature and men have established the canon—the body of literature that is said to be worth reading. Speaking a bit broadly, in this male-dominated literature men are good if they are strong and active, whereas women are good if they are weak and passive. Thus, in the world of fairy tales the admirable male is the energetic hero Jack the Giant Killer, but the admirable female is the passive Sleeping Beauty. Active women, such as the wicked stepmother or (a disguised form of the same thing) the witch, are generally villainous. (There are, of course, exceptions, such as Gretel, in "Hansel and Gretel.") A woman hearing or reading the story of Sleeping Beauty or of Little Red Ridinghood (rescued by the powerful woodcutter) must, it is argued, respond differently from a man. For instance, a woman may be brainwashed into admiring Sleeping Beauty, but only at great cost to her mental well-being. A more resistant female reader may recognize in herself no kinship with the beautiful passive Sleeping Beauty and may respond to the story indignantly. Another way to put it is this: The male reader perceives a romantic story, but the female reader perceives a story of tyranny.

For a discussion of the ways in which, it is argued, women *ought* to read, you may want to look at Judith Fetterley's book, *The Resisting Reader.* Briefly, Fetterley's point is that women should resist the meanings (that is, the visions of how women ought to behave) that males bury in their books. "To read the canon of what is currently considered classic American literature is perforce to identify as male," Fetterley says. "It insists on its universality at the same time that it defines that universality in specifically male terms." In resisting the obvious meanings, Fetterley argues, women may discover more significant meanings. For instance, Fetterley argues that Faulkner's "A Rose for Emily"

> is a story not of a conflict between the South and the North or between the old order and the new; it is a story of the patriarchy North and South, new and old,

and of the sexual conflict within it. As Faulkner himself has implied, it is a story of a woman victimized and betrayed by the system of sexual politics, who nevertheless has discovered, within the structures that victimize her, sources of power for herself…. "A Rose for Emily" is the story of how to murder your gentlemen caller and get away with it. (34–35)

Fetterley goes on to argue that society made Emily a "lady"; that is, society dehumanized her by elevating her. For instance, Emily's father, seeking to shape her life, stood in the doorway of their house and drove away her suitors. So far as he was concerned, Emily was a nonperson, a creature whose own wishes were not to be regarded; he alone would shape her future. Because society (beginning with her father) made her a "lady"—a creature so elevated that she is not taken seriously as a passionate human being—she is able to kill Homer Barron and not be suspected. Here is Fetterley speaking of the passage in which the townspeople crowd into her house when her death becomes known:

> When the would-be "suitors" finally get into her father's house, they discover the consequences of his oppression of her, for the violence contained in the rotted corpse of Homer Barron is the mirror image of the violence represented in the tableau, the back-flung front door flung back with a vengeance. (42)

Feminist criticism has been concerned not only with the depiction of males and females in a male-determined literary canon and also with female responses to these images, but with yet another topic: women's writing. Many excellent writers of fiction, poetry, and drama have been neglected, it has been argued, simply because they were women. Feminists have further argued that certain forms of writing are especially the province of women—for instance, journals, diaries, and letters—and, predictably, these forms have not been given adequate space in the traditional, male-established canon.

In your own writing, you may or may not adopt one of the points of view just summarized, but inevitably you will adopt *some* point of view, consciously or not; that is, your response to a work will be partly conditioned by your experience even when you try to be objective. Let's look next at two kinds of critical writing that concentrate on the ways in which works of literature are constructed. These methods of criticism emphasize the work as an independent creation, a self-contained unity, something to be studied in itself, not as part of a historical context or an author's life. The emphasis is on the *form* of the work, the relationships between the parts: the construction of the plot, the contrasts between characters, the functions of rhymes, the point of view, and so on. Hence, such criticism is called **formalist criticism.**

Such criticism is, so to speak, *intrinsic* criticism, rather than extrinsic, for it concentrates on the work, independent of its background or its writer. Formalist criticism, of course, begins with a personal response to the literary work, but it goes on to try to account for the response by closely examining the work. It assumes that the author shaped the poem, play, or story so fully that the work guides our responses. The assumption that "meaning" is fully and completely presented within the text is not much in favor today, when many literary critics argue that the active or subjective reader (for instance, Fetterley's "resisting reader") and not the author of the text makes the "meaning." Still, even if one grants that the reader is active, not passive or coolly objective, one may argue that the author is active, too, constructing a text that controls the reader's responses. Of course, during the process of writing about our responses, we may find that our responses change. Presumably, we see with increasing clarity what the work is really like and what it really means.

In any case, formalist criticism tries to explain how and why the work produces its final effect. Like all other criticism, such criticism does not claim to offer its reader a response equal to reading the original work. It claims, however, to explain—at least in some measure—how the construction of the literary work produces a particular response. A critical essay does not claim to do what a literary work itself does, any more than an owner's manual claims to be an automobile. It claims only to show how the thing works, how it produces our responses. In practice, formalist criticism usually takes one of two forms, explication and analysis.

TWO COMMON APPROACHES

Explication

A line-by-line or episode-by-episode commentary on what is going on in a text is an **explication** (literally, unfolding or spreading out). It takes some skill to work one's way along without saying, "In line one ..., in the second line ..., in the third line ...." One must sometimes boldly say something like, "The next stanza begins with ... and then introduces ...." And, of course, one can discuss the second line before the first line if that seems to be the best way of handling the passage.

An explication does not deal with the writer's life or times, and it is not a paraphrase, a rewording—though it may include paraphrase—but a commentary revealing your sense of the meaning of the work. To this end it calls attention, as it proceeds, to the implications of words, the function of rhymes, the shifts in point of view, the development of contrasts, and any other contributions to the meaning.

A Sample Explication: Langston Hughes's "Harlem"

The following short poem is by Langston Hughes (1902–1967), an African-American writer who was born in Joplin, Mississippi, lived part of his youth in Mexico, spent a year at Columbia University, served as a merchant seaman, and worked in a Paris nightclub, where he showed some of his poems to Dr. Alain Locke, a strong advocate of African-American literature. When he returned to the United States, Hughes went on to publish fiction, plays, essays, and biographies; he also founded theaters, gave public readings, and was, in short, an important force.

Harlem

What happens to a dream deferred?

> Does it dry up
> like a raisin in the sun?
> Or fester like a sore—
> And then run?
> Does it stink like rotten meat?
> Or crust and sugar over—
> like a syrupy sweet?
>
> Maybe it just sags
> like a heavy load.
>
> *Or does it explode?*

Different readers will respond at least somewhat differently to any work. On the other hand, since writers want to communicate, they try to control their readers' responses, and they count on their readers to understand the denotations of words as they understand them. Thus, Hughes assumed that his readers knew that Harlem was the site of a large African-American community in New York City. A reader who confuses the title of the poem with Haarlem in the Netherlands will wonder what this poem is saying about the tulip-growing center in northern Holland. Explication is based on the assumption that the poem contains a meaning and that by studying the work thoughtfully we can unfold the meaning or meanings. (The point—which has been disputed—will be brought up again at the end of this discussion of explication.)

Let's assume that the reader understands Hughes is talking about Harlem, New York, and that the "dream deferred" refers to the unfulfilled hopes of African-Americans who live in a dominant white society. But Hughes does not say "hopes," he says "dream," and he does not say "unfulfilled," he says "deferred." You might ask yourself exactly what differences there are between these words. Next, after you have read the poem several times, you might think about which expression is better in the context, "unfulfilled hopes" or "dream deferred," and why.

Working toward an Explication of "Harlem"

Let's turn to an explication of the poem, a detailed examination of the whole. Here are the jottings of one student:

Harlem

These annotations chiefly get at the structure of the poem, the relationship of the parts. The student notices that the poem begins with a line set off by itself and ends with a line set off by itself, and he also notices that each of these lines is a question. Further, he indicates that each of these two lines is emphasized in other ways: the first begins farther to the left than any of the other lines—as though the other lines are subheadings or are in some way subordinate—and the last is italicized.

Some Journal Entries

The student who made these annotations later wrote an entry in his journal:

Feb. 18. Since the title is "Harlem," it's obvious that the "dream" is by African-American people. Also, obvious that Hughes thinks that if the "dream" doesn't become real there may be riots ("explode"). I like "raisin in the sun" (maybe because I like the play), and I like the business about "a syrupy sweet" -- much more pleasant than the festering sore and the rotten meat. But if the dream becomes "sweet,"

what's wrong with that? Why should something "sweet"
explode?

Feb. 21. Prof. McCabe said to think of structure or form of
a poem as a sort of architecture, a building with a foundation, floors, etc., topped by a roof -- but since we read a
poem from top to bottom, it's like a building upside down.
Title is foundation (even though it's at top); last line is
roof, capping the whole. As you read, you add layers. Foundation of "Harlem" is a question (first line). Then, set
back a bit from foundation, or built on it by white space, a
tall room (7 lines high, with 4 questions); then, on top of
this room, another room (two lines, one statement, not a
question). Funny; I thought that in poems all stanzas are
the same number of lines. Then -- more white space, so another unit -- the roof. Man, this roof is going to fall in -- "explodes." Not just the roof, maybe the whole house.

Feb. 21, pm. I get it; one line at start, one line at end;
both are questions, but the last sort of says (because it is
in italics) that it is the most likely answer to the question of the first line. The last line is also a question,
but it's still an answer. The big stanza (7 lines) has 4
questions: 2 lines, 2 lines, 1 line, 2 lines. Maybe the
switch to 1 line is to give some variety, so as not to be
dull? It's exactly in the middle of the poem. I get the
progress from raisin in the sun (dried, but not so
terrible), to festering sore and to stinking meat, but I
still don't see what's so bad about "a syrupy sweet." Is
Hughes saying that after things are very bad they will get
better? But why, then, the explosion at the end?

Feb 23. "Heavy load" and "sags" in next-to-last stanza seems
to me to suggest slaves with bales of cotton, or maybe poor
cotton pickers dragging big sacks of cotton. Or maybe people
doing heavy labor in Harlem. Anyway, very tired. Different
from running sore and stinking meat earlier; not disgusting,
but pressing down, deadening. Maybe worse than a sore or
rotten meat -- a hard, hopeless life. And then the last line.
Just one line, no fancy (and disgusting) simile. Boom! Not
just pressed down and tired, like maybe some racist whites
think (hope?) blacks will be? Bang! Will there be survivors?

Drawing chiefly on these notes, the student jotted down some key ideas
to guide him through a draft of an analysis of the poem. (The organization of

the draft posed no problem; the student simply followed the organization of the poem.)

11 lines; short, but powerful; explosive
Question (first line)
answers (set off by space and also indented)
"raisin in the sun": shrinking
"sore"   } *disgusting*
"rotten meat"
"syrupy sweet": relief from disgusting comparisons
Final question (last line): explosion?
explosive (powerful) because:
short, condensed, packed
in italics
stands by self —like first line
no fancy comparison; very direct

The Final Draft

Here is the final essay:

Langston Hughes's "Harlem"

"Harlem" is a poem that is only eleven lines long, but it is charged with power. It explodes. Hughes sets the stage, so to speak, by telling us in the title that he is talking about Harlem, and then he begins by asking "What happens to a dream deferred?" The rest of the poem is set off by being indented, as though it is the answer to his question. This answer is in three parts (three stanzas, of different lengths).

In a way, it's wrong to speak of the answer, since the rest of the poem consists of questions, but I think Hughes means that each question (for instance, does a "deferred" hope "dry up / like a raisin in the sun?") really is an answer, something that really has happened and that will happen again. The first question, "Does it dry up / like a raisin in the sun?" is a famous line. To compare hope to a raisin dried in the sun is to suggest a terrible shrinking. The next two comparisons are to a "sore" and to "rotten meat." These comparisons are less clever, but they are very effective because they are disgusting. Then, maybe because of the disgusting comparisons, he gives a comparison that is not at all disgusting. In this comparison he says that maybe the "dream deferred" will "crust over -- / like a syrupy sweet."

The seven lines with four comparisons are followed by a stanza of two lines with just one comparison:

Maybe it just sags
like a heavy load.

So if we thought that this postponed dream might finally turn into something "sweet," we were kidding ourselves. Hughes comes down to earth, in a short stanza, with an image of a heavy load, which probably also calls to mind images of people bent under heavy loads, maybe of cotton, or maybe just any sort of heavy load carried by African-Americans in Harlem and elsewhere.

The opening question ("What happens to a dream deferred?") was followed by four questions in seven lines, but now, with "Maybe it just sags / like a heavy load" we get a statement, as though the poet at last has found an answer. But at the end we get one more question, set off by itself and in italics: _"Or does it explode?"_ This line itself is explosive for three reasons: it is short, it is italicized, and it is a stanza in itself. It's also interesting that this line, unlike the earlier lines, does <u>not</u> use a simile. It's almost as though Hughes is saying, "O.K.

```
we've had enough fancy ways of talking about this terrible
situation; here it is, straight."
```

TOPIC FOR DISCUSSION

The student's explication suggests that the comparison with "a syrupy sweet" deliberately misleads the reader into thinking the ending will be happy, and it thus serves to make the real ending even more powerful. In class another student suggested that Hughes may be referring to African-Americans who play Uncle Tom, people who adopt a smiling manner in order to cope with an oppressive society. Which explanation do you prefer, and why? What do you think of combining the two?

Does some method or principle help us decide which interpretation is correct? Can one, in fact, talk about a "correct" interpretation, or only about a plausible or implausible interpretation and an interesting or uninteresting interpretation?

Note: Another explication (of W. B. Yeats's "The Balloon of the Mind") appears in Chapter 7.

Analysis

Explication is a method used chiefly in the study of fairly short poems. Of course, if one has world enough and time, one can set out to explicate all of *Moby-Dick* or *Wuthering Heights* or *Hamlet;* more likely, one will explicate only a paragraph or at most a page in a novel or a speech or two in a play. In writing about works longer than a page or two, a more common approach than explicating is **analyzing** (literally, separating into parts in order to understand). An analysis may consider only the functions of the setting in *Wuthering Heights* or the comedy in *Hamlet* or the differences and resemblances between Willy Loman and King Lear or the changes Shakespeare made when he turned his source into *Julius Caesar.*

Analysis, of course, is not a process used only in talking about literature. It is commonly applied in thinking about almost any complex matter. Martina Navratilova plays a deadly game of tennis. What makes it so good? How does her backhand contribute? What does her serve do to her opponent? Another example: A discussion about the morality of condemning killers to death will distinguish at least between those killers whose actions are premeditated and those whose actions are not. And in the first class it might distinguish between professional killers who carefully contrive a death, killers who are irrational except in their ability to contrive a death, and robbers who contrive a property crime and who kill only when they believe that killing is necessary in order to complete the intended crime. One can hardly talk usefully about capital punishment without making some such analysis of killers. And so it makes sense if you are writing about literature—say, about Gatsby's "dream" in Fitzgerald's *The Great Gatsby*—to try to see the components of the dream. One critic begins a discussion of it thus:

> Gatsby's dream divides into three basic and related parts: the desire to repeat the past, the desire for money, and the desire for incarnation of "unutterable visions" in the material earth.
>
> Ernest H. Lockridge, *Twentieth Century Interpretations of "The Great Gatsby"* (Englewood Cliffs, N.J., 1968), p. 11.

And, of course, the essayist goes on to study these three components in detail.

Although Chapters 1 and 2 include specimens of analytic criticism, another example may be useful here.

Suppose you have noticed that singers of blues often sing about traveling. Maybe you recall the lines,

> When a woman takes the blues
> She tucks her head and cries
> But when a man catches the blues,
> He catches a freight and rides,

and you wonder, among other things, "Why all this talk of traveling?" You decide you want to look into something along these lines, and so you search your memory of blues, play whatever records are available, read some anthologies that print blues lyrics, and generally try to set your thoughts in order. You find that blues often talk about traveling but that the travel is not all of the same sort, and you begin to analyze (separate into parts) the blues that use this motif. You begin to jot down words or phrases:

```
disappointed lover

travel to a job

from the South

fantasy travel

back to the South

life is a trip

my first trip out of the state

jail
```

You are making a scratch outline, for you are establishing categories, fiddling with them until you have established categories as nearly coordinate as possible; and you are indicating the order in which you will discuss them. You rearrange them as you refine your thinking because your essay will not record your thought processes—with all the false steps—as they occurred; the finished essay will record your best thoughts in the order that you judge to be best for a reader. Then perhaps you find it useful to describe your categories a bit more fully:

1. Travel as an escape from unhappy love
2. Travel as an economic necessity when jobs are not available at home
3. Travel as an escape from the South to the North
4. Travel as an escape from the North back to the South
5. Travel as sheer wishful thinking, an image of escape from the unhappiness of life until death releases one
6. Travel as an image of the hard job of living, as in "It's a long old road, but I'm gonna find the end"
7. Enforced travel—to prison

You have now taken the theme of travel and separated it into various parts, not for the fun of inventing complications but for the sake of educating yourself and your reader. Having made these or similar distinctions, you can go on to say some interesting things about one or all of these superficially similar but really rather different motifs of travel. You have had to divide "travel" into parts before you can answer the question you began with: "Why all this talk about traveling?" Perhaps your answer—your point or your **thesis**—is that talking about travel is a way of talking about life.

Once you have established your categories and tentatively settled on the order in which you will treat them, your job is half done. You have arrived at a thesis, assembled evidence to persuade the reader to accept the thesis, and begun to organize your essay. Possibly your finished essay will make the following points, in the order given but with convincing detail (perhaps some quotations from blues) to support them:

1. Singers of blues sing of traveling, but the travel is of various sorts. (Note: In your opening paragraph you may want to announce your thesis and to indicate the organization your paper will have. Such a paragraph will be a help to both the writer and the reader. These matters need not be stated formally unless your instructor asks you to do so.)

2. Often people travel because of economic, social, or even physical pressure (to get a job; to get to a more congenial environment in the urban North—or back to the rural South; to go to jail).

3. Most often, however, and perhaps in the most memorable songs, it is for another reason: It is an attempt to reduce the pain of some experiences, especially betrayed love, and the hearer senses that the attempt cannot succeed.

4. In such songs it is usually the men who travel, because they are more mobile than women (women are left to take care of the children), but whether it is the man who has deserted the woman or the woman who has deserted the man, both are pathetic figures because even the deserter will be haunted by the memory of the beloved.

5. All these variations on the theme of travel overlap, and almost always you sense that the trip—whether to the North or the South, to a job or to jail, to a man or to a woman, or to nowhere in particular—is an image or metaphor for the trip through life, the long, painful road that everyone must walk.

Comparison: An Analytic Tool

Analysis frequently involves comparing: Things are examined for their resemblances to and differences from other things. Strictly speaking, if one emphasizes the differences rather than the similarities, one is contrasting rather than comparing, but we need not preserve this distinction; we can call both processes *comparing*.

Although your instructor may ask you to write a comparison of two works of literature, the *subject* of the essay is the works; comparison is simply an effective analytic technique to show some of the qualities in the works. You might compare Chopin's use of nature in "The Story of an Hour" (page 12) with the use of nature in another story, in order to reveal the subtle differences between the stories, but a comparison of works utterly unlike can hardly tell the reader or the writer anything.

Something should be said about organizing a comparison, say between the settings in two stories, between two characters in a novel (or even between a character at the end of a novel and the same character at the beginning), or between the symbolism of two poems. Probably, a student's first thought after making some jottings is to discuss one half of the comparison and then go on to the second half. Instructors and textbooks (though not this one) usually condemn such an organization, arguing that the essay breaks into two parts and that the second part involves a good deal of repetition of categories set up in the first part. Usually, they recommend that the students organize their thoughts differently, somewhat along these lines:

1. First similarity
   a. first work (or character, or characteristic)
   b. second work
2. Second similarity
   a. first work
   b. second work
3. First difference
   a. first work
   b. second work
4. Second difference
   a. first work
   b. second work

and so on, for as many additional differences as seem relevant. If one wishes to compare *Huckleberry Finn* with *The Catcher in the Rye,* one may organize the material thus:

1. First similarity: the narrator and his quest
   a. Huck
   b. Holden
2. Second similarity: the corrupt world surrounding the narrator
   a. society in *Huck*
   b. society in *Catcher*
3. First difference: degree to which the narrator fulfills his quest and escapes from society
   a. Huck's plan to "light out" to the frontier
   b. Holden's breakdown

Another way of organizing a comparison and contrast:

1. First point: the narrator and his quest
   a. similarities between Huck and Holden
   b. differences between Huck and Holden
2. Second point: the corrupt world
   a. similarities between the worlds in *Huck* and *Catcher*
   b. differences between the worlds in *Huck* and *Catcher*
3. Third point: degree of success
   a. similarities between Huck and Holden
   b. differences between Huck and Holden

A comparison need not employ either of these structures. There is even the danger that an essay employing either of them may not come into focus until the essayist stands back from the seven-layer cake and announces in the concluding paragraph that the odd layers taste better. In one's preparatory thinking, one may want to make comparisons in pairs (good-natured humor: the clown in *Othello,* the clownish grave-digger in *Hamlet;* social satire: the clown in *Othello,* the grave-digger in *Hamlet;* relevance to main theme: ...; length of role: ...; comments by other characters: ...), but one must come to some conclusions about what these add up to before writing the final version. This final version should not duplicate the thought processes; rather, it should be organized so as to make the point—the thesis—clearly and effectively. After reflection, one may believe that although there are superficial similarities between the clown in *Othello* and the clownish grave-digger in *Hamlet,* there are essential differences; then in the finished essay one probably will not wish to obscure the main point by jumping back and forth from play to play, working through a series of similarities and differences. It may be better to discuss the clown in *Othello* and then to point out that, although the grave-digger in *Hamlet* resembles him in A, B, and C, the grave-digger also has other functions (D, E, and F) and is of greater consequence to *Hamlet* than the clown is to *Othello*. Some repetition in the second half of the essay ("The grave-digger's puns come even faster than the clown's....") will bind the two halves into a meaningful whole, making clear the degree of similarity or difference. The point of the essay presumably is not to list pairs of similarities or differences but to illuminate a work or works by making thoughtful comparisons.

Although in a long essay one cannot postpone until page 30 a discussion of the second half of the comparison, in an essay of, say, fewer than ten pages nothing is wrong with setting forth one half of the comparison and then, in light of it, the second half. The essay will break into two unrelated parts if the second half makes no use of the first or if it fails to modify the first half, but not if the second half looks back to the first half and calls attention to differences that the new material reveals. Students ought to learn how to write an essay with interwoven comparisons, but they ought also to know that a comparison may be written in another, simpler and clearer way.

The following summary, paragraph by paragraph, of Stanley Kauffmann's comparison of film versions of Joyce's *Ulysses* and *Finnegans Wake* gives an idea of how a comparison can be treated. Kauffmann's essay, published in the *New American Review #2*, is, of course, filled with concrete details that here are omitted, but the gist of the eleven paragraphs is as follows:

1. Because subjectivity fascinates filmmakers, it is natural that Joyce's two great novels of subjectivity would be filmed. One film is good, the other poor.
2. The poor film is *Ulysses,* a book that summarizes a vast amount of life.
3. The film of *Ulysses* has two motifs: tolerance and sexual candor. But these are only minor parts of the novel.
4. The film cannot be said to be faithful to the novel. True, it adds almost nothing; but it omits an enormous amount.
5. Some things, of course, simply cannot be filmed, and so let us look at what is present rather than what is absent in the film. The opening is good, but ..., and ..., and ... are poor.
6. In general, the acting is poor.
7. On the other hand, the film of *Finnegans Wake* is pretty successful, capturing the effect of a dream.
8. Though a bit long and with some of the faults of the film of *Ulysses,* the film of *Finnegans Wake* is interesting, imaginative, and inventive.
9. The director uses subtitles, an effective device because Joyce's words (often puns) are "visual objects."
10. The actors effectively convey in their lines the sense of a dream.
11. The film of *Finnegans Wake* captures the mythical quality that the film of *Ulysses* fails to capture.

As this skeleton of the essay shows, Kauffmann introduces both halves of the comparison in his opening paragraph. Paragraphs 2–6 concentrate on one half (the film of *Ulysses*); paragraphs 7–8 concentrate on the second half of the comparison, but they remind the reader of the first half; paragraphs 9–10 discuss more fully the second—more important—film; and paragraph 11, the conclusion, offers a final judgment on both films.

Finally, a reminder: the purpose of a comparison is to call attention to the unique features of something by holding it up against something similar but significantly different. You can compare Macbeth with Banquo (two men who hear a prophecy but who respond differently), or Macbeth with Lady Macbeth (a husband and wife, both eager to be monarchs but differing in their sense of the consequences), or Hamlet and Holden Caulfield (two people who see themselves as surrounded by a corrupt world), but you can hardly compare Holden with Macbeth or with Lady Macbeth—there simply aren't enough points of resemblance to make it worth your effort to call attention to subtle differences. If the differences are great and apparent, a comparison is a waste of effort. ("Blueberries are different from elephants. Blueberries do not have trunks. And elephants do not grow on bushes.") Indeed, a comparison between essentially and evidently unlike things can only obscure, for by making the comparison the writer implies that significant similarities do exist, and readers can only wonder why they do not see them. The essays that do break into two halves are essays that make uninstructive comparisons: the first half tells the reader about five qualities in Charles Dickens, the second half tells the reader about five different qualities in Virginia Woolf.

A Note on Writing a Summary

One other point: The essay on "The Story of an Hour" in Chapter 2 does not include a *summary* because the writer knew that all of her readers were thoroughly familiar with Chopin's story. Sometimes, however, it is advisable to summarize the work you are writing about, thus reminding a reader who has not read the work recently, or even informing a reader who may never have read the work. A review of a new work of literature or of a new film, for instance, usually includes a summary, on the assumption that readers are unfamiliar with it.

A summary is a brief restatement or condensation of the plot. Consider this summary of Chopin's "The Story of an Hour."

> A newspaper office reports that Brently Mallard has been killed in a railroad accident. When the news is gently broken to Mrs. Mallard by her sister Josephine, Mrs. Mallard weeps wildly and then shuts herself up in her room, where she sinks into an armchair. Staring dully through the window, she sees the signs of spring, and then an unnameable sensation possesses her. She tries to reject it but finally abandons herself to it. Renewed, she exults in her freedom, in

the thought that at last the days will be her own. She finally comes out of the room, embraces her sister, and descends the stairs. A moment later her husband—who in fact had not been in the accident—enters. Mrs. Mallard dies—of the joy that kills, according to the doctors' diagnosis.

Here are a few principles that govern summaries:

1. A summary is much briefer than the original. It is not a paraphrase—a word-by-word translation of someone's words into your own. A paraphrase is usually at least as long as the original, whereas a summary is rarely longer than one-fourth of the original and is usually much shorter. A novel may be summarized in a few paragraphs, or even in one paragraph.

2. A summary usually achieves its brevity by omitting almost all of the concrete details of the original and by omitting minor characters and episodes. Notice that the summary of "The Story of an Hour" omits the friend of the family, omits specifying the signs of spring, and omits the business of the sister imploring Mrs. Mallard to open the door.

3. A summary is as accurate as possible, given the limits of space.

4. A summary is normally written in the present tense. Thus "A newspaper office reports ..., Mrs. Mallard weeps ...."

5. Because a summary is openly based on someone else's writing and you do not claim that it presents your own ideas or even your own words, you need not use quotation marks around any words that you take from the original. Thus, after some such lead-in as "Kate Chopin's 'The Story of an Hour' may be summarized thus," you need not say such things as "Chopin then goes on to tell us that Mrs. Mallard ...."

6. If the summary is brief (say, fewer than 250 words), it may be given as a single paragraph. If you are summarizing a long work, you may feel that a longer summary is needed. In this case your reader will be grateful to you if you divide the summary into paragraphs. As you draft your summary, you may find natural divisions. For instance, the scene of the story may change midway, providing you with the opportunity to use two paragraphs. Or you may want to summarize a five-act play in five paragraphs.

Summaries have their place in essays, but remember that a summary is not an analysis; it is only a summary.

FINDING A TOPIC

All literary works afford their own topics for analysis, and all essayists must set forth their own theses, but a few useful generalizations may be made. You can often find a thesis by asking one of two questions:

1. *What is this doing?* That is, why is this scene in the novel or play? Why is Beckett's *Waiting for Godot* in two acts, rather than one or three? Why the biblical allusions in *Waiting for Godot?* Why is the clown in *Othello?* Why are these lines unrhymed? Why is this stanza form employed? What is the significance of the parts of the work? (Titles are often highly significant parts of the work: Ibsen explained that he called his play *Hedda Gabler* rather than *Hedda Tesman* because "She is to be regarded rather as her father's daughter than as her husband's wife." Ibsen's *Ghosts*, Kesey's *One Flew over the Cuckoo's Nest*, and Roth's *Great American Novel* would be slightly different things if they had other titles. Beckett's *En attendant Godot*—*Waiting for Godot*—was originally entitled *En attendant*, that is, *Waiting*. Why the change?)

2. *Why do I have this response?* Why do I find this poem clever or moving or puzzling? How did the author make this character funny or dignified or pathetic? How did he or she communicate the idea that this character is a bore without boring me? Why am I troubled by the representation of women in this story? Why do I regard as sexist this lover's expression of his love?

The first of these questions, "What is this doing?" requires that you identify yourself with the author, wondering, for example, whether this opening scene is the best possible for this story. The second question, "Why do I have this response?" requires that you trust your feelings. If you are amused or bored or puzzled or annoyed, assume that these responses are appropriate and follow them up, at least until a rereading of the work provides other responses.

The chapters on fiction, drama, poetry, film, and the essay try to provide the relevant critical vocabulary; they also try to do two other things: suggest the sorts of problems critics write about, and offer paragraphs that can serve as models of critical writing. After reading the chapter on fiction, for example, you should have not only an idea of what plot, symbolism, and setting are but also an idea of how some people write about them. It is primarily from those chapters and from your instructor and, above all, from your own responses to literature that you should get help in developing your sense of appropriate topics, but a few examples are offered here.

Caution: For the sake of clarity, these topics are stated baldly. They are rough beginnings and need to be shaped into theses. Consider the difference between "Hamlet's Relationship to Horatio" (an unshaped topic) and the thesis you might work out: "Although Hamlet admires Horatio's stoic temperament and values his companionship, Hamlet's temperament is more heroic."

Sample Topics in Fiction

PLOT

"Death as a Device to Link Episodes in *Huckleberry Finn*"

"The Appropriateness of the Ending of *Lord of the Flies*"

THEME

"Does the End of *Huckleberry Finn* Violate the Meaning of the Rest of the Work?"

"The 'Phoniness' of Middle-Class Morality in *The Catcher in the Rye*"

"Race Relations in Ellison's 'Battle Royal'"

"The Female as Victim in Melville's 'The Tartarus of Maids'"

"Paralysis in Joyce's *Dubliners*"

"Love and Marriage in the Short Fiction of Virginia Woolf"

"Original Sin in Flannery O'Connor's 'A Good Man Is Hard to Find'"

CHARACTER

(Sometimes a mere character sketch may be acceptable; more often, one will study character to see how it contributes to the theme or how it helps define another character.)

"Huck Finn's Distinctive Language"

"A Comparison Between the Widow Douglas in *Tom Sawyer* and the Widow Douglas in *Huckleberry Finn*"

"What Holden Caulfield Is *Really* Like"

"Holden Caulfield: Adolescent Snob or Suffering Saint?"

"Why Does the Narrator in 'The Yellow Wallpaper' Become Insane"

"Dilsey and Joe Christmas: The Poles of Faulkner's Conception of the Role of African-Americans"

FORESHADOWING

(Really an aspect of plot and character.)

"Are We Adequately Prepared for Huck's Decision to 'Light Out for the Territory'?"

"Suspense and Surprise in ..."

"The Humor of the Unexpected"

"Preparation for the Ending in Jackson's 'The Lottery'"

SETTING

"The River versus Civilization in *Huckleberry Finn*"

"The Doctor's Office and the Pig-Parlor in Flannery O'Connor's 'Revelation'"

"The Function of the Setting in ..."

SYMBOLISM

"The River in *Huckleberry Finn*"

"Walls in 'Bartleby'"

"Light in O'Connor's 'Revelation'"

"Water in Chopin's *The Awakening*"

POINT OF VIEW

"If *Huckleberry Finn* Were Narrated by the Widow Douglas Instead of by Huck, ..."

"Objectivity in Hemingway's 'Hills Like White Elephants'"

"The Unreliable Narrator in ..."

Sample Topics in Drama

When writing about a play, you may find a topic similar to one of those given in the preceding paragraphs. But in addition to those centering on theme, character, foreshadowing, setting, and symbolism, you may find the following examples useful:

IRONY

"Unconscious Irony in *Macbeth*"

"Conscious Irony in Shaw's *Major Barbara*"

TRAGEDY

"Macbeth: Hero or Villain?"

"A Comparison Between King Oedipus and Willy Loman"

"Willy Loman and Arthur Miller's Theory of Tragedy"

"Is Nora Helmer a Tragic Figure?"

"*The Emperor Jones*: Eugene O'Neill and the African-American as Tragic Hero"

COMEDY

"The Comic in the Tragic: Beckett's *Waiting for Godot*"

"The Comic Portrayal of Villainy in ..."

"Racist Implications in the Characterization of the Comic African-American"

PLOT

"Surprise versus Suspense in *Macbeth*"

"Coincidence in *A Doll's House*"

"Flashbacks in *Death of a Salesman*"

"Foreshadowing in *Raisin in the Sun*"

GESTURE

"Appropriate Gestures for Macbeth in the Banquet Scene"

"Suggestions of Laurel and Hardy and of Chaplin in *Waiting for Godot*"

Sample Topics in Poetry

VOICE

"The Unawareness of Egotism: The Duke in 'My Last Duchess'"

"New England Voices in Frost's Poems"

"Emily Dickinson's Ironic Self-Deprecation"

DICTION

"The Use of Colloquialisms in Frost"

"The Language of the Blues in a Poem by Langston Hughes"

"Patterns of African-American Speech in Amiri Baraka"

FIGURATIVE LANGUAGE

"Scientific Imagery as a Vehicle for Passion"

"Images of Destructive Passion in Adrienne Rich"

"Organic Metaphors in a Poem by Whitman"

SYMBOLISM

"Frost's Woods and Stars"

"Biblical Symbolism in a Spiritual"

STRUCTURE

"Logic and Illogic in …"

"Paradox in …"

"The Movement from Anger to Resignation in …"

"The Development of the Theme, Stanza by Stanza, in …"

IRONY

"Understatement as a Means of Protest in American Folk Ballads "

"The Speaker's Conscious versus Unconscious Irony in Browning's 'My Last Duchess'"

PATTERNS OF SOUND

"Rhyme and Reason in ..."

"The Not-So-Free Verse of 'When Lilacs Last in the Dooryard Bloom'd'"

"The Influence of the Blues on Some Modern Poets"

Topics for essays on film often resemble those for essays on fiction and drama, but because of special problems, discussion of the matter is postponed until Chapter 8, "Writing about Films."

CONSIDERING THE EVIDENCE

Once your responses have led you to a topic ("The Clown in *Othello*") and then to a thesis ("The clown is relevant"), be certain that you have all the evidence. Usually this means that you should study the context of the material you are discussing. For example, if you are writing about *The Catcher in the Rye,* before you argue that because Holden distrusts the adult world, "old" is his ultimate word of condemnation, remember that he speaks of "old Phoebe" and of "old Thomas Hardy," both of whom he values greatly. Before you argue that the style of *Romeo and Juliet* is highly formal, remember that it includes such lines as "Where's Potpan, that he helps not to take away? He shift a trencher! He scrape a trencher!" (The play *does* have a good deal of highly formal writing, and an essay can be written on it, but the essayist should be aware that the play has other styles, too.) Before you argue that the imagery in *Romeo and Juliet* associates the lovers with light and death with dark, remember that not every image of light and dark works in this way. At the beginning of the play several extended passages associate the infatuated Romeo with darkness. The discrepancy can be explained; it must be explained.

ORGANIZING THE MATERIAL

"'Begin at the beginning,' the King said very gravely, 'and go on till you come to the end: then stop.'" This is how your paper should seem to the reader, but it need not have been drafted thus. In fact, unless you are supremely gifted, you will (like the rest of us) have to work very hard to make things easy for the reader.

After locating a topic, converting it into a thesis, and weighing the evidence, a writer has the job of organizing the material into a coherent whole, a sequence of paragraphs that holds the reader's interest (partly because it sets forth material clearly) and that steadily builds up an effective argument. Notice that in the essay on irony (pp. 24–25) in Kate Chopin's "The Story of an

Hour," the student wisely moves from the lesser ironies to the chief irony. To begin with the chief irony and end with the lesser ironies would almost surely be anticlimactic.

The organization of an essay will, of course, depend on the nature of the essay: An essay on foreshadowing in *Macbeth* probably will be organized chronologically (material in the first act will be discussed before material in the second act), but an essay on the character of Macbeth may conceivably begin with the end of the play, discussing Macbeth as he is in the fifth act, and then may work backward through the play, arriving at last at the original Macbeth, so to speak, of the beginning of the play. (This is not to suggest that such an organization be regularly employed in writing about a character—only that it might be employed effectively.) Or suppose one is writing about whether Macbeth is a victim of fate. The problem might be stated, and the essayist might go on to take up one view and then the other. Which view should be set forth first? Probably it will be best to let the reader first hear the view that will be refuted, so that you can build to a climax.

The important point is not that there is only one way to organize an essay, but that an essayist find the way that seems best for the particular topic and argument. Once you think you know more or less what you want to say, you will usually, after trial and error, find what seems the best way of communicating it to a reader. A scratch outline (see p. 39) will help you find your way, but don't assume that once you have settled on an outline the organization of your essay finally is established. After you read the draft that you base on your outline, you may realize that a more effective organization will be more helpful to your reader—which means that you must move paragraphs around, revise your transitions, and, in short, produce another draft.

COMMUNICATING JUDGMENTS

Because a critical essay is a judicious attempt to help a reader see what is going on in a work or in a part of a work, the voice of the critic usually sounds, on first hearing, impartial; but good criticism includes—at least implicitly—evaluation. The critic may say not only that the setting changes (a neutral expression) but also that "the novelist aptly shifts the setting" or "unconvincingly describes ..." or "effectively juxtaposes ...." These evaluations are supported with evidence. The critic has feelings about the work under discussion and reveals them, not by continually saying "I feel" and "this moves me," but by calling attention to the degree of success or failure perceived. Nothing is wrong with occasionally using "I," and noticeable avoidances of it—"it is seen that," "this writer," "the present writer," "we," and the like— suggest an offensive sham modesty; but too much talk of "I" makes a writer sound like an egomaniac.

Consider this sentence from the opening paragraph in a review of George Orwell's *1984*.

> I do not think I have ever read a novel more frightening and depressing; and yet, such are the originality, the suspense, the speed of writing and withering indignation that it is impossible to put the book down.

Fine—provided that the reviewer goes on to offer evidence that enables readers to share his or her evaluation of *1984*.

One final remark on communicating judgments: Write sincerely. Any attempt to neglect your own thoughtful responses and replace them with fabrications designed to please an instructor will surely fail. It is hard enough to find the words that clearly communicate your responses; it is almost impossible to find the words that express your hunch about what your instructor expects your responses to be. George Orwell shrewdly commented on the obvious signs of insincere writing: "When there is a gap between one's real and one's declared aims, one turns as it were instinctively to long words and exhausted idioms, like a cuttlefish squirting out ink."

REVIEW: HOW TO WRITE AN EFFECTIVE ESSAY

All writers must work out their own procedures and rituals (John C. Calhoun liked to plow his farm before writing), but the following suggestions may provide some help. The writing process may be divided into four stages—Pre-writing, Drafting, Revising, and Editing—though as the following discussion admits, the stages are not always neatly separate.

1. Pre-Writing

Read the work carefully. You may, on this first reading, want to highlight or annotate certain things, such as passages that please or that puzzle, or you may prefer simply to read it through. In any case, on a second reading you will certainly want to annotate the text and to jot down notes either in the margins or in a journal. You probably are not focusing on a specific topic, but rather are taking account of your early responses to the work.

If you have a feeling or an idea, jot it down; don't assume that you will remember it when you get around to drafting your essay. Write it down so that you will be sure to remember it and so that in the act of writing it down you can improve it. Later, after reviewing your notes (whether in the margins or in a journal) you'll probably find that it's a good idea to transfer your best points to three-by-five inch cards, writing on one side only. By putting the material on cards, you can easily group related points later.

2. Drafting

After reviewing your notes and sorting them out, you will probably find that you have not only a topic (a subject to write about) but a thesis (a point to be made, an argument). Get it down on paper. Perhaps begin by jotting down your thesis and under it a tentative outline. (If you have transferred your preliminary notes to index cards, you can easily arrange the cards into a tentative organization.)

If you are writing an explication, the order probably is essentially the order of the lines or of the episodes. If you are writing an analysis, you may wish to organize your essay from the lesser material to the greater (to avoid anticlimax) or from the simple to the complex (to ensure intelligibility). If you are discussing the roles of three characters in a story, it may be best to build up to the one of the three that you think the most important. If you are comparing two characters, it may be best to move from the most obvious contrasts to the least obvious.

At this stage, however, don't worry about whether the organization is unquestionably the best possible organization for your topic. A page of paper with some ideas in some sort of sequence, however rough, will encourage you that you do have something to say. If you have doubts, by all means record them. By writing down your uncertainties, you will probably begin to feel your way toward tentative explanations of them.

Almost any organization will help you get going on your draft; that is, it will help you start writing an essay. The process of writing will itself clarify and improve your preliminary ideas. If you are like most people, you can't do much precise thinking until you have committed to paper at least a rough sketch of your initial ideas. Later, you can push and polish your ideas into shape, perhaps even deleting all of them and starting over, but it's a lot easier to improve your ideas once you see them in front of you than it is to do the job in your head. On paper, one word leads to another; in your head, one word often blocks another.

Just keep going; you may realize, as you near the end of a sentence, that you no longer believe it. Okay; be glad that your first idea led you to a better one, and pick up your better one and keep going with it. What you are doing is, in a sense, by trial and error pushing your way not only toward clear expression but toward sharper ideas and richer responses.

Although we have been talking about drafting, most teachers rightly regard this first effort at organizing one's notes and turning them into an essay not as a first draft but as a zero draft, really a part of pre-writing. When you reread it, you will doubtless find passages that need further support, passages that seem out of place, and passages that need clarification. You will also find passages that are better than you thought at the outset you could produce. In any case, on rereading the zero draft you will find things that will require you to go back and check the work of literature and to think further about what you have said about it. After rereading the literary work and your draft, you are in a position to write something that can rightly be called a first draft.

3. Revising

Try to allow at least a day to elapse before you start to revise your zero draft and another day before you revise your first draft. If you come to the material with a relatively fresh eye, you may see, for example, that the thesis needs to be announced earlier or more clearly or that certain points need to be supported by concrete references—perhaps by brief quotations from the literary work. A review by your peers will give you a good sense of which things need clarification and of whether your discussion is adequately organized.

4. Editing

Small-scale revision, such as checking the spelling, punctuation, and accuracy of quotations, is usually called *editing*. Even when you get to this stage, you may unexpectedly find that you must make larger revisions. In checking a quotation, for instance, you may find that it doesn't really support the point you are making, so you may have to do some substantial revising.

Time has run out. Type or write a clean copy, following the principles concerning margins, pagination, and documentation set forth later in this book. If you have borrowed any ideas, be sure to give credit to your sources. Finally, proofread and make corrections as explained on pages 220–221.

The whole process of writing about literature, then, is really a process of responding and of revising one's responses—not only one's responses to the work of literature but also to one's own writing about those responses. When you jot down a note and then jot down a further thought (perhaps even rejecting the earlier note) and then turn this material into a paragraph and then revise the paragraph, you are in the company of Picasso, who said that in painting a picture he advanced by a series of destructions. You are also following Mrs. Beeton's famous recipe:

First catch your hare, then cook it.

Part Two

4
Writing about Essays

The word *essay* entered the English language in 1597, when Francis Bacon called a small book of ten short prose pieces *Essays*. Bacon borrowed the word from Michel de Montaigne, a French writer who in 1580 had published some short prose pieces under the title *Essais*—that is, "testings" or "attempts," from the French verb *essayer,* "to try." Montaigne's title indicated that his graceful and personal jottings—the fruit of pleasant study and meditation—were not fully thought-out treatises but rather sketches that could be amplified and amended.

If you keep a journal, you are working in Montaigne's tradition. You jot down your tentative thoughts, perhaps your responses to a work of literature, partly to find out what you think and how you feel. Montaigne said, in the preface to his book, "I am myself the subject of my book," and in all probability you are the real subject of your journal. Your entries, recorded responses to other writers and your reflections on those responses, require you to examine yourself.

THE ESSAYIST'S PERSONA

Many of the essays that give readers the most pleasure are, like entries in a journal, chiefly reflective. An essay of this kind sets forth the writer's attitudes or states of mind, and the reader's interest in the essay is almost entirely in the way the writer sees things. It's not so much *what* the writers see and say as *how* they say what they see. Even in narrative essays—essays that recount events, for example, a bit of biography—our interest is more in the essayists' *responses* to the events than in the events themselves. When we read an essay, we almost say, "So that's how it feels to be you," and "Tell me more about the way you see things." The bit of history is less important than the memorable presence of the writer.

When you read an essay, try to imagine the kind of person who wrote it, the kind of person who seems to be speaking it. Then slowly reread the essay, noticing *how* the writer conveyed this personality or persona or "voice" (even while he or she was writing about a topic "out there"). The writer's persona may be revealed, for example, by common or uncommon words, by short or long sentences, by literal or figurative language, or by offering familiar or erudite examples.

Let's take a simple, familiar example of words that establish a persona. Lincoln begins the Gettysburg Address with "Four score and seven years ago." He might have said "Eighty-seven years ago"—but the language would have lacked the biblical echo, and the persona would have been that of an ordinary person rather than that of a man who has about him something of the tone of an Old Testament prophet. This religious tone is entirely fitting, since President Lincoln was speaking at the dedication of a cemetery for "these hallowed dead" and was urging the audience to give all of their energies to ensure that the dead men had not died in vain. By such devices as the choice of words, the length of sentences, and the sorts of evidence offered, an author sounds to the reader solemn or agitated or witty or genial or severe. If you read Martin Luther King's "I Have a Dream," you will notice that he begins his essay (originally it was a speech, delivered at the Lincoln Memorial on the one-hundredth anniversary of Lincoln's Emancipation Proclamation) with these words: "Five score years ago ...." King is deliberately echoing Lincoln's words, partly in tribute to Lincoln but also to help establish himself as the spiritual descendent of Lincoln and, further back, of the founders of the Judaeo-Christian tradition.

Tone

Only by reading closely can we hear in the mind's ear the writer's tone—whether it is ironic or earnestly straightforward, indignant or genial. Perhaps you have heard the line from Owen Wister's novel *The Virginian:* "When you call me that, smile." Words spoken with a smile mean something different from the same words forced through clenched teeth. But while speakers can communicate or, we might say, can guide the responses of their audience by body language and gestures, by facial expressions, and by changes in tone of voice, writers have only words in ink on paper. As a writer, you are learning control of tone as you learn to take pains in your choice of words, in the way you arrange sentences, and even in the punctuation marks you may find yourself changing in your final draft. These skills will pay off doubly if you apply them to your reading by putting yourself in the place of the writer whose work you are reading. As a reader, you must make some effort to "hear" the writer's tone as part of the meaning the words communicate. Skimming is not adequate to that task. Thinking carefully about the works means, first of all, reading them carefully, listening for the sound of the speaking voice so that you can respond to the persona—the personality or character the author presents in the essay.

WRITING ABOUT AN ESSAYIST'S STYLE

Since much of the pleasure we receive from an essay is derived from the essayist's style—the *how* with which an essayist conveys an attitude toward some aspect of reality that is revealed—your instructor may ask you to analyze the writer's style.

Read the following essay by Joan Didion. While reading it, annotate it wherever you are inclined (you may want to express responses in the margin and to underline puzzling words or passages that strike you as especially effective or as especially clumsy). Then reread the essay; since you will now be familiar with the essay as a whole, you may want to make further annotations, such as brief comments on Didion's use of repetition or of short and long sentences.

Joan Didion, a fifth-generation Californian, was born in Sacramento in 1934. In 1956 she was graduated from the University of California, Berkeley, and in the same year she published her first story and won a contest sponsored by *Vogue* magazine. Since then she has written essays, stories, screenplays, and novels. All of her writing, she says, is an "act of saying *I,* of imposing oneself upon other people, of saying *listen to me, see it my way, change your mind.*"

Los Angeles Notebook
Joan Didion

There is something uneasy in the Los Angeles air this afternoon, some unnatural stillness, some tension. What it means is that tonight a Santa Ana will begin to blow, a hot wind from the northeast whining down through the Cajon and San Gorgonio Passes, blowing up sandstorms out along Route 66, drying the hills and nerves to the flash point. For a few days now we will see smoke back in the canyons, and hear sirens in the night. I have neither heard nor read that a Santa Ana is due, but I know it, and almost everyone I have seen today knows it too. We know it because we feel it. The baby frets. The maid sulks. I rekindle a waning argument with the telephone company, then cut my losses and lie down, given over to whatever it is in the air. To live with the Santa Ana is to accept, consciously or unconsciously, a deeply mechanistic view of human behavior.

I recall being told, when I first moved to Los Angeles and was living on an isolated beach, that the Indians would throw themselves into the sea when the bad wind blew. I could see why. The Pacific turned ominously glossy during a Santa Ana period, and one woke in the night troubled not only by the peacocks screaming in the olive trees but by the eerie absence of surf. The heat was surreal. The sky had a yellow cast, the kind of light sometimes called "earthquake weather." My only neighbor would not come out of her house for days, and there were no lights at night, and her husband roamed the place with a machete. One day he would tell me that he had heard a trespasser, the next a rattlesnake.

"On nights like that," Raymond Chandler once wrote about the Santa Ana,   3
"every booze party ends in a fight, meek little wives feel the edge of the carving knife and study their husband's necks. Anything can happen." That was the kind of wind it was. I did not know then that there was any basis for the effect it had on all of us, but it turns out to be another of these cases in which science bears out folk wisdom. The Santa Ana, which is named for one of the canyons it rushes through, is a *foehn* wind, like the *foehn* of Austria and Switzerland and the *hamsin* of Israel. There are a number of persistent malevolent winds, perhaps the best known of which are the mistral of France and the Mediterranean sirocco, but a *foehn* wind has distinct characteristics: it occurs on the leeward slope of a mountain range and, although the air begins as a cold mass, it is warmed as it comes down the mountain and appears finally as a hot dry wind. Whenever and wherever a *foehn* blows, doctors hear about headaches and nausea and allergies, about "nervousness," about "depression." In Los Angeles some teachers do not attempt to conduct formal classes during a Santa Ana because the children become unmanageable. In Switzerland the suicide rate goes up during the *foehn,* and in the courts of some Swiss cantons the wind is considered a mitigating circumstance for crime. Surgeons are said to watch the wind, because blood does not clot normally during a *foehn*. A few years ago an Israeli physicist discovered that not only during such winds, but for the ten or twelve hours which precede them, the air carries an unusually high ratio of positive to negative ions. No one seems to know exactly why that should be; some talk about friction and others suggest solar disturbances. In any case the positive ions are there, and what an excess of positive ions does, in the simplest terms, is make people unhappy. One cannot get much more mechanistic than that.

Easterners commonly complain that there is no "weather" at all in South-   4
ern California, that the days and the seasons slip by relentlessly, numbingly bland. That is quite misleading. In fact the climate is characterized by infrequent but violent extremes: two periods of torrential subtropical rains which continue for several weeks and wash out the hills and send subdivisions sliding toward the sea; about twenty scattered days a year of the Santa Ana, which, with its incendiary dryness, invariably means fire. At the first prediction of a Santa Ana, the Forest Service flies men and equipment from northern California into the southern forests, and the Los Angeles Fire Department cancels its ordinary non-firefighting routines. The Santa Ana caused Malibu to burn the way it did in 1956, and Bel Air in 1961, and Santa Barbara in 1964. In the winter of 1966–67 eleven men were killed fighting a Santa Ana fire that spread through the San Gabriel Mountains.

Just to watch the front-page news out of Los Angeles during a Santa Ana is   5
to get very close to what it is about the place. The longest single Santa Ana pe-

riod in recent years was in 1957, and it lasted not the usual three or four days but fourteen days, from November 21 until December 4. On the first day 25,000 acres of the San Gabriel Mountains were burning, with gusts reaching 100 miles an hour. In town, the wind reached Force 12, or hurricane force, on the Beaufort Scale; oil derricks were toppled and people ordered off the downtown streets to avoid injury from flying objects. On November 22 the fire in the San Gabriels was out of control. On November 24 six people were killed in automobile accidents, and by the end of the week the Los Angeles *Times* was keeping a box score of traffic deaths. On November 26 a prominent Pasadena attorney, depressed about money, shot and killed his wife, their two sons, and himself. On November 27 a South Gate divorcée, twenty-two, was murdered and thrown from a moving car. On November 30 the San Gabriel Fire was still out of control, and the wind in town was blowing eighty miles an hour. On the first day of December four people died violently, and on the third the wind began to break.

It is hard for people who have not lived in Los Angeles to realize how radically the Santa Ana figures in the local imagination. The city burning is Los Angeles's deepest image of itself: Nathanael West perceived that, in *The Day of the Locust;* and at the time of the 1965 Watts riots what struck the imagination most indelibly were the fires. For days one could drive the Harbor freeway and see the city on fire, just as we had always known it would be in the end. Los Angeles weather is the weather of catastrophe, of apocalypse, and, just as the reliably long and bitter winters of New England determine the way life is lived there, so the violence and the unpredictability of the Santa Ana affect the entire quality of life in Los Angeles, accentuate its impermanence, its unreliability. The wind shows us how close to the edge we are.

[1968]

Annotations and Journal Entries

While reading the essay a second time, one student planning to write on Didion's style here marked the first paragraph thus:

There is something uneasy in the Los Angeles air this afternoon, some unnatural stillness, some tension. What it means is that tonight a Santa Ana will begin to blow, a hot wind from the northeast whining down through the Cajon and San Gorgonio Passes, blowing up sandstorms out along Route 66, drying the hills and the nerves to the flash point. For a few days now we will see smoke back in the canyons, and hear sirens in the night. I have neither heard nor read that a Santa Ana is due, but I know it, and almost everyone I have seen today knows it too. We know it because we feel it. The baby frets. The maid sulks. I rekindle a waning argument with the telephone company, then cut my losses and lie down, given over to whatever it is in the air. To live with the Santa Ana is to accept, consciously or unconsciously, a deeply mechanistic view of human behavior.

He marked other paragraphs in more or less the same way, and later in the day wrote the following entry in his journal:

<u>Tuesday.</u> She really seems to get the effect of this terrible, oppressive wind. Didion repeats a lot ("something ... some ... some," all in the first sentence). I think she is trying to give us the feel of a wind that won't let up, that keeps hammering at us and driving us crazy. But what persona do I find in this essay? I'm not sure. Sometimes she seems school-teacherish, with that lecture on <u>foehn</u> winds. And in paragraph 4 when she says "This is quite misleading," that's a little sharp. Maybe the wind is getting her down!!

<u>Tuesday night.</u> I'm still not all that wild about the tone in "That is quite misleading," but I guess "school-teacherish" isn't quite the way to describe Didion on the whole. How many school teachers read Raymond? She <u>does</u> sound a bit teachery in the first sentence of the last paragraph ("It is hard for people who have not lived in Los Angeles to realize that ...."), but I guess that a writer sometimes <u>has</u> to give a little lecture. Maybe when she says "It is hard, etc." she is really trying to be helpful, reassuring us that if we don't realize whatever her point is, we aren't therefore idiots. She knows that lots of her readers don't know much about L.A. so she is being helpful.

Later, drawing largely on his annotations in the text and on his entries in his journal, this student jotted down the following notes in preparation for drafting an essay on Didion's style in "Los Angeles Notebook":

persona (as revealed by style?)
    rather personal ("I recall being told," in parag. 1)
    sometimes a bit of the school teacher
        (for instance on <u>foehn</u> wind, in 3
        "This is quite misleading" in 4)
    but: very interesting; very informative; a <u>good</u> teacher
        she seems to know what she is talking about; details
        about <u>foehn</u> wind in par. 4; facts about what the San-
        ta Ana did to Malibu in 1956, Bel Air in 1961, Santa
        Barbara in 1964. Also facts about longest Santa Ana
        (14 days, in 1957) in parag. 5.
style (chief characteristics that I see)
    some long sentences and some short sentences
        long sentences: Second: 45 words; prob. longest in
            essay; no, longest is next-to-last, 53 words!!!

```
         The point? Long, blowing, continuing wind? Cer-
      tainly seems so in 3d sentence, with wind "whin-
      ing, blowing, drying"; it just keeps going on and
      on.
   short sentences: "We know it because we feel it. The
      baby frets. The maid sulks."
         The point? Impatience? Inability to think, to ac-
            complish anything that takes a little time?
            General nervousness?
repetition of words: "something," "some," "some" in first
   par. In 3, "about" appears three times in one
   sentence -- and also three "ands" here. So, length
   plus repetition = suggestion of the driving, continu-
   ing wind.
```

A Sample Essay on Joan Didion's Style

Ultimately, the student wrote the following short essay. You'll notice that it draws heavily on the notes on style and hardly at all on the notes on persona. Notes written during pre-writing are a source to draw on. Resist the temptation to work in, at all costs, everything you've produced.

```
          Joan Didion's Style: Not Hot Air

   In "Los Angeles Notebook" Joan Didion has a point to
make. A sentence at the end of her first paragraph states
the point concisely: "To live with the Santa Ana is to ac-
cept, consciously or unconsciously, a deeply mechanistic
view of human behavior." But she doesn't simply make the
point; her essay tries to make the point effectively, to
make us feel the truth of what she says. I think she
succeeds, partly because she knows what she is talking about
(she gives lots of details about the destructive effects of
the wind) and partly because she uses certain stylistic de-
vices, especially very short and very long sentences, and
repetition.
   Her first sentence is probably of average length, but it
```

repeats "some" (once in the form of "something") three times:

> There is something uneasy in the Los Angeles air this afternoon, some unnatural stillness, some tension.

The sentence is not monotonous, but the repetition perhaps makes it seem a bit longer than it really is, and the repetition suggests a lack of change, a lack of progress. As the reader soon finds, it helps to suggest the driving and unchanging wind. The second sentence, forty-five words long, makes the point clear:

> What it means is that tonight a Santa Ana will begin to blow, a hot wind from the northeast whining down through the Cajon and San Gorgonio Passes, blowing up sandstorms out along Route 66, drying the hills and the nerves to the flash point.

The length of the sentence, and the use of <u>whining</u>, <u>blowing</u>, and <u>drying</u> -- continuous actions -- makes the sentence go on and on, giving an effect of the constant wind.

The length of even this unusually long sentence is exceeded by the next-to-last sentence in the essay, fifty-three words about the catastrophic weather of Los Angeles. But this next-to-last sentence, which again suggests the relentless wind, is followed by a sentence of only eleven words, and in fact Didion earlier in the essay writes a number of fairly short or even very short sentences. These short sentences, like the long ones, contribute to the reader's response. If the long sentences suggest the wind, the short sentences suggest the nervousness, crankiness, or fidgetiness of the person who experiences the wind, or who even only senses the coming of the wind: "We know it because we feel it. The baby frets. The maid sulks." These choppy sentences seem to fret and sulk.

In "Los Angeles Notebook" Didion gives us many facts

about the destructive effect of the Santa Ana, which, she
explains, is a <u>foehn</u> wind. Her essay is informative and she
is a good teacher, but her most effective method of teaching
is not the use of facts but the use of a style that helps
the reader to feel the impact of the <u>foehn</u>.

SUMMING UP: GETTING IDEAS FOR WRITING ABOUT ESSAYS

1. What kind of essay is it? Is it chiefly a presentation of facts (for example, an exposition, a report, or a history), or is it an argument or a meditation?

2. What does it seem to add up to? If the essay is chiefly meditative or speculative, how much emphasis is placed on the persona? That is, if the essay is a sort of thinking-out-loud, is your interest chiefly in the announced or ostensible topic, or in the writer's mood and personality? If the essay is chiefly a presentation of facts, does it also have a larger implication? For instance, if it narrates a happening (history), does the reader draw an inference—find a meaning—in the happening? If the essay is chiefly an argument, what is the thesis? How is the thesis supported? (Is it supported, for example, by induction, deduction, analogy, or emotional appeal?) Do you accept the assumptions (explicit and implicit)?

3. What is the tone of the essay? Is it, for example, solemn, or playful? Is the tone consistent? If not, how do the shifts affect your understanding of the writer's point or your identification of the writer's persona?

4. What sort of *persona* does the writer create, and how does the writer create it? (For example, does the writer use colloquial language or technical or formal language? Short sentences or long ones? Personal anecdotes? Quotations from authorities?)

5. What is especially good (or bad) about the essay? Is it logically persuasive? Or entertaining? Or does it introduce an engaging persona? Or (if it is a narrative) does it tell a story effectively, using (where appropriate) description, dialogue, and commentary, and somehow make you feel that this story is worth reporting?

5

Writing about Fiction: The World of the Story

PLOT AND CHARACTER

Plot has two chief meanings: (1) what happens, the gist of the narrative, and (2) the writer's arrangement of the material into a story. Thus, in the first sense all tellings of the life of Lincoln have the same plot, but in the second sense a writer who begins with the assassination and then gives the earlier material is setting forth a plot that differs from one given by a writer who begins at the beginning.

Let's take the first sense—the gist of the happenings—first. A summary of the plot of a short story may be as short as a sentence. One reader summarized the plot of Nathaniel Hawthorne's "Young Goodman Brown" (printed in Appendix A) as follows:

```
Brown, having journeyed into the wood where he sees
respectable citizens partaking in a ceremony of witchcraft,
returns to Salem, a man who has lost his faith in humanity.
```

Here is a somewhat longer summary, also by a student:

```
At sunset Brown leaves his wife and journeys from Salem into
a forest, where he meets an older man, sees (or dreams of)
various respectable townspeople who turn out to be engaged in
a witches' meeting. He realizes that his wife is about to be
inducted into the villainous band. At dawn Brown returns to
Salem, a gloomy man who has lost his faith in his neighbors
and his wife.
```

Of course, two summaries of the same story may differ, according to length and according to which details and episodes strike the writer as essential, but most readers can probably agree that a given summary is or is not accurate. Remember, a summary is *not* an interpretation. It simply tries to give the gist of what happens. Thus, a summary of the plot of "Young Goodman Brown" will *not* include such a sentence as "Hawthorne suggests that all people are evil" or "Hawthorne implies that Brown misjudges his neighbors." An essay may, of course, make such statements—in fact, almost surely your instructor will insist that you go beyond a summary and offer an interpretation—but keep in mind that a summary briefly retells the plot; it does not offer an interpretation.

It is usual to say that a plot has an **introduction,** a **complication,** and a **resolution;** that is, it gets under way, then some difficulty or problem or complexity arises (usually a **conflict** of opposed wills or forces), and finally there is some sort of settling down. A somewhat metaphoric way of putting it is to say that the plot can often be seen as the tying and then the untying of a knot; the end is the **dénouement** (French for "untying").

Still another way of looking at the organization of the happenings in many works of fiction is to see the plot as a pyramid or triangle. The German critic Gustav Freytag, in *Techniques of the Drama* (1863), introduced this conception in examining the five-act structure of plays, but it can be applied to some fiction, too. In this view, we begin either with an unstable situation or with an apparently stable situation that is soon disrupted; that is, some difficulty or problem or complexity arises (usually a **conflict** of opposed wills or forces). The early happenings, with their increasing tension, constitute a **rising action,** which culminates in a **climax** or **crisis** or **turning point.** (The word *climax* comes from a Greek word meaning "ladder." Originally, the climax was the entire rising action, but the word has come to mean the high point or end of the rising action.) What follows the decisive moment is the **falling action,** which ends in a stable situation—a situation that the reader takes to be final. Of course, the characters need not die; the reader feels, however, that nothing more is to be said about them. Here is a diagram showing Freytag's Pyramid. Remember, however, that a story *need* not have this structure.

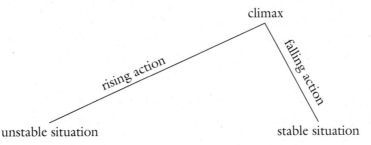

climax

rising action

falling action

unstable situation

stable situation

The structure of Hawthorne's "Young Goodman Brown" might be discussed in these terms:

1. *Stable situation—soon to be upset:* Brown and Faith dwell lovingly in Salem.
2. *Rising action:* Brown departs from Salem, meets the older man, sees Goody Cloyse, and so on.
3. *Climax:* Brown cries out, "With heaven above, and Faith below, I will yet stand firm against the devil!" but he is overcome by the sound of Faith's voice and by the sight of the pink ribbon, and he becomes "maddened with despair."
4. *Falling action:* Brown returns to Salem, shrinks from his neighbors, coldly encounters his wife.
5. *Stable situation:* Brown lives many years in Salem, but all of the years are sorrowful.

"Young Goodman Brown" has a fair amount of physical action—for instance, a trip to the forest and an assembling of witches—but most readers would probably agree that the most important "action" is the conflict that rages in Brown's mind, or, to put it slightly differently, the physical journey from Salem to a forest and back to Salem is less important than the change that takes place within Brown's mind. Early fiction tends to have a good deal of physical action—wanderings, strange encounters, births, and deaths. But in some fiction, little seems to happen. These apparently plotless stories, however, usually involve a mental action—a significant perception, a decision, a failure of the will—and the process of this mental action is the plot.

The sense of causality is in part rooted in **character.** Things happen, in most good fiction, at least partly because the people have certain personalities or characters (moral, intellectual, and emotional qualities) and, given their natures, because they respond plausibly to other personalities. What their names are and what they look like may help you understand them, but probably the best guide to characters is what they do. As we get to know more about their drives and goals—especially the choices they make—we enjoy seeing the writer complete the portraits, finally presenting us with a coherent and credible picture of people in action. In this view, plot and character are inseparable. Plot is not simply a series of happenings, but happenings that come out of character, that reveal character, and that influence character. Henry James puts it thus: "What is character but the determination of incident? What is incident but the illustration of character?" But, of course, characters are not defined only by what they do. The narrator often describes them, and the characters' words and dress reveal aspects of them.

You may want to set forth a character sketch, describing some person in the story or novel. You will probably plan to convey three things:

appearance,

personality, and

character—"character" here meaning not a figure in a literary work but the figure's moral or ethical values.

Of course, "character" in this sense may not be utterly distinct from "personality," but personality is more a matter of psychology than of ethics. For example, wit, irritability, and fastidiousness can be regarded as parts of personality, but generosity, cowardice, and temperance can be regarded as parts of character or of morality. The distinction is not always clear, but it is evident enough when we speak of someone as "a diamond in the rough." We probably mean that the person is morally solid (a matter of character) though given to odd or even rude expressions of personality.

In preparing a character sketch, take these points into consideration:

1. What the person says (but remember that what he or she says need not be taken at face value; the person may be hypocritical or self-deceived or biased)
2. What the person does
3. What others (including the narrator of the story) say about the person
4. What others *do* (their actions may help indicate what the person could do but does not do)
5. What the person looks like—face, body, clothes. These may help convey the personality, or they may in some measure help disguise it.

Writing about a Character

A character sketch (remember—we have made a distinction between character and personality, but when one speaks of a "character sketch" one means all aspects of a figure in a work of literature, *not* simply the moral sense), such as "Holden Caulfield: Adolescent Snob or Suffering Saint?" may be complex and demanding, especially if the character (the figure) is complex. Notice that in the example just referred to, the writer sees that Holden might (at least at first glance) be interpreted in two very different ways, a snob or a saint. In fact, the student who wrote the essay argued that Holden has touches of the adolescent snob but is chiefly a suffering saint.

An essay on a character, you will recall, is necessarily in some degree an interpretation, and, thus, even such an essay has a thesis or argument holding it together. Usually, however, you will want to do more than set forth your view of a character. Probably, you will discuss the character's function or contrast him or her with other characters or trace the development of personality. (One of the most difficult topics, the character of the narrator, will be discussed later in this chapter, under the heading "Point of View.") You probably will still want to keep in mind the five suggestions for getting at a character (as well as others on page 69), but you will also want to go further, relating your findings to additional matters of the sort we will examine now.

ORGANIZING AN ANALYSIS OF A CHARACTER

As you read and reread, you will highlight and annotate the text and will jot down notes, recording (in whatever order they come to you) your thoughts about the character you are studying. Reading with a view toward writing, you'll want to

1. jot down traits as they come to mind ("kind," "forgetful," "enthusiastic"); and
2. look back at the text, searching for supporting evidence (characteristic actions, brief supporting quotations), and of course you will also look for counter-evidence so that you may modify your earlier impressions.

Brainstorming leads to an evaluation and a shaping of your ideas. Evaluating and shaping lead to a tentative outline. A tentative outline leads to the search for supporting evidence—the material that will constitute the body of your essay.

When you set out to write a first draft, review your annotations and notes, and see if you can summarize your view of the character in one or two sentences:

> X is ....

or

> Although X is ..., she is also ....

That is, try to formulate a thesis sentence or a thesis paragraph—a proposition that you will go on to support.

You want to let your reader know early, probably in your first sentence—and almost certainly by the end of your first paragraph—which character you are writing about and what your overall thesis is.

The body of your essay will be devoted to supporting your thesis. If you have asserted that although so-and-so is cruel and domineering he nevertheless is endowed with a conscience, you will go on in your essay to support those assertions with references to passages that demonstrate them. This support does *not* mean that you tell the plot of the whole work; an essay on a character is by no means the same as a summary of the plot. Since you must support your generalizations, you will have to make brief references to specific episodes that reveal his personality, and almost surely you will quote an occasional word or passage.

An essay on a character may be organized in many possible ways. Much will depend on your purpose and thesis. For instance, you may want to show how the character develops—gains knowledge or matures or disintegrates. Or you may want to show what the character contributes to the story or play as a whole. Or, to give yet another example, you may want to show that the character is unbelievable. Still, although no single organization is always right, two methods are common and effective.

One effective way of organizing an essay on a character is to let the organization of your essay follow closely the sequence of the literary work; that is, you might devote a paragraph to the character as we first perceive him or her and then in subsequent paragraphs go on to show that this figure is later seen to be more complex than he or she at first appears. Such an essay may trace your changing responses.

A second effective way of organizing an essay on a character is to set forth, early in the essay, the character's chief traits—let's say the chief strengths and two or three weaknesses—and then go on to study each trait you have listed. The organization would (in order to maintain the reader's interest) probably begin with the most obvious points and then move on to the less obvious, subtler points. The body of your essay, in any case, is devoted to offering evidence that supports your generalizations about the character.

What about a concluding paragraph? The concluding paragraph ought *not* to begin with the obviousness of "Thus, we see," or "In conclusion," or "I recommend this story because ...." In fact, after you have given what you consider to be a sound sketch of the character, it may be appropriate simply to quit. Especially if your essay has moved from the obvious traits to the more subtle and more important traits, and if your essay is fairly short (say, fewer than 500 words), a reader may not need a conclusion. Further, why blunt what you have just said by adding an unnecessary and merely repetitive summary? If you do feel that a conclusion is necessary, you may find it effective to write a summary of the character, somewhat as you did in your opening. For the conclusion, relate the character's character to the entire literary work; that is, try to give the reader a sense of the role that the character plays.

A Sample Essay on a Character: "Holden's Kid Sister"

A student decided to write about Phoebe, Holden Caulfield's sister in J. D. Salinger's *The Catcher in the Rye*. Before writing, he reread the book, highlighting certain passages about Phoebe. He then reviewed the text and jotted down some key ideas, reproduced here.

```
Phoebe Josephine Caulfield
    Holden's kid sister
        playful, funny, fun to be with
        likes movies
        invents new name (Weatherfield)
        good dancer
        academically good ("smart"; "good in all subjects")
```

> Actually, Holden says this, and as he somewhere
> says, he's a terrible liar -- but here he's proba-
> bly telling the truth. He wouldn't lie about her.
> (Does this point have to be proved?)
> good listener (that's what H. needs; it seems that
>   almost everyone else is trying to <u>tell</u> him some
>   phoney stuff, but P. accepts him)
> good listener <u>but</u> she doesn't always agree with him
>   or approve of what he's doing.
>   Example: disapproves of his leaving school
>   BUT though she's upset by it, she sticks with him
>   Other examples needed?
> She's loyal -- and she loves him. Does anyone else
>   love him?

This material provided much of the first draft, which was submitted to peer review. The student then revised the draft, partly in accordance with the suggestions offered and partly in the light of his own further thinking. Here is the final version.

Holden's Kid Sister

Phoebe Josephine Caulfield, Holden's ten-year-old sister in J. D. Salinger's <u>The Catcher in the Rye,</u> is a child with a mind of her own. She doesn't care for her middle name, and so on the first page of one of her many notebooks she gives herself a new one: "Phoebe Weatherfield Caulfield." She is, we gather, playful and imaginative, but she is also in touch with reality, and able to get along well in the world. She has friends, and at school she is "good in all subjects." The quality that most impresses a reader, however, is not her academic success but her loyalty to Holden, and even when she criticizes Holden she does so out of deep love for him.

Since Holden is the narrator of the book, all that we know of Phoebe is seen through his eyes, but there is no reason to doubt his comments about her. Fairly early in the book, in Chapter 10, he gives us a long description, in the course of which he says that she is "pretty and smart," a redhead, "skinny," and (more important, of course) "affectionate." Later Holden tells us that she shares his taste in movies, and that she is a perfect partner when she dances with him. That is, Phoebe is on Holden's wave-length; the two can move in harmony, and not only when they dance. For instance, she is a good listener, and Holden desperately needs someone who can listen to him, since most of the people in his world are big talkers and are trying to impose their own values on him.

This is not to say, however, that Phoebe approves of all of Holden's actions. When she learns that he has left school, she is upset with him, but the reader always feels that any criticism she makes proceeds from her love for Holden. She is so loyal to him that she wants to leave school and go with him when he tells her he plans to run away from New York and hitchhike to the West. Her loyalty, her refusal to leave him, causes him to abandon his desperate plan to flee.

Her sincerity and her love for Holden are not enough to restore him to mental health (at the end of the book we learn that he "got sick and all," and is now in some sort of asylum), but the reader knows that if any character in the book can provide the human warmth that Holden requires, that character is his bright, strong-willed, loving "kid sister."

A few comments on this essay:

1. The title is informative and at least moderately interesting—more interesting, for example, than "Phoebe Caulfield."

2. The writer does not cite pages because the instructor did not ask him to do so, but if your instructor asks you to give references, use the form prescribed. (On citations, see pages 233–245.)

3. The opening paragraph announces the topic, gives a brief description of Phoebe (her age, her imaginativeness) and ends by focusing on her most important trait, her love for Holden.

4. The body of the essay (paragraphs 2 and 3) offers a few additional minor details, but chiefly it supports (by means of the comment on dancing) the earlier generalization that Phoebe is uniquely in harmony with Holden. It does not summarize the plot, but it does refer to certain episodes, and it interprets them in order to show how they reveal Phoebe's character.

5. The final paragraph, the fourth, offers additional support (her plan to run away with Holden), and it concludes with a glance at the conclusion of the novel. Thus the essay more or less echoes the chronology of the book, but these last sentences are not mere plot-telling. Rather, they solidify the writer's view of Phoebe's character and her importance to Holden.

FORESHADOWING

The writer of fiction provides a coherent world in which the details work together. **Foreshadowing,** which eliminates surprise or at least greatly reduces it and thus destroys a story that has nothing except a surprise ending to offer, is a powerful tool in the hands of the writer of serious fiction. Even in such a story as Faulkner's "A Rose for Emily," in which we are surprised to learn near the end that Miss Emily has slept beside the decaying corpse of her dead lover, from the outset we expect something strange; that is, we are not surprised by the surprise, only by its precise nature. The first sentence of the story tells us that after Miss Emily's funeral (the narrator begins at the end) the townspeople cross her threshold "out of curiosity to see the inside of her house, which no one save an old manservant ... had seen in at least ten years." As the story progresses, we see Miss Emily prohibiting people from entering the house, and we hear that after a certain point no one ever sees Homer Barron again, that "the front door remained closed," and (a few paragraphs before the end of the story) that the townspeople "knew that there was one room in that region above the stairs which no one had seen in forty years." The paragraph preceding the revelation that "the man himself lay in bed" is devoted to a description of Homer's dust-covered clothing and toilet articles. In short, however much we are unprepared for the precise revelation, we are prepared for some strange thing in the house; and, given Miss Emily's purchase of poison and Homer's disappearance, we have some idea of what will be revealed.

Joyce's "Araby" is another example of a story in which the beginning is a preparation for all that follows. Consider the first two paragraphs:

> North Richmond Street, being blind, was a quiet street except at the hour when the Christian Brothers' school set the boys free. An uninhabited house of

two storeys stood at the blind end, detached from its neighbours in a square ground. The other houses of the street, conscious of decent lives within them, gazed at one another with brown imperturbable faces.

The former tenant of our house, a priest, had died in the back drawing-room. Air, musty from having been long enclosed, hung in all the rooms, and the waste room behind the kitchen was littered with old useless papers. Among these I found a few paper-covered books, the pages of which were curled and damp: *The Abbot*, by Walter Scott, *The Devout Communicant* and *The Memoirs of Vidocq*. I liked the last best because its leaves were yellow. The wild garden behind the house contained a central apple-tree and a few straggling bushes under one of which I found the late tenant's rusty bicycle pump. He had been a very charitable priest; in his will he had left all his money to institutions and the furniture of his house to his sister.

Of course the full meaning of the passage will not become apparent until you have read the entire story. In a sense, a story has at least three lives:

when we read the story, sentence by sentence, trying to turn the sequence of sentences into a consistent whole;

when we have finished reading the story and we think back on it as a whole, even if we think no more than "That was a waste of time"; and

when we reread a story, knowing already even as we read the first line how it will turn out at the end.

Let's assume that you have not read the whole of "Araby." On the basis only of a reading of the first two paragraphs, what might you highlight or underline? Here are the words that one student marked:

blind	musty
quiet	kitchen was littered
set the boys free	leaves were yellow
brown imperturbable faces	wild garden ... apple-tree
priest	charitable priest

No two readers will come up with exactly the same list (if you live on North Richmond Street, you will probably underline it and put an exclamation mark in the margin; if you attended a parochial school, you'll probably underline "Christian Brothers' school"), but perhaps most readers, despite their varied experience, would agree that Joyce is giving us a picture of what he elsewhere called the "paralysis" of Ireland. How the story will turn out is, of course, unknown to a first-time reader. Perhaps the paralysis will increase, or perhaps it will be broken. Joyce goes on adding sentence to sentence, trying to shape the reader's response, and the reader goes on reading, making meaning out of the sentences.

As we read further in the story, we are not surprised to learn that the boy for a while manufactured quasi-religious experiences (religion being dead—remember the dead priest and his rusty bicycle pump). In his ears, shop-boys sing "litanies," his girl friend's name springs to his lips "in strange prayers," and his vision of her is a "chalice" that he carries "safely through a throng of foes." He plans to visit a bazaar, and he promises to bring her a gift; but after he has with some difficulty arrived at the bazaar, he is vastly disappointed by the trivial conversation of the attendants, by the counting of the day's receipts (money-changers in the temple), and by the darkness ("the upper part of the hall was now completely dark"). The last line of the story runs thus: "Gazing up into the darkness I saw myself as a creature driven and derided by vanity; and my eyes burned with anguish and anger." Everything in the story coheres; the dead-end street, the dead priest, the rusty pump—all are perfect preludes to this story about a boy's recognition of the nothingness that surrounds him. The "vanity" that drives and derides him is not only the egotism that moved him to think he could bring the girl a fitting gift but also the nothingness that is spoken of in the biblical "Vanity of vanities, all is vanity."

In preparing to write about foreshadowing, you will reread the story; now that you know how it ends, you will be able to see how certain early details are relevant to the ending. Underline or highlight these, and perhaps jot down brief notes in the margins, such as "images of emptiness" or "later turns out ironically." At a later stage in the process of writing, you probably will find it useful to jot down on a sheet of paper key phrases from the text and to annotate them with such comments as "The first of many religious images" and "same image appears later."

What is the best way to organize an essay on foreshadowing? Probably you will work through the evidence chronologically, though your initial paragraph may discuss the end and indicate that the remainder of the essay will be concerned with tracing the way in which the author prepares the reader for this end and simultaneously maintains the right amount of suspense. If the suspense is too slight, we stop reading, not caring what comes next. If it is too great, we are perhaps reading a story in which the interest depends entirely on some strange happening rather than a story with sufficiently universal application to make it worthy of a second reading.

Your essay may study the ways in which details gain in meaning as the reader gets farther into the story. Or it may study the author's failure to keep details relevant and coherent, the tendency to introduce material for its momentary value at the expense of the larger design. An essay on an uneven story may do both: it may show that although there are unfortunate irrelevancies, considerable skill is used in arousing and interestingly fulfilling the reader's expectations. If you feel that the story is fundamentally successful, the organization of your thoughts may reflect your feelings. After an initial paragraph stating the overall position, you may discuss the failures and then go on at greater length to discuss the strengths, ending strongly on your main point. If you feel that the story is essentially a failure, perhaps first discuss its merits briefly and then go on to your main point—the unsatisfactory nature of the story. To reverse this procedure would be to leave the reader with an impression contrary to your thesis.

SETTING AND ATMOSPHERE

Foreshadowing normally makes use of **setting.** The setting or environment in the first two paragraphs of Joyce's "Araby" is not mere geography, not mere locale: it provides an **atmosphere,** an air that the characters breathe, a world in which they move. Narrowly speaking, the setting is the physical surroundings—the furniture, the architecture, the landscape, the climate—and these often are highly appropriate to the characters who are associated with them. Thus, in Emily Brontë's *Wuthering Heights* the passionate Earnshaw family is associated with Wuthering Heights, the storm-exposed moorland, whereas the mild Linton family is associated with Thrushcross Grange in the sheltered valley below. Hawthorne's "Young Goodman Brown" also has two settings, Salem in the daytime and a nearby forest at night. A reader of the story probably consciously or unconsciously comes to believe that Salem is associated with order, decency, the good, and the dark forest with chaos and evil.

Broadly speaking, setting includes not only the physical surroundings but a point or several points in time. The background against which we see the characters and the happenings may be specified as morning or evening, spring or fall, and this temporal setting in a good story will probably be highly relevant; it will probably be part of the story's meaning, perhaps providing an ironic contrast (think of the festive, carnival setting in Poe's "The Cask of Amontillado," a story of a murder) or perhaps exerting an influence on the characters.

Some comments on familiar examples from Thomas Hardy's novels may clarify the significance of setting. In *Tess of the D'Urbervilles* we are told of a place called Flintcomb Ash, where "the whole field was in color a desolate drab; it was a complexion without features, as if a face, from chin to brow, should be only an expanse of skin. The sky wore, in another color, the same likeness; a white vacuity of expression with the lineaments gone." Or, near the end of the novel, when, just before her arrest, Tess lies upon a great stone slab at Stonehenge, she is associated with all the victims of history and prehistory. Dorothy Van Ghent calls attention to the role that the earth plays in *Tess.* She writes of

> the long stretches of earth that have to be trudged in order that a person may get from one place to another, the slowness of the business, the irreducible reality of it (for one has only one's feet), its grimness of soul-wearing fatigue and

shelterlessness and doubtful issue at the other end of the journey where nobody may be at home.

The English Novel, (New York, 1953), p. 201

Van Ghent goes on to say, in discussing *The Mayor of Casterbridge:*

> The Roman ruins round about the town of Casterbridge are a rather ... complicated metaphor, for they are works of man that have fallen into earth; they speak mutely of the anonymity of human effort in historical as well as in geological times; their presence suggests also the classic pattern of the Mayor's tragedy, the ancient repetitiveness of self-destruction; and they provide thus a kind of guarantee or confirming signature of the heroism of the doomed human enterprise.

The English Novel, p. 202

Note: Although your instructor may ask you to write a paragraph describing the setting, more often he or she will want something more complicated, such as an essay on the *function* of the setting. For such an essay, you may find it useful to begin with a paragraph or two describing the setting or settings, but be sure to go on to analyze the significance of this material.

SYMBOLISM

Writers of fiction do not write only about things that have happened to them. They write about things they have seen or heard, and also about thoughts and emotions.

Inevitably, writers use symbols. Symbols are neither puzzles nor colorful details but are among the concrete embodiments that give the story whatever accuracy it has. Joyce's dead-end street, dead priest, apple tree (suggestive of the Garden of Eden, now fallen?), and rusty bicycle pump all help define very precisely the condition of a thoroughly believable Dublin. In Hemingway's *Farewell to Arms* the river in which Frederic Henry swims when he deserts the army is as material as the guns he flees, but it also probably suggests to a reader that Henry is symbolically cleaning himself of war. In Chopin's "Ripe Figs" (page 3) the "tender" leaves mentioned at the outset of the story may suggest Babette's immaturity; the ripening figs may suggest a stage in her maturity; and the chrysanthemums mentioned at the end of the story may suggest the two older women, Maman and Frosine, enjoying an autumnal blossoming, a "second bloom," so to speak. If so, we can say that these things are symbolic; they are themselves, but they also stand for something more than themselves. Finally, in Hawthorne's "Young Goodman Brown" Salem and the nearby forest are themselves and (as was mentioned a moment ago in the discussion of setting and atmosphere) they also probably come to stand for good versus evil, or order versus disorder.

At this point it's appropriate to mention that at least to some degree readers will differ in their interpretations of symbolic elements. For example, although most readers of "Young Goodman Brown" probably will agree that the older man symbolizes the Devil, they may disagree about whether this Devil is an objective reality or is a figment of Brown's own disordered (corrupt?) imagination. Consider further Hawthorne's emphasis both on darkness and on fiery red in the forest. Readers may agree that the darkness in the forest symbolizes evil or at least moral confusion, but they may not agree on whether the bright red flames that illuminate the evil-doers stand for some sort of highly visible or clear-cut evil. Is Hawthorne establishing a contrast between two kinds of evil—evil that (in our moral darkness) we do not understand is evil, and evil that clearly and brightly is perceived as evil? Or is he simply using the flames as flames?

Given the ambiguity of symbols, it's good to remember that whatever their implications, symbols usually are also very specific. Mary McCarthy, in an essay on symbolism, points out that symbols are not odd things stuck into a story but are things that properly belong in the world of the story. She effectively illustrates her point with an example from Tolstoy's *Anna Karenina*.

> ... Toward the beginning of the novel, Anna meets the man who will be her lover, Vronsky, on the Moscow-St. Petersburg express; as they meet, there has been an accident; a workman has been killed by the train. This is the beginning of Anna's doom, which is completed when she throws herself under a train and is killed; and the last we see of Vronsky is in a train with a toothache; he is off to the wars. The train is necessary to the plot of the novel, and I believe it is also symbolic both of the iron forces of material progress that Tolstoy hated so and that played a part in Anna's moral destruction, and also of those iron laws of necessity and consequence that govern human action when it remains on the sensual level.
>
> One can read the whole novel, however, without being conscious that the train is a symbol; we do not have to "interpret" to feel the import of doom and loneliness in the train's whistle—the same import we ourselves can feel when we hear a train whistle blow in the country even today.
>
> *On the Contrary* (New York 1962), p. 236

The symbols are a part of the world of the story, contributing to its sense of immediacy or reality, as well as radiating suggestions or (to use Henry James's figure) casting long shadows. In Hardy's *Jude the Obscure,* for example, the pigeons that Jude and Sue are forced to sell are symbols of Jude's and Sue's caged existence, but they are also pigeons that Jude and Sue are forced to sell. Furthermore, other references to birds in the novel function similarly, as do the passages dealing with the trapped rabbit. Birds and rabbits are a part of Jude's world, meaningful on the realistic level but resonant, too. An essayist who discusses symbolism in a piece of fiction will probably want to examine the degree to which the symbols are integral and interrelated.

A Sample Essay on Atmosphere as Symbol: "Darkness in *Dubliners*"

The next example, a fine essay by a student, points out that the repeated references to darkness in Joyce's *Dubliners* are an important part of the meaning of the book. Among the strengths of the essay are these strategies:

1. The title and the first paragraph of the essay give the reader an idea of what will follow.
2. The next paragraph discusses the first story in the book, and the third paragraph discusses the last story. The essayist wisely avoids plodding through fifteen stories by choosing the first and the last stories she implies that all of the stories share the motif.
3. The fourth paragraph sets forth the general implications of darkness, and it is followed by a fairly detailed paragraph analyzing the motif in one story.
4. In the concluding paragraph the essayist concedes that the references to darkness are literal as well as symbolic, but she quietly insists that the symbolic implications are there, too.

Although this title doesn't announce the thesis, it at least announces the topic.

Thesis is stated early.

Darkness in Dubliners

The fifteen short stories in Joyce's collection called Dubliners are not simply fifteen separate stories, or even fifteen stories united only by being about people in the city for which the book is named. The unity is greater than physical locale: there is a unity of theme, which Joyce himself said was "paralysis,"[1] and this sense of paralysis is conveyed not only by what the characters do-- or, more often, what they do not do-- but also by Joyce's insistence on the dark sky, or the darkness inside a room, in most of the stories. Darkness, especially of night, seems

The essay is not a research paper, but the student has done some digging, and gives credit to the source. (For another way of indicating a source, see pages 234–245.)

------

[1]Letter to the publisher, quoted in Harry Levin, James Joyce (London: Faber and Faber, 1944), p. 29.

to surround the characters, hindering them from any advance and representing their mental condition.

Overall view; then narrows to reasonable choice of "the very first story."

Most of the stories are set in a dark street or a dark room. For example, the very first story, "The Sisters," begins as follows:

Quotation provides evidence, and lets us hear Joyce for a moment.

> There was no hope for him this time; it was the third stroke. Night after night I had passed the house (it was vacation time) and studied the lighted square of the window: and night after night I had found it lighted in the same way, faintly and evenly.

Useful brief quotations; longer ones are not needed.

As the story continues, we find that a priest has at last died. The narrator visits the house "after sunset" (a time of day that itself suggests the death of the day) and he learns that the dead priest "was quite resigned" and "was a disappointed man." Near the end of the story we learn that the priest was mentally sick, and was once found "sitting up by himself in the dark in his confession-box." In short, the priest's mind was darkened, and this is revealed in the episode of the confession-box and in the several references to night, a time when men do not usually work or make progress. Death and darkness are associated, and Dublin seems to be a dying city.

Reasonable choice of a second example.

If we jump, for a moment, across the entire book, to some sentences in the last paragraph of the last story, "The Dead," we find remarkable connections with the first story. Again it is night, and again we get references to a dim light surrounded by darkness. This time a man is in his bedroom, looking out of a window on a snowy night. The final paragraph includes such expressions as "He watched sleepily the flakes, silver and dark, falling obliquely against the lamplight," "journey westward," "the dark central plain," "their last end," "falling," "buried," and "the living and the dead." In this story the whole of Dublin is wrapped in night and in a cover of snow, and the chief character falls asleep. Here as in the first story about the dead priest, the literal time of day -- night -- contributes to the sense of death or paralysis. The people in Dublin seem to live in darkness -- that is, in frustration and spiritual emptiness.

In almost all the stories, the darkness is made the more ominous by feeble lights that seem to try to overcome it but of course fail to do so. In the first story, for example, the window was lighted "night after night," but at last the time came when the priest died and the blinds were drawn. The only light inside is from candles burning at the dead man's head; this light is not seen from the street, where the window is lit only by "tawny gold" light reflected from the clouds. Inside, the narrator "groped" his way to a chair, and then learns of the episode in the confession-box. Darkness takes over. Sometimes the images of light against the dark are not literal, as in the previous instances, but are figurative. In

Brief quotations offered as evidence.

Skillful pulling together of the material so far.

Generalization has been amply supported.

We are inclined to take the writer's word about "all the stories" because we have been convinced by the previous discussion of two stories.

"The Dead," for instance, we get this figurative description of Gabriel: "The dull fires of his lust began to glow angrily in his veins." Here again life or vitality is associated with light ("fire"). As in the other stories, the light does not last, for Gabriel's lust soon disappears and he falls asleep in the night. In another story, "Ivy Day in the Committee Room," the fire is literal; some minor politicians are discussing an election in a room with a dying fire, and it is clear that they are the corrupt or dying left-overs of what was once a genuinely patriotic movement. We are told that the weather is unpleasant and that "the short day had grown dark." Several times we are told that the room is dark, the fire being inadequate. We learn from the dialogue that there is bribery, suspicion, selfishness, a total lack of idealism. In short, the physical locale -- a darkening room, fitfully illuminated by a dying fire -- is a way of representing the people who live in it.

Because it would be tedious to go through each story, describing the special sorts of darkness that appear in almost all, this paper will study a single story, "Araby," in a bit more detail. The gist of the plot is that a young boy, in love with a girl, promises to bring her something from a fair called Araby, but when he gets to the fair, just before closing time, he finds that his romantic visions of himself as a heroic lover, and of the fair as a sort of enchanted place, are demol-

Judicious references to evidence in other stories.

Essayist offers a reasonable justification for the procedure.

Plot summary is brief and useful, not mere padding.

ished by the tawdriness of the fair. This short summary gives only one hint, in the reference to closing time, of the role that darkness plays in creating the atmosphere that helps to shape the characters, but in fact the story is filled with references to darkness.

Evidence from the text.

The narrator played in "dark muddy lanes," "dark dripping gardens," and "dark odorous stables," and he admires the girl from inside of his room, where he has pulled the shade "down to within an inch of the sash so that I could not be seen." On the day he is to go to the fair to bring back his trophy, his uncle does not get home until nine o'clock, and therefore the boy does not get to the fair until ten to ten, when "the greater part of the hall was in darkness." This is the way the story ends:

Fairly long quotation is not padding; it is evidence.

> I heard a voice call from one of the galleries that the light was out. The upper part of the hall was now completely dark.
>   Gazing up into the darkness I saw myself as a creature driven and derided by vanity; and my eyes burned with anguish and anger.

The narrator's sense of disillusionment is perfectly represented by the statement of the voice that "the light was out." The voice is stating a simple fact about the light in the hall, but the reader understands its relation to the narrator's state of mind. In the last sentence of the story, the narrator looks into the dark and sees nothing: his rich illusions,

or delusions, have vanished, and he is surrounded by nothing, for he now has nothing
within him.

Essayist raises a possible objection, and refutes it.

Dublin probably is often dark; certainly
night comes to Dublin as it comes to every
other city, and one might try to argue that
Joyce is merely being accurate in his depiction of dark days, and of nights. But when one
rereads the stories, and notices how few are
set in the daylight, and how often the darkness is stressed, and how appropriate it is to
the spiritually impoverished characters in the
book, one realizes that Joyce is doing more
than giving realistic pictures of Dublin at a

Quiet reaffirmation of thesis.

certain time of day. His descriptions of dark
streets, dark rooms, and of fitful bits of
illumination, are also descriptions of a state
of mind that dominates the Dubliners in
Dubliners.

POINT OF VIEW

The Dublin in *Dubliners* and the England in *Jude* are the Dublin and England that Joyce and Hardy thought existed, but it must be remembered that although an author *writes* a story, someone else *tells* it. The story is seen from a particular **point of view,** and this point of view in large measure determines our response to the story. A wide variety of terms has been established to name differing points of view, but the following labels are among the commonest. We may begin with two categories: third-person points of view (in which the narrator is, in the crudest sense, not a participant in the story) and first-person points of view (in which the "I" who narrates the story plays a part in it).

Third-Person Narrators

The **third-person point of view** itself has several subdivisions. At one extreme is the **omniscient narrator,** who knows everything that is going on and can tell us the inner thoughts of all the characters. The omniscient narrator may editorialize, pass judgments, reassure the reader, and so forth, in which case he or she may sound like the author. Here is Hardy's editorially omniscient narrator in *Tess of the D'Urbervilles,* telling the reader that Tess was mistaken in imagining that the countryside proclaimed her guilt:

> But this encompassment of her own characterization, based upon shreds of convention, peopled by phantoms and voices antipathetic to her, was a sorry and mistaken creation of Tess's fancy—a cloud of moral hobgoblins by which she was terrified without reason.

Still, even this narrator is not quite Hardy; he does not allude to his other books, his private life, or his hope that the book will sell. If he is Hardy, he is only one aspect of Hardy, quite possibly a fictional Hardy, a disembodied voice with particular characteristics.

Another sort of third-person narrator, **selective omniscient,** takes up what Henry James called a "center of consciousness," revealing the thoughts of one of the characters but (for the most part) seeing the rest of the characters from the outside only. Wayne Booth, in a thoughtful study of Jane Austen's *Emma,* explains the effectiveness of selective omniscience in this novel. He points out that Emma is intelligent, witty, beautiful, and rich. But she is flawed by pride, and, until she discovers and corrects her fault, she almost destroys herself and her friends. How may such a character be made sympathetic, so that we will hope for the happy conclusion to the comedy? "The solution to the problem of maintaining sympathy despite almost crippling faults," Booth says,

> was primarily to use the heroine herself as a kind of narrator, though in third person, reporting on her own experience…. By showing most of the story through Emma's eyes, the author insures that we shall travel with Emma rather than stand against her. It is not simply that Emma provides, in the unimpeachable evidence of her own conscience, proof that she has many redeeming qualities that do not appear on the surface; such evidence could be given with authorial commentary, though perhaps not with such force and conviction. Much more important, the sustained inside view leads the reader to hope for good fortune for the character with whom he travels, quite independently of the qualities revealed.
>
> *The Rhetoric of Fiction* (Chicago, 1961), pp. 245–246

Booth goes on to point out in a long and careful analysis that "sympathy for Emma can be heightened by withholding inside views of others as well as by granting them of her."

In writing about point of view, one tries to suggest what the author's choice of a particular point of view contributes to the story. Wayne Booth shows how Jane Austen's third-person point of view helps keep sympathetic a character who otherwise might be less than sympathetic. Notice that Booth states the problem—how to draw an intelligent but proud woman so that the reader will wish for a happy ending—and he presents his answer convincingly, moving from "It is not simply ..." to "Much more important ..." (To reverse the order would cause a drop in interest.) He then moves from a discussion of the inside treatment of Emma to the outside treatment of the other characters, thus substantiating and enlarging his argument.

Possibly one could reverse this procedure, beginning with a discussion of the treatment of the characters other than Emma and then closing in on Emma, but such an essay may seem slow in getting under way. The early part may appear unfocused. The reader will for a while be left wondering why in an essay on point of view in *Emma* the essayist does not turn to the chief matter, the presentation of the central character.

The third-person narrator, then, although not in the ordinary sense a character in the story, is an important voice in the story, who helps give shape to it. Another type of third-person narrator is the so-called **effaced narrator.** (Some critics use the term **dramatic point of view** or **objective point of view.**) This narrator does not seem to exist, for (unlike the editorially omniscient narrator) he or she does not comment in his or her own voice and (unlike the omniscient and selective omniscient narrators) does not enter any minds. It is almost improper to speak of an effaced narrator as "he" or "he or she," for no evident figure is speaking. The reader hears dialogue and sees only what a camera or a fly on the wall would see. The following example is from Hemingway's "The Killers":

> The door of Henry's lunchroom opened and two men came in. They sat down at the counter.
> "What's yours?" George asked them.
> "I don't know," one of the men said. "What do you want to eat, Al?"
> "I don't know," said Al. "I don't know what I want to eat."

But even an effaced narrator has, if we think a moment, a kind of personality. The story the narrator records may seem "cold" or "scientific" or "reportorial" or "objective," and such a **tone** or voice (attitude of the narrator, as it is detected) may be an important part of the story. Rémy de Gourmont's remark, quoted in Ezra Pound's *Literary Essays,* is relevant: "To be impersonal is to be personal in a special kind of way.... The objective is one of the forms of the subjective."

In writing about a third-person narrator, speak of "the narrator" or "the speaker," not of "the author."

First-Person Narrators

To turn to **first-person**, or **participant, points of view:** The "I" who narrates the story (recall that at the end of "Araby" the narrator says, "I saw myself as a creature driven and derided by vanity") may be a major character in it (as he is in "Araby," in *The Catcher in the Rye,* and in Mark Twain's *Huckleberry Finn*), or may be a minor character, a mere witness (Dr. Watson narrates tales about Sherlock Holmes, Nick Carraway narrates the story of Gatsby in *The Great Gatsby*). Of course, the narrator, even when a relatively minor character, is still a character, and, therefore, in some degree the story is about him or her. Although *The Great Gatsby* is primarily about Gatsby, it is also about Nick's changing perception of Gatsby.

First-person narrators may not fully understand their own report. Take Huck Finn in *The Adventures of Huckleberry Finn.* In one passage Huck describes the "astonishing things" performed at a circus he witnessed, including a drunk who badgered the ringmaster until he was permitted to try to ride a horse. Of course, the drunk turns out to be an expert performer and is part of the circus act, but Huck thinks the ringmaster was genuinely deceived by a performer who "had got up that joke all out of his own head." In using Huck as the narrator, Mark Twain uses an **innocent eye,** a device in which a good part of the effect consists in the discrepancy between the narrator's imperfect awareness and the reader's superior awareness. Mark Twain makes much more important use of the device in another passage in *Huckleberry Finn,* when Huck is listening to Jim, an escaped slave:

> Jim talked out loud all the time while I was talking to myself. He was saying how the first thing he would do when he got to a free state he would go to saving up money and never spend a single cent, and when he got enough he would buy his wife, which was owned on a farm close to where Miss Watson lived; and then they would both work to buy the two children, and if their master wouldn't sell them, they'd get an Ab'litionist to go and steal them.
>
> It most froze me to hear such talk. He wouldn't ever dared to talk such talk in his life before. Just see what a difference it made in him the minute he judged he was about free. It was according to the old saying, "Give a nigger an inch and he'll take an ell." Thinks I, this is what comes of my not thinking. Here was this nigger, which I had as good as helped to run away, coming right out flat-footed and saying he would steal his children—children that belonged to a man I didn't even know; a man that hadn't ever done me no harm.
>
> I was sorry to hear Jim say that, it was such a lowering of him.

Of course, we hear *unconscious* irony in Huck's words, especially in his indignation that Jim "would steal his children—children that belonged to a man I didn't even know."

Although we sometimes feel that a first-person narrator (Conrad's Marlow in several novels is an example) is a very thinly veiled substitute for the author, the words of a first-person narrator require the same kind of scrutiny that we give to the words of the other characters in a story or play. The reader must deduce the personality from what is said. For instance, the narrator of "Araby" never tells us that he was a good student, but, from such a passage as the following, we can deduce that he was a bookish boy until he fell in love: "I watched my master's face pass from amiability to sternness; he hoped I was not beginning to idle."

A first-person narrator is not likely to give us the help that an editorially omniscient narrator gives. We must deduce from this passage from "Araby" that the narrator's uncle drinks too much: "At nine o'clock I heard my uncle's latchkey in the hall-door. I heard him talking to himself and heard the hall-stand rocking when it had received the weight of his overcoat. I could inter-pret these signs." In a first-person narrative it is sometimes difficult for the reader to interpret the signs. In a sense the author has given the reader two stories: the story the narrator tells and the story of a narrator telling a story.

An essay on point of view in a first-person story will probably character-ize the narrator at some length. For instance, it will point out that the narra-tor is a not-too-bright adult who is eagerly telling a new acquaintance some-thing about life in this town. The essay will then go on to show how this narrator's character colors the story that he or she tells. The essay will, for in-stance, explain that because the narrator is rather simple, he does not under-stand that he is in fact recounting a story about murder and not—as he thinks—a curious accident; that is, the essay will discuss how the reader's re-sponse resembles or differs from the narrator's.

In writing about point of view in a first-person narrative, such as *Huck-leberry Finn,* after an introductory remark to the effect that Huckleberry Finn narrates the story, use the character's name or a pronoun ("Huck fails to see …") in speaking of the narrator.

Caution: Essays on narrative point of view have a way of slipping into es-says on what the story is about. Of course, point of view *is* relevant to the theme of the story, but if you are writing about point of view, keep this focus in sight, explaining, for instance, how it shapes the theme.

THEME: VISION OR DISCOURSE?

Because modern fiction makes subtle use of it, point of view can scarcely be neglected in a discussion of **theme**—what a story is about. Perhaps unfairly, modern criticism is usually unhappy with suggestions of the author's voice in older fiction. We would rather see than be lectured. We are less impressed by "It was the stillness of an implacable force brooding over an inscrutable inten-tion" (from Conrad's *Heart of Darkness*) than by this passage from the same book:

Black shapes crouched, lay, sat between the trees, leaning against the trunks, clinging to the earth, half coming out, half effaced within the dim light, in all the attitudes of pain, abandonment, and despair. Another mine on the cliff went off, followed by a slight shudder of the soil under my feet. The work was going on. The work! And this was the place where some of the helpers had withdrawn to die.

The second quotation, but not the first, gives us the sense of reality that we have come to expect from fiction. (Still, this is a critical assumption that can be questioned.) Hardy's novels in particular have been censured on this account; the modern sensibility is uneasy when it hears Hardy's own voice commenting on the cosmic significance of the happenings, as when in *Tess of the D'Urbervilles* the narrator says: "In the ill-judged execution of the well-judged plan of things, the call seldom produces the comer, the man to love rarely co-incides with the hour for loving." The passage goes on in this vein at some length. Even in passages of dialogue, we sometimes feel that we are getting not a vision of life but a discourse on it, as in this famous exchange between Tess and her brother:

> "Did you say the stars were worlds, Tess?"
> "Yes."
> "All like ours?"
> "I don't know; but I think so. They sometimes seem to be like the apples on our stubbard-tree. Most of them splendid and sound—a few blighted."
> "Which do we live on—a splendid one or a blighted one?"
> "A blighted one."

We prefer the picture of the field at Flintcomb Ash, the pigeons, the rab-bits, Stonehenge. Partly, we feel that overt commentary (even when put into the mouths of the characters) leaves the world of fiction and invites us to judge it separately as philosophy. Partly the difficulty is that twentieth-century novelists and readers have come to expect the novel to do something different from what Hardy and his contemporaries expected it to do. As Virginia Woolf puts it in "Mr. Bennett and Mrs. Brown," the novelists before World War I "made tools and established conventions which do their business. But those tools are not our tools, and that business is not our business. For us those conventions are ruin, those tools are death." Van Ghent concisely gives the modern objection: when the philosophic vision

> can be loosened away from the novel to compete in the general field of abstract truth—as frequently in Hardy—it has the weakness of any abstraction that statis-tics and history and science may be allowed to criticize; whether true or false for one generation or another, or for one reader or another, or even for one person-al mood or another, its status as truth is relative to conditions of evidence and belief existing outside the novel and existing there quite irrelevant to whatever body of particularized life the novel itself might contain.
>
> *The English Novel,* p. 197

Van Ghent goes on to explain that the philosophic vision has its proper place in the novel when it is "local and inherent there through a maximum of organic dependencies." She illustrates her point by quoting this passage from *Tess*, which describes the coming of morning after Tess's horse has been accidentally stabbed to death by the shaft of a mail cart.

> The atmosphere turned pale, the birds shook themselves in the hedges, arose, and twittered, the lane showed all its white features, and Tess showed hers, still whiter. The huge pool of blood in front of her was already assuming the iridescence of coagulation; and when the sun rose, a million prismatic hues were reflected from it. Prince lay alongside still and stark, his eyes half open, the hole in his chest looking scarcely large enough to have let out all that had animated him.

Part of Van Ghent's comment runs thus:

> With the arousal and twittering of the birds we are aware of the oblivious manifold of nature stretching infinite and detached beyond the isolated human figure; the iridescence of the coagulating blood is, in its incongruity with the dark human trouble, a note of the same indifferent cosmic chemistry that has brought about the accident; and the smallness of the hole in Prince's chest, that looked "scarcely large enough to have let out all that had animated him," is the minor remark of that irony by which Tess's great cruel trial appears as a vanishing incidental in the blind waste of time and space and biological repetition. Nevertheless, there is nothing in this event that has not the natural "grain" of concrete fact; and what it signifies—of the complicity of doom with the most random occurrence, of the cross-purposing of purpose in a multiple world, of cosmic indifference and of moral desolation—is a local truth of a particular experience and irrefutable as the experience itself.
>
> *The English Novel*, pp. 198–99

Determining and Discussing the Theme

First, we can distinguish between *story* and *theme* in fiction. Story is concerned with "How does it turn out? What happens?" Theme is concerned with "What does it add up to? What motif holds the happenings together? What does it make out of life, and, perhaps, what wisdom does it offer?"* In a good work of fiction, the details add up, or, to use Flannery O'Connor's words, they are "controlled by some overall purpose." In F. Scott Fitzgerald's *The Great Gatsby*, for example, are many references to popular music, especially to jazz. These references contribute to our sense of the reality in Fitzger-

---

*A theme in a literary work is sometimes distinguished from a *thesis*, an arguable message such as "People ought not to struggle against Fate." The theme, it might be said, is something like "The struggle against Fate" or "The Process of Maturing" or "The Quest for Love." In any case, the formulation of a theme normally includes an abstract noun or a phrase, but it must be remembered that such formulations as those in the previous sentence are finally only shorthand expressions for highly complex statements. For further comments on theme, see pp. 122–124 and 189–191.

ald's depiction of America in the 1920s, but they do more: They help comment on the shallowness of the white middle-class characters, and they sometimes (very gently) remind us of an alternative culture. One might study Fitzgerald's references to music with an eye toward getting a deeper understanding of what the novel is about.

Preliminary Notes and Two Sample Essays on the Theme of Shirley Jackson's "The Lottery"

Here are the notes and the final essays of two students who chose to write about the theme of Jackson's "The Lottery." (The story is printed in Appendix A of this book.)

The first student, after reading and rereading the story, jotted down the following notes as a sort of preliminary outline. Some of the notes were based on passages he had underlined. Notice that the jottings include some material specifically on the story and other material—references to the outside world—that is relevant to what the student takes to be the theme of the story. When he reviewed his notes before starting on a first draft, the student deleted some of them, having decided that they were not especially useful for his essay. Still, they were worth jotting down; only in retrospect can a writer clearly see which notes are useful.

```
Is Jackson saying that human nature is evil? Prob. no; here,
   people just follow a tradition, and don't examine it. Mr.
   Warner defends lottery, saying "There's always been a
   lottery." No real argument in defense of it.
We are least conscious of the things we take for granted; I
   recall someone's saying "a fish is not aware of water
   until it is out of it."
examples of blindly following society's customs
   compulsory schooling (how many people ever even remotely
      think of schooling their children at home?)
   school is 5 days a week; why not 4 or 6? Bachelor's de-
      gree is 4 years; why not 3 or 5?
   segregation (until 1960s; still in S. Africa)
   women not permitted to drive in Saudi Arabia
   women must wear veil in Saudi Arabia
   eating of meat; might a vegetarian society not look with
      horror at our habit of eating meat?
   slavery (thought to be "natural" by almost all societies
      until nineteenth century)
thoughtless following of custom in "The Lottery"
   exact words of ritual lost, but still necessary to ad-
      dress "each person approaching"
   original box gone, but present box said to be made of
      parts of previous box
```

lottery an established ritual: "The lottery was conducted
    ~~as~~ were the square dances, the teenage club, the
    Halloween program ~~by~~ Mr. Summers, who had time and
    energy to devote to civic activities." <u>Important:</u> the
    lottery is a civic activity, a social action, a <u>sum-
    mer</u> (pun?) ritual.
Evil? Certainly yes, since killing an innocent, but no one
    in the story says it's evil.
BUT Adams does say that in the north village "they're
    talking of giving up the lottery," and his wife says
    "Some places have already quit lotteries."
Also: a girl whispers, "I hope it's not Nancy," so at
    least one person feels uneasy about the whole thing
Are these people evil? No, they seem pretty decent. They
    just don't much question what they are doing, and they do
    something terrible
the box
    black = death?
    made out of pieces of old box
    "faded," "splintered badly": does this symbolize a need
        for a new tradition?
the papers
    earlier, wood chips. At end, wind blows away slips of
        paper. Symbolic of life fluttering away? (Prob. not)
the three-legged stool
    symbolic? If so, of what?
possible title
    The Violent Lottery
    The Irrational Lottery
    We All Participate in "The Lottery"
    The Meaning of the Lottery

A lot of the material here is good, though some of it would be more
suited for an essay on symbolism, and it is chiefly this material that the writer
wisely deleted in preparing to draft an essay on the theme of Jackson's story.
After writing a draft and then revising it, the author submitted the revision to
a group for peer review. Ultimately, he turned in the following essay.

We All Participate in "The Lottery"

The townsfolk in Shirley Jackson's "The Lottery" engage
in a horrible ritual. They stone an innocent person to

death. It would be horrible enough if the person they stoned were guilty of some crime, and stoning was a form of capital punishment that the society practiced, but in the case of "The Lottery" the person is not guilty of any crime. Tessie Hutchinson simply has the bad luck to pick the wrong slip of paper from a box, a paper marked with a black spot.

The people in this unnamed town every year hold a lottery, to find a victim. On the whole, they seem to believe that the lottery is necessary, or is natural; at least they hardly question it. True, Mr. Adams says that in the north village "they're talking of giving up the lottery," and his wife says that "Some places have already quit lotteries," but that's about as much as one hears of anybody questioning this institution of society. Probably most of the people in the village would agree with Old Man Warner, who says that people who talk about giving up the lottery are a "pack of crazy fools." He adds, "There's <u>always</u> been a lottery," and that seems to be about the best answer that anyone can give. Of course the people don't take any special pleasure in the lottery, and there is at least one expression of sympathy, when a girl says, "I hope it's not Nancy." On the whole, however, the people seem to believe that the lottery must be held, and someone has to die.

It's important to notice that the lottery is one of the "civic activities," that is, it is part of the regular life of these people, part (so to speak) of the air they breathe. For the most part they don't question the lottery any more than we question compulsory education, the length of the school year, or the eating of meat. When one thinks about it, one might ask why the government should have the power to compel parents to send children to school, or, for that matter, why a child shouldn't have the right to leave school whenever he or she feels like it. Why should children have almost no rights? People simply don't bother to think about this issue, or about many others. For instance, I can imagine that a member of a vegetarian society—say a Hindu Brahmin society—must be horrified by the way almost all Americans think nothing of raising animals (bringing life into the world) for the sole purpose of eating them. We just accept these things, without thinking, but from the view of another culture they may be horrible customs.

What Jackson seems to be saying to her readers is this: "Unthinkingly you follow certain conventions. These conventions seem to you to be natural, and for the most part they are harmless, but some of them are barbaric and destructive." That is, Jackson is telling us to examine our lives, and to stop assuming that all of our customs are right. Some of the beliefs we share today may, in time, come to be seen to be as evil as slavery or murder.

Now for the notes and the essay by a second student. This writer came to a very different conclusion about the theme of "The Lottery." After reading this student's notes and her essay, you may want to compare the two essays. Do you find one essay more interesting than the other? More persuasive? If so, why? You may feel that even though the essays come to different conclusions, the two essays are equally interesting and equally valid.

```
surprise and shock
    shock
        violence (at end)
        esp. shocking because violence comes from people who
            seem normal and decent
        (only a few expressions of hesitation; Mr. and Mrs.
            Adams)
        Jackson claimed violence was normal (quote passage)
    (talk of giving up lotteries)
    surprise
        we don't know, until late, what's going on;
        on rereading, we see lots of clues about what will
            happen
            Example: references to stones
```

Meanings?
    lottery = the draft in wartime?
    lottery = community violence? Example: War (??)
    lottery = violent U.S. society??
       "   " <u>any</u> violent custom; bad tradition?
   human nature corrupt? sinful? (Note name of Adams, also
      Graves) (other significant names: Summers, Warner);
      human tendency to look for a scapegoat. Is it true?

Jackson quoted on her meaning: "violence and general inhu-
      manity" but do we have to believe her?
   Maybe just a horror story, without "meaning" *Example of such a story?*
   <u>Are</u> normal people willing to kill without great provoca-
   tion?

Possible titles
   Shirley Jackson on Human Nature
   Do We All Participate in "The Lottery"?
   How Fair is Shirley Jackson's Lottery?
   Is "The Lottery" Fair?

When you read the essay, you'll notice that for a title the author settled on the last of her four tentative titles. The first title, "Shirley Jackson on Human Nature," is too broad since the essay is not on all of Jackson's work but on only one story. The second tentative title, "Do We All Participate in 'The Lottery'?", is acceptable, but it sounds a bit clumsy, so the choice apparently came down to the last two titles or to some entirely new title that the writer might discern during the process of revising her drafts.

Notice also that some points mentioned in the preliminary notes—for instance, the reference to Mr. Summers and to Mr. Warner—are omitted from the essay. And some points scarcely mentioned in the outline are emphasized in the essay. In drafting and revising the essay, the writer found that certain things weren't relevant to her point, and so she dropped them and found that others required considerable amplification.

Is "The Lottery" Fair?

Probably all readers are surprised by the ending of
Shirley Jackson's "The Lottery." But the story does more
than offer a surprise. It shocks, because it seems to say
that people who are perfectly ordinary, just like ourselves,
are capable of killing an innocent neighbor for apparently
no reason at all. On rereading the story, we can see that

Jackson has carefully prepared for the ending, and we can admire her skill. For instance, the second paragraph tells us that "Bobby Martin had already stuffed his pockets full of stones, and the other boys soon followed his example, selecting the smoothest and roundest stones" (863). We almost feel, when we reread the story, that we should not have been surprised. But even after we see that the ending has been foreshadowed, we remain shocked by the violence, and by what the story says about human beings. But exactly what <u>does</u> it say about them? And does it say anything that strikes us as true?

If we assume that the story <u>does</u> say something about life, and is not simply a meaningless shocker, we may come up with several possible interpretations. Is Jackson saying that Americans seem peaceful and neighborly but really are quite willing to engage in violence? (Although she does not clearly set the story in an identifiable region, she clearly sets it in a small town in the United States.) Certainly newspapers every day tell us of violent acts, but the violent acts are usually of an individual (a mad killer, or a rapist) or are of nature (an earthquake, a tornado).

Of course someone might conceivably argue that this story, which is about a community, is a sort of allegory about the United States as a whole. It was written in 1948, only three years after the end of World War II, and someone might claim that it is about American willingness to use violence, that is, to go to war. Or one might even say that it is about the wartime draft, which was a sort of lottery that chose certain people whose lives were risked.

But to see the story as a reference to World War II seems very strained. Nothing in the story suggests a conscious conflict between groups, as, for instance, Jackson could have suggested if members of this town were allied against another town. And though the story certainly is set in the United States, nothing in the story calls attention to a particularly <u>American violence.</u>

Another way of thinking about "The Lottery" is to see it as a story about all human beings -- not just Americans -- who unthinkingly submit to destructive traditions. This interpretation can be better supported than the first interpretation. For instance, at least two people in the story briefly question the tradition of the lottery. Steve Adams says, "Over in the north village they're talking of giving up the lottery," and a moment later his wife adds, "Some places have already quit lotteries" (866). But of course the story tells us that this community does not give up the lottery; in fact, we are particularly shocked to learn, near the end, that Steve Adams is "in the front of the crowd of villagers" (868) when they attack Tessie Hutchinson.

It's obvious that the story is about a terrible tradition that is accepted with relatively little objection, but we can still ask what connection the story has with our own lives. What traditions do we engage in that are so deadly? The wartime draft has already been mentioned, but even pacifists probably would grant that most of the people who engage in war are aware that war is terrible, and thus they are unlike Jackson's villagers. The story may be about the deadliness of certain traditions, but a reader is left wondering which of our traditions are represented in Jackson's lottery. Racism and sexism have had terrible effects, but it is hard to relate the lottery, which picks a victim at random, to discrimination against people of a certain color or a certain sex.

A third view, and one that I think is somewhat sounder than the first two views, is that the story is about human nature. Although most people are decent, they are also capable of terrible irrational violence. In Christian terms this is explained by Original Sin, a sinfulness that we have inherited from Adam. Jackson certainly allows for the possibility of some sort of Biblical interpretation, since, as we have seen, Mr. Adams is one of the leaders of the assault, and he is accompanied by Mr. Graves. The original sin of the first Adam led to death, and thus to the grave.

Shirley Jackson herself from time to time offered comments on the story. According to Judy Oppenheimer, in <u>Private Demons: The Life of Shirley Jackson,</u> when the fiction editor of <u>The New Yorker</u> asked her if "there was anything special she was trying to convey," she said, "Not really." When the editor pressed her, and asked if the story "made its point by an ironic juxtaposition of ancient superstition and modern setting," Jackson said "Sure, that would be fine," since she didn't like to discuss her work (128). Her fullest comment, according to Oppenheimer, was given to a columnist who was writing for the <u>San Francisco Chronicle:</u>

> I suppose I hoped, by setting a particularly brutal rite
> in the present and in my own village, to shock the read-
> ers with a graphic demonstration of the pointless vio-
> lence and general inhumanity of their own lives. (qtd. in
> Oppenheimer 131)

There are obvious problems with accepting this comment. First of all, as has been mentioned, Jackson offered contradictory comments on the meaning of the story. She seems not to have worried about being consistent. Second, the words she used by way of introducing her intention -- "I suppose I hoped" -- indicate that she herself was not entirely clear about what she had intended. Third, even if she did correct-

ly state her intention, she may not have fulfilled it adequately.

Certainly the story shows people who seem quite decent
but who with only a little hesitation participate in a barbaric ritual. Perhaps Jackson did intend to say in her story
that this is what we are also like. And since the story is
related to ancient rituals in which societies purify themselves by finding a scapegoat, Jackson seems to be saying
that all people, no matter how normal or decent they seem,
engage in violence that they think purifies them or is at
least in some way necessary for their own wellbeing. But
just because Jackson <u>said</u> something like this, and said it
in a gripping story, it isn't necessarily true. Despite all
of the realistic detail -- for instance Mrs. Hutchinson's desperate charge that "It isn't fair"-- the final picture of
life that "The Lottery" gives does not seem to me to be at
all realistic, and therefore I don't think the story says
anything about life. The story surprises and it shocks, for
instance like Poe's "The Fall of the House of Usher." Maybe
it even shows "The pointless violence and general inhumani-
ty" in the lives of Jackson's neighbors, but does it reflect
the lives of her readers? Do apparently normal, decent people routinely engage in barbaric behavior? I'm not like
these people, and I doubt that Jackson and her neighbors
were like them either. "The Lottery" is a cleverly plotted
story, but the more you look at it, and the more you admire
the skillful foreshadowing, the more it seems to be a clever
trick, and the less it seems to be related to life.

Works Cited

Jackson, Shirley. "The Lottery." <u>The Harper Anthology of
Fiction.</u> Ed. Sylvan Barnet. New York: Harper, 1991.
862-68.

Oppenheimer, Judy. <u>Private Demons: The Life of Shirley Jackson.</u> New York: Putnam's, 1988.

SUMMING UP: GETTING IDEAS FOR WRITING ABOUT FICTION

Here are some questions that may help stimulate ideas about stories. Not every question is relevant to every story, but if after reading a story and thinking about it you then run your eye over these questions, you will probably find some questions that will help you think further about the story—that will help you get ideas.

As has been said in earlier chapters, it's best to do your thinking with a pen or pencil in hand. If some of the following questions seem to you to be especially relevant to the story you will be writing about, jot down—freely, without worrying about spelling—your initial responses, interrupting your writing only to glance again at the story when you feel the need to check the evidence.

PLOT

1. Does the plot grow out of the characters, or does it depend on chance or coincidence? Did something at first strike you as irrelevant that later you perceived as relevant? Do some parts continue to strike you as irrelevant?

2. Does surprise play an important role, or does foreshadowing? If surprise is very important, can the story be read a second time with any interest? If so, what gives it this further interest?

3. Does chance play a role? If so, is chance used to begin, complicate, or resolve the work? Is the story improbable? If so, is it, therefore, unsatisfying?

4. What conflicts does the story include? Physical, intellectual, moral, or emotional conflicts of one character against another? Of one character against the setting, or against society? Conflicts within a single character? Is the chief conflict between clear-cut good and evil, or is it more complex?

5. Are certain episodes narrated out of chronological order? If so, were you puzzled? Annoyed? Why might the author have chosen that order?

6. Are certain situations repeated? If so, what do you make of the repetitions?

CHARACTER

1. Which character chiefly engages your interest? Why?
2. What purposes do minor characters serve? Do you find some who by their similarities and differences help define each other or help define the major character? How else is a particular character defined—by his or her words, actions (including thoughts and emotions), dress, setting, narrative point of view? Do certain characters act differently in the same or in a similar situation?
3. How does the author reveal character? By explicit authorial (editorial) comment, for instance, or by revelation through dialogue? Through depicted action? Through the actions of other characters? How are the author's methods especially suited to the whole of the story?
4. Is the behavior plausible; that is, are the characters well motivated?
5. If a character changes, why and how does he or she change? (You may want to jot down each event that influences a change.) Or did you change your attitude toward a character not because the character changes but because you came to know the character better?
6. Are the characters round or flat? Are they complex, or are they highly typical (for instance, one-dimensional representatives of a social class or age)? Are you chiefly interested in a character's psychology, or does the character strike you as standing for something, such as honesty or the arrogance of power?
7. How has the author caused you to sympathize with certain characters? How does your response—your sympathy or lack of sympathy—contribute to your judgment of the conflict?

POINT OF VIEW

1. Who tells the story? How much does the narrator know? Does the narrator strike you as reliable? What effect is gained by using this narrator?
2. How does the point of view help shape the theme? After all, the basic story of "Little Red Ridinghood"—what happens—remains unchanged whether told from the wolf's point of view or the girl's, but (to simplify grossly) if we hear the story from the wolf's point of view, we may feel that the story is about terrifying yet pathetic compulsive behavior; if from the girl's point of view, about terrified innocence.
3. It is sometimes said that the best writers are subversive, forcing us to see something that we do not want to see—something that is true but that violates our comfortable conventional ideas. Does this story oppose our comfortable conventional views?
4. Does the narrator's language help you construct a picture of the nar-

rator's character, class, attitude, strengths, and limitations? (Jot down some evidence—for instance, colloquial or formal expressions, ironic comments, figures of speech.) How far can you trust the narrator? Why?

SETTING

1. Do you have a strong sense of the time and place? Is the story very much about, say, New England Puritanism, or race relations in the South in the late nineteenth century, or midwestern urban versus small-town life? If time and place are important, how and at what points in the story has the author conveyed this sense? If you do not strongly feel the setting, do you think the author should have made it more evident?
2. What is the relation of the setting to the plot and the characters? (For instance, do houses or rooms or their furnishings say something about their residents?) Would anything be lost if the descriptions of the setting were deleted from the story or the setting were changed?

SYMBOLISM

1. Do certain characters or certain objects seem to you to stand for something in addition to themselves? Does the setting—whether a house, a farm, a landscape, a town, a period—have an extra dimension?
2. If you do believe that the story has symbolic elements, do you think they are adequately integrated within the story, or do they strike you as being too obviously stuck in?

STYLE

1. How has the point of view shaped or determined the style?
2. How would you characterize the style? Simple? Understated? Figurative? Or what, and why?
3. Do you think the style is consistent? If it isn't—for instance, if shifts are made from simple sentences to highly complex ones—what do you make of the shifts?

THEME

1. Is the title informative? What does it mean or suggest? Did the meaning seem to change after you read the story? Does the title help you formulate a theme? If you had written the story, what title would you have used?
2. Do certain passages—dialogue or description—seem to you to point especially toward the theme? Do you find certain repetitions of words

or pairs of incidents highly suggestive and helpful in directing your thoughts toward stating a theme? Flannery O'Connor, in *Mystery and Manners,* says, "In good fiction, certain of the details will tend to accumulate meaning from the action of the story itself, and when that happens, they become symbolic in the way they work." Does this story work that way?

3. Is the meaning of the story embodied in the whole story, or does it seem stuck in, for example, in certain passages of editorializing?

4. Suppose someone asked you to state the theme of the story. Could you? And if you could, would you say the theme of a particular story reinforces values you hold, or does it to some degree challenge them? Or is the concept of a theme irrelevant to this story?

WRITING FICTION ABOUT FICTION

Your instructor may ask you to write a short story, perhaps even a story in the style of one of the authors you have studied or a story that is in some way a variation of—perhaps a modernization of, or a response to—one of the stories you have studied. If you have read Poe's "The Cask of Amontillado," for instance, you might rewrite the story, setting it in the present and telling it from the point of view of the victim instead of the point of view of the murderer. And you might vary the plot so that the would-be murderer is outwitted by the man who (he thinks) is so stupid.

Such an exercise, which requires you to read and reread a model, will teach you a good deal about the ways in which your author uses language and the conventions of fiction. In short, you will learn much about the art of the short story. One thing you will surely learn is that writing a story is difficult; another is that it can be fun.

Here is an example, written by Lola Lee Loveall for a course taught by Diana Muir at Solano Community College. Ms. Loveall's story is a response to Kate Chopin's "The Story of an Hour" (p. 12). Notice that Loveall's first sentence is close to her source—a good way to get started, but by no means the only way; notice, too, that elsewhere in her story she occasionally echoes Chopin—for instance, in the references to the treetops, the sparrows, and the latchkey. A reader enjoys detecting these echoes.

What is especially interesting, however, is that before she conceived her story, Loveall presumably said to herself something like, "Well, Chopin's story is superb, but suppose we shift the focus a bit. Suppose we think about what it would be like *from the husband's point of view* to live with a woman who suffered from 'heart trouble,' a person whom one had to treat with 'great care'" (Chopin's words, in the first sentence of "The Story of an Hour"). "And what about Mrs. Mallard's sister, Josephine—so considerate of Mrs. Mallard? What, exactly, would *Mr.* Mallard think of her? Wouldn't he see her as a pain in the neck? And what might he be prompted to do? That is, how might this character in this situation respond?" And so Loveall's characters and her plot began to take shape. As part of the game, she committed herself to writing a plot that in its broad outline resembled Chopin's by being highly ironic. But read it for yourself.

```
Lola Lee Loveall
English 6
```

The Ticket
(A Different View of "The Story of an Hour")

Knowing full well his wife was afflicted with heart trouble, Brently Mallard wondered how he was going to break the news about the jacket. As he strode along his boots broke through the shallow crust from the recent rain, and dust kicked up from the well-worn wagon road came up to flavor his breathing. At least, the gentle spring rain had settled the dusty powder even as it had sprinkled his stiffly starched shirt which was already dampened from the exertion of stamping along. The strenuous pace he set himself to cover the intervening miles home helped him regain his composure. Mr. Brently Mallard was always calm, cool, and confident.

However, he hadn't been this morning when he stepped aboard the train, took off his jacket and folded it neatly beside him, and settled in his seat on the westbound train. He had been wildly excited. Freedom was his. He was Free! He was off for California, devil take the consequences! He would be his old self again, let the chips fall where they may. And he would have been well on his way, too, if that accursed ticket agent hadn't come bawling out, "Mr. Mallard, you left your ticket on the counter!" just when Mallard himself had spied that nosy Jan Ardan bidding her sister good-

bye several car lengths down the depot. How could he be so
unfortunate to run into them both twice this morning? Earlier, they had come into the bank just as the banker had extended the thick envelope.

"You understand, this is just an advance against the estate for a while?"

Only Mallard's persuasiveness could have extracted that
amount from the cagey old moneybags.

Mallard had carefully tucked it into his inside pocket.

This was the kind of spring day to fall in love -- or
lure an adventurer to the top of the next hill. Sparrows
hovered about making happy sounds. Something about their
movements reminded Mallard of his wife -- quick, fluttering,
then darting away.

He had loved her at first for her delicate ways. They had
made a dashing pair -- he so dark and worldly, she so fragile
and fair -- but her delicacy was a trap, for it disguised the
heart trouble, bane of his life. Oh, he still took her a sip
of brandy in bed in the morning as the doctor had suggested,
although, of course, it wasn't his bed anymore. He had moved
farther down the hall not long after her sister, Josephine,
came to help, quick to come when Mrs. Mallard called, even
in the middle of the night. After one such sudden appearance
one night -- "I thought I heard you call" -- he had given up
even sharing the same bed with his wife, although there had
been little real sharing there for some time.

"No children!" the doctor had cautioned.

Mallard concentrated harder on the problem of the missing
jacket. What to say? She would notice. Maybe not right away,
but she would be aware. Oh, he knew Louise's reaction. She
would apparently take the news calmly, then make a sudden
stab toward her side with her delicate hands, then straight-

en and walk away -- but not before he observed. A new jacket
would cost money. Discussing money made the little drama
happen more often, so now Mr. Mallard handled all the finan-
cial affairs, protecting her the best he could. After all,
it was her inheritance, and he took great care with it, but
there were the added costs: doctors, Josephine living with
them, the medications, even his wife's brandy. Why, he
checked it daily to be sure it was the proper strength. Of
course, a man had to have a few pleasures, even if the cards
did seem to fall against him more often than not. He manful-
ly kept trying.

Everyone has a limit, though, and Mr. Mallard had reached
his several days ago when the doctor had cautioned him
again.

"She may go on like she is for years, or she may just
keel over any time. However, the chances are she will gradually go downhill and need continual care. It is impossible
to tell."

Mallard could not face "gradually go downhill." His man-
hood revolted against it. He was young, full of life. Let
Josephine carry the chamber pot! After Louise's demise
(whenever that occurred!) the simple estate which she had
inherited reverted to Josephine. Let her earn it. Also, good
old friend Richards was always about with a suggestion here
or a word of comfort there for Louise. They'd really not
care too much if Mallard were a long time absent.

As he drew nearer his home, Mallard continued to try to
calm his composure, which was difficult for he kept hearing
the sound of the train wheels as it pulled away, jacket, envelope, and all, right before his panic-stricken eyes: CALI-
FORNIA; California; california; california.

DUTY! It was his duty not to excite Louise. As he thought

of duty he unconsciously squared his drooping shoulders, and the image of Sir Galahad flitted across his mind.

The treetops were aglow in the strange afterlight of the storm. A shaft of sunlight shot through the leaves and fell upon his face. He had come home.

He opened the front door with the latchkey. Fortunately, it had been in his pants pocket.

Later, the doctors did not think Mr. Mallard's reaction unusual, even when a slight smile appeared on the bereaved husband's face. Grief causes strange reactions.

"He took it like a man." they said.

Only later, when the full significance of his loss reached him, did he weep.

6

Writing
about Drama

The college essays you write about plays will be similar in many respects to analytic essays about fiction. Unless you are writing a review of a performance, you probably won't try to write about all aspects of a play. Rather, you'll choose some significant topic. For instance, if you are writing about Tennessee Williams's *The Glass Menagerie,* you might compare the aspirations of Jim Connor and Tom Wingfield, or you might compare Tom's illusions with those of his sister, Laura, and his mother, Amanda. Or you might examine the symbolism, perhaps limiting your essay to the glass animals but perhaps extending it to include other symbols, such as the fire escape, the lighting, and the Victrola. Similarly, if you are writing an analysis, you might decide to study the construction of one scene of a play, or, if the play does not have a great many scenes, even the construction of the entire play.

A list of questions on pages 139–141 may help you find a topic for the particular play you choose.

A SAMPLE ESSAY

The following essay discusses the structure of *The Glass Menagerie.* It mentions various characters, but, since its concern is with the arrangement of scenes, it does not (for instance) examine any of the characters in detail. An essay might well be devoted to examining (for example) Williams's assertion that "There is much to admire in Amanda, and as much to love and pity as there is to laugh at," but an essay on the structure of the play is probably not the place to talk about Williams's characterization of Amanda.

Preliminary Notes

After deciding to write on the structure of the play, with an eye toward seeing the overall pattern, the student reread *The Glass Menagerie*, jotted down some notes briefly summarizing each of the seven scenes, with an occasional comment, and then typed them. On rereading the typed notes, he added a few observations in handwriting.

nagging

1. begins with Tom talking to audience;
   ~~says he is a magician~~
   America, in 1930s
        "shouting and confusion"
   Father deserted
   Amanda nagging; ~~is she a bit cracked?~~
   Tom: bored, angry
   Laura: embarrassed, depressed

2. Laura: quit business school; sad, but
   Jim's name is mentioned, so,
   lighter tone introduced

out-and-out battle —

3. Tom and Amanda argue
   Tom almost destroys glass menagerie
   Rage: Can things get any worse?

reconciliation, and false hopes — then final collapse

4. T and A reconciled
   T to try to get a "gentleman caller"

5. T tells A that Jim will visit
   things are looking up

6. Jim arrives; L terrified
   still, Aman thinks things can work out

7. Lights go out (foreshadowing dark ending?)
   Jim a jerk, clumsy; breaks unicorn, but L doesn't seem to
   mind. Maybe he *is* the right guy to draw her into normal
   world. Jim reveals he is engaged:
        "Desolation."
   Tom escapes into merchant marine, but can't escape memo-
        ries. Speaks to audience.
        L. blows out candles (does this mean he forgets her?
        No, because he is remembering her right now. I don' t
        get it, if the candles are supposed to be symbolic.)

These notes enabled the student to prepare a rough draft, which he then submitted to some classmates for peer review. (On peer review, see pages 22–23.)

Notice that the final version of the essay, printed below, is *not* merely a summary (a brief retelling of the plot). Although it does indeed include summary, it chiefly is devoted to showing *how* the scenes are related.

Title is focused; it announces topic and thesis.

The Solid Structure of

<u>The Glass Menagerie</u>

Opening paragraph closes in on thesis.

In the "Production Notes" Tennessee Williams calls <u>The Glass Menagerie</u> a "memory play," a term that the narrator in the play also uses. Memories often consist of fragments of episodes which are so loosely connected that they seem chaotic, and therefore we might think that <u>The Glass Menagerie</u> will consist of very loosely related episodes. However, the play covers only one episode and though it gives the illusion of random talk, it really has a firm structure and moves steadily toward a foregone conclusion.

Reasonable organization; the paragraph touches on the beginning and the end.

Brief but effective quotations.

Tennessee Williams divides the play into seven scenes. The first scene begins with a sort of prologue and the last scene concludes with a sort of epilogue that is related to the prologue. In the prologue Tom addresses the audience and comments on the 1930s as a time when America was "blind" and was a place of "shouting and confusion." Tom also mentions that our lives consist of expectations, and though he does not say that our expectations are unfulfilled, near the end of the prologue he quotes a postcard that his father wrote to the family he deserted: "Hello -- Goodbye." In the epilogue Tom tells us that he followed his "father's footsteps," deserting the family.

And just before the epilogue, near the end of
Scene VII, we see what can be considered an-
other desertion: Jim explains to Tom's sister
Laura that he is engaged and therefore cannot

Useful generalization based on earlier details.

visit Laura again. Thus the end is closely
related to the beginning, and the play is the
steady development of the initial
implications.

Chronological organiza- tion is reasonable. Open- ing topic sentence lets readers know where they are going.

The first three scenes show things going
from bad to worse. Amanda is a nagging mother
who finds her only relief in talking about the
past to her crippled daughter Laura and her
frustrated son Tom. When she was young she was
beautiful and was eagerly courted by rich
young men, but now the family is poor and this
harping on the past can only bore or infuriate
Tom and embarrass or depress Laura, who have
no happy past to look back to, who see no happy future, and who can only be upset by Amanda's insistence that they should behave as she
behaved long ago. The second scene deepens the

Brief plot summary supports thesis.

despair: Amanda learns that the timorous Laura
has not been attending a business school but
has retreated in terror from this confronta-
tion with the contemporary world. Laura's
helplessness is made clear to the audience,
and so is Amanda's lack of understanding. Near
the end of the second scene, however, Jim's
name is introduced; he is a boy Laura had a
crush on in high school, and so the audience
gets a glimpse of a happier Laura and a sense
that possibly Laura's world is wider than the

stifling tenement in which she and her mother and brother live. But in the third scene things get worse, when Tom and Amanda have so violent an argument that they are no longer on speaking terms. Tom is so angry with his mother that he almost by accident destroys his sister's treasured collection of glass animals, the fragile lifeless world which is her refuge. The apartment is literally full of the "shouting and confusion" that Tom spoke of in his prologue.

Useful summary and transition.

The first three scenes have revealed a progressive worsening of relations; the next three scenes reveal a progressive improvement in relations. In Scene IV Tom and his mother are reconciled, and Tom reluctantly -- apparently in an effort to make up with his mother -- agrees to try to get a friend to come to dinner so that Laura will have "a gentleman caller." In Scene V Tom tells his mother that Jim will come to dinner on the next night, and Amanda brightens, because she sees a possibility of security for Laura at last. In Scene VI Jim arrives, and despite Laura's initial terror, there seems, at least in Amanda's mind, to be the possibility that things will go well.

The seventh scene, by far the longest, at first seems to be fulfilling Amanda's hopes. Despite the ominous fact that the lights go out because Tom has not paid the electric bill, Jim is at ease. He is an insensitive oaf, but that doesn't seem to bother Amanda,

and almost miraculously he manages to draw
Laura somewhat out of her sheltered world.
Even when Jim in his clumsiness breaks the
horn of Laura's treasured glass unicorn, she
is not upset. In fact, she is almost relieved
because the loss of the horn makes the animal
less "freakish" and he "will feel more at home
with the other horses." In a way, of course,
the unicorn symbolizes the crippled Laura, who
at least for the moment feels less freakish
and isolated now that she is somewhat reunited
with society through Jim. But this is a play
about life in a blind and confused world, and
though in a previous age the father escaped,
there can be no escape now. Jim reveals that
he is engaged, Laura relapses into "desolation," Amanda relapses into rage and bitter-
ness, and Tom relapses into dreams of escape.
In a limited sense Tom does escape. He leaves
the family and joins the merchant marine, but
his last speech or epilogue tells us that he
cannot escape the memory of his sister: "Oh,
Laura, Laura, I tried to leave you behind me,
but I am more faithful than I intended to be!"

The essayist is thinking and commenting, not merely summarizing the plot.

And so the end of the last scene brings us
back again to the beginning of the first
scene: we are still in a world of "the blind"
and of "confusion." But now at the end of the
play the darkness is deeper, the characters
are lost forever in their unhappiness as Laura
"blows the candles out," the darkness being
literal but also symbolic of their
extinguished hopes.

Numerous devices, such as repeated refer-

Useful, thoughtful summary of thesis.

ences to the absent father, to Amanda's youth, to Laura's Victrola and of course to Laura's glass menagerie help to tie the scenes together into a unified play. But beneath these threads of imagery, and recurring motifs, is a fundamental pattern that involves the movement from nagging (Scenes I and II) to open hostilities (Scene III) to temporary reconciliation (Scene IV) to false hopes (Scenes V and VI) to an impossible heightening of false hopes and then, in a swift descent, to an inevitable collapse (Scene VII). Tennessee Williams has constructed his play carefully. G. B. Tennyson says that a "playwright must 'build' his speeches, as the theatrical expression has it" (13). But a playwright must do more, he must also build his play out of scenes. Like Ibsen, if Williams had been introduced to an architect he might have said, "Architecture is my business too."

Works Cited

Documentation

Tennyson, G. B. <u>An Introduction to Drama.</u> New York: Holt, 1967.

Williams, Tennessee. <u>The Glass Menagerie. Literature for Composition.</u> Ed. Sylvan Barnet et al. 3rd ed. New York: Harper, 1992. 722-767.

The danger in writing about structure, especially if one proceeds by beginning at the beginning and moving steadily to the end, is that one will simply tell the plot. This essay on *The Glass Menagerie* manages to say things about the organization of the plot even as it tells the plot. It has a point, hinted at in the pleasantly paradoxical title, developed in the body of the essay, and wrapped up in the last line.

TYPES OF PLAYS

Most of the world's great plays written before the twentieth century may be regarded as one of two kinds: **tragedy** or **comedy.** Roughly speaking, tragedy dramatizes the conflict between the vitality of the single life and the laws or limits of life. The tragic hero reaches a height, going beyond the experience of others but at the cost of his or her life. Comedy dramatizes the vitality of the laws of social life. In comedy, the good life is seen to reside in the shedding of an individualism that isolates, in favor of a union with a genial and enlightened society. These points must be amplified a bit before we go on to the point that, of course, any important play does much more than can be put into such crude formulas.

Tragedy

Tragic heroes usually go beyond the standards to which reasonable people adhere; they do some fearful deed that ultimately destroys them. This deed is often said to be an act of *hubris,* a Greek word meaning something like "overweening pride." It may involve, for instance, violating a taboo, such as that against taking life. But if the hubristic act ultimately destroys the man or woman who performs it, it also shows that person (paradoxically) to be in some way more fully a living being—a person who has experienced life more fully, whether by heroic action or by capacity for enduring suffering—than the other characters in the play. Othello kills Desdemona, Lear gives away his crown and banishes his one loving daughter, Antony loses his share of the Roman Empire; but all of these men seem to live more fully than the other characters in the plays—for one thing, they experience a kind of anguish unknown to those who surround them and who outlive them. (If the hero does not die, he or she usually is left in some deathlike state, as is the blind Oedipus in *King Oedipus.*)

In tragedy, we see humanity pushed to an extreme; in agony and grief the hero enters a world unknown to most and reveals magnificence. After his or her departure from the stage, we are left in a world of littler people. The closing lines of almost any of Shakespeare's tragedies may be used to illustrate the point. *King Lear,* for example, ends thus:

> The oldest hath borne most: we that are young
> Shall never see so much, nor live so long.

What has just been said may (or may not) be true of most tragedies, but it certainly is not true of all. If you are writing about a tragedy, you might consider whether the points just made are illustrated in your play. Is the hero guilty of *hubris?* Does the hero seem a greater person than the others in the play? An essay examining such questions probably requires not only a character sketch but also some comparison with other characters.

Tragedy commonly involves **irony** of two sorts: unconsciously ironic deeds and unconsciously ironic speeches. **Ironic deeds** have some consequence more or less the reverse of what the doer intends. Macbeth thinks that by killing Duncan he will gain happiness, but he finds that his deed brings him sleepless nights. Brutus thinks that by killing Caesar he will bring liberty to Rome, but he brings tyranny. In an unconsciously **ironic speech,** the speaker's words mean one thing to him or her but something more significant to the audience, as when King Duncan, baffled by Cawdor's treason, says:

> There's no art
> To find the mind's construction in the face:
> He was a gentleman on whom I built
> An absolute trust.

At this moment Macbeth, whom we have already heard meditating the murder of Duncan, enters. Duncan's words are true, but he does not apply them to Macbeth, as the audience does. A few moments later Duncan praises Macbeth as "a peerless kinsman." Soon Macbeth will indeed become peerless, when he kills Duncan and ascends to the throne.* Sophocles's use of ironic deeds and speeches is so pervasive, especially in *King Oedipus,* that **Sophoclean irony** has become a critical term. Here is a critic summarizing the ironies of *King Oedipus:*

> As the images unfold, the enquirer turns into the object of enquiry, the hunter into the prey, the doctor into the patient, the investigator into the criminal, the revealer into the thing revealed, the finder into the thing found, the savior into the thing saved ("I was saved, for some dreadful destiny"), the liberator into the thing released ("I released your feet from the bonds which pierced your ankles" says the Corinthian messenger), the accuser becomes the defendant, the ruler the subject, the teacher not only the pupil but also the object lesson, the example.
>
>   Bernard Knox, "Sophocles' Oedipus," in *Tragic Themes in Western Literature,* ed. Cleanth Brooks (New Haven, 1955), pp. 10–11

Notice, by the way, the neatness of that sentence; it is unusually long but it does not ramble, it does not baffle, and it does not suggest a stuffy writer. The verb *turns* governs the first two-thirds; and after the second long parenthesis, when the messenger's speech may cause the reader to forget the verb, the writer provides another verb, *becomes.*

When the deed backfires or has a reverse effect, such as Macbeth's effort

---

*Dramatic irony (ironic deeds or happenings, and unconsciously ironic speeches) must be distinguished from *verbal irony,* which is produced when the speaker is *conscious* that his or her words mean something different from what they say. In *Macbeth* Lennox says: "The gracious Duncan / Was pitied of Macbeth. Marry, he was dead! / And the right valiant Banquo walked too late. / ... / Men must not walk too late." He *says* nothing about Macbeth having killed Duncan and Banquo, but he *means* that Macbeth has killed them.

to gain happiness has, we have what Aristotle called a **peripeteia,** or a **reversal.** When a character comes to perceive what has happened (Macbeth's "I have lived long enough: my way of life / Is fall'n into the sere, the yellow leaf"), he experiences (in Aristotle's language) an **anagnorisis,** or **recognition.** Strictly speaking, for Aristotle the recognition was a matter of literal identification, for example, that Oedipus was the son of a man he killed. In *Macbeth,* the recognition in this sense is that Macduff, "from his mother's womb / Untimely ripped," is the man who fits the prophecy that Macbeth can be conquered only by someone not "of woman born."

In his analysis of drama Aristotle says that the tragic hero comes to grief through his **hamartia,** a term sometimes translated as **tragic flaw** but perhaps better translated as **tragic error.** Thus, it is a great error for Othello to trust Iago and to strangle Desdemona, for Lear to give away his kingdom, and for Macbeth to decide to help fulfill the prophecies. If we hold to the translation "flaw," we begin to hunt for a fault in their characters; and we say, for instance, that Othello is gullible, Lear self-indulgent, Macbeth ambitious, or some such thing. In doing this, we may overlook their grandeur. To take a single example: Iago boasts he can dupe Othello because

> The Moor is of a free and open nature
> That thinks men honest that but seem to be so.

We ought to hesitate before we say that a man who trusts men because they seem to be honest has a flaw.

When writing about tragedy, probably the commonest essay topic is on the tragic hero. Too often the hero is judged mechanically: He or she must be noble, must have a flaw, must do a fearful deed, must recognize his flaw, must die. The previous paragraph suggests that Shakespeare's practice makes doubtful one of these matters, the flaw. Be similarly cautious about accepting the rest of the package unexamined. (This book has several times urged you to trust your feelings; don't assume that what you have been taught about tragedy—in these pages or elsewhere—must be true and that you should, therefore, trust such assertions even if they go against your own responses to a given play.) On the other hand, if "tragedy" is to have any meaning—any use as a term—it must have some agreed-upon attributes.

An essay that seeks to determine whether a character is a tragic character ought at its outset to make clear its conception of tragedy and the degree of rigidity, or flexibility, with which it will interpret some or all of its categories. For example, it may indicate that although nobility is a *sine qua non,* nobility is not equivalent to high rank. A middle-class figure with certain mental or spiritual characteristics may, in such a view, be an acceptable tragic hero.

An essay closely related to the sort we have been talking about measures a character by some well-known theory of tragedy. For example, one can measure Willy Loman, in *Death of a Salesman,* against Miller's essays on tragedy or against Aristotle's remarks on tragedy. The organization of such an essay is usually not a problem: Isolate the relevant aspects of the theoretical statement, and then examine the character to see if, point by point, he illustrates them. But remember that even if Willy Loman fulfills Arthur Miller's idea of a tragic figure, you need not accept him as tragic; conversely, if he does not fulfill Aristotle's idea, you need not deny him tragic status. Aristotle may be wrong.

Comedy

Although a comedy ought to be amusing, the plays that are called comedies are not just collections of jokes. Rather, they are works that are entertaining throughout and that end happily.

In comedy, the fullest life is seen to reside within enlightened social norms: At the beginning of a comedy we find banished dukes, unhappy lovers, crabby parents, jealous husbands, and harsh laws; but at the end we usually have a unified and genial society, often symbolized by a marriage feast to which everyone, or almost everyone, is invited. Early in *A Midsummer Night's Dream,* for instance, we meet quarreling young lovers and a father who demands that his daughter either marry a man she does not love or enter a convent. Such is the Athenian law. At the end of the play the lovers are properly matched, to everyone's satisfaction.

Speaking broadly, most comedies fall into one of two classes: **satiric comedy** and **romantic comedy.** In satiric comedy the emphasis is on the obstructionists—the irate fathers, hardheaded businessmen, and other members of the Establishment who at the beginning of the play seem to hold all the cards, preventing joy from reigning. They are held up to ridicule because they are repressive monomaniacs enslaved to themselves, acting mechanistically (always irate, always hardheaded) instead of responding genially to the ups and downs of life. The outwitting of these obstructionists, usually by the younger generation, often provides the resolution of the plot. Jonson, Molière, and Shaw are in this tradition; their comedy, according to an ancient Roman formula, "chastens morals with ridicule"; that is, it reforms folly or vice by laughing at it. In romantic comedy (one thinks of Shakespeare's *Midsummer Night's Dream, As You Like It,* and *Twelfth Night*) the emphasis is on a pair or pairs of delightful people who engage our sympathies as they run their obstacle race to the altar. Obstructionists are found here too, but the emphasis is on festivity.

Essays on comedy often examine the nature of the humor. Why is an irate father, in this context, funny? Or why is a young lover, again in this context, funny? Commonly, one will find that at least some of the humor is in the disproportionate nature of their activities (they get terribly excited) and in their inflexibility. In both of these qualities they are rather like the cat in animated cartoons who repeatedly chases the mouse to his hole and who repeatedly bangs his head against the wall. The following is a skeleton of a possible essay on why Jaques in *As You Like It* is amusing:

> Jaques is insistently melancholy. In the Eden-like Forest of Arden, he sees only the dark side of things.
>
> His monomania, however, is harmless to himself and to others; because it causes us no pain, it may entertain us.
>
> Indeed, we begin to look forward to his melancholy speeches. We delight in hearing him fulfill our expectations by wittily finding gloom where others find mirth.
>
> We are delighted, too, to learn that this chastiser of others has in fact been guilty of the sort of behavior he chastises.
>
> At the end of the play, when four couples are wed, the inflexible Jaques insists on standing apart from the general rejoicing.

Such might be the gist of an essay. It needs to be supported with details, and it can be enriched, for example, by a comparison between Jaques's sort of jesting and Touchstone's; but it is at least a promising draft of an outline.

In writing about comedy you may be concerned with the function of one scene or character, but whatever your topic, you may find it helpful to begin by trying to decide whether the play is primarily romantic or primarily satiric (or something else). One way of getting at this is to ask yourself to what degree you sympathize with the characters. Do you laugh *with* them, sympathetically, or do you laugh *at* them, regarding them as at least somewhat contemptible?

Tragicomedy

The word *tragicomedy* has been used to denote (1) plays that seem tragic until the happy ending, (2) plays that combine tragic and comic scenes, and (3) plays that combine the anguish of tragedy with the improbable situations and unheroic characters and funny dialogue of comedy. It is this last sort of tragicomedy (also called "black comedy") that will occupy us here because it has attracted most of the best dramatists of our time, for example, Beckett, Genet, and Ionesco. They are the dramatists of the Absurd in two senses: the irrational and the ridiculous. These writers differ from one another and from play to play, but they all are preoccupied with the loneliness of people in a world without the certainties afforded by God or by optimistic rationalism. This loneliness is heightened by a sense of impotence derived partly from an awareness of our inability to communicate in a society that has made language meaningless, and partly from an awareness of the precariousness of our existence in an atomic age.

Landmarks on the road to people's awareness of their littleness are Darwin's *The Origin of Species* (1859), which reduced human beings to the product of "accidental variations"; Marx's writings, which attributed people's sense of alienation to economic forces and thus implied that people had no identity they could properly call their own; and Freud's writings, which by charting people's unconscious drives and anarchic impulses induced a profound distrust of the self.

The result of such developments in thought seems to be that a "tragic sense" in the twentieth century commonly means a despairing or deeply uncertain view, something very different from what it meant in Greece and in Elizabethan England. This uncertainty is not merely about the cosmos or even about character or identity. In 1888, in the Preface to *Miss Julie*, Strindberg called attention to the new sense of the instability of character:

> I have made the people in my play fairly "characterless." The middle-class conception of a fixed character was transferred to the stage, where the middle class has always ruled. A character there came to mean an actor who was always one and the same, always drunk, always comic or always melancholy, and who needed to be characterized only by some physical defect such as a club foot, a wooden leg, or a red nose, or by the repetition of some such phrase such as, "That's capital," or "Barkis is willin'."… Since the persons in my play are modern characters, living in a transitional era more hurried and hysterical than the previous one at least, I have depicted them as more unstable, as torn and divided, a mixture of the old and the new.

Along with the sense of characterlessness, or at least of the mystery of character, developed in the drama (and in the underground film and novel) was a sense of plotlessness or of the fundamental untruthfulness of the traditional plot that moved by cause and effect. Ionesco, for example, has said that a play should be able to stop at any point; it ends only because—as in life—the audience at last has to go home to bed. Moreover, Ionesco has allowed directors to make heavy cuts, and he has suggested that endings other than those he wrote are possibilities. After all, in a meaningless world one can hardly take a dramatic plot seriously.

Every play is different from every other play; each is a unique and detailed statement, and the foregoing paragraphs give only the broadest outlines—tragedies, comedies, and tragicomedies seen at a distance, as it were. The analyst's job is to try to study the differences, as well as the similarities, in an effort (in Henry James's words) "to appreciate, to appropriate, to take intellectual possession, to establish in fine a relation with the criticized thing and make it one's own."

ASPECTS OF DRAMA

Theme

The best way to make a work of art one's own is (again in Henry James's words) "to be one of the people on whom nothing is lost." If we have perceived the work properly, we ought to be able to formulate its **theme,** its underlying idea, and perhaps we can even go so far as to say its moral attitudes, its view of life, its wisdom. Some critics, it is true, have argued that the concept of theme is meaningless. They hold that *Macbeth,* for example, gives us only an extremely detailed history of one imaginary man. In this view, *Macbeth* says nothing to you or me; it only says what happened to some imaginary man. Even *Julius Caesar* says nothing about the historical Julius Caesar or about the nature of Roman politics. On this we can agree; no one would offer Shakespeare's play as evidence of what the historical Caesar said or did. But surely the view that the concept of theme is meaningless and that a work tells us only about imaginary creatures is a desperate one. We *can* say that we see in *Julius Caesar* the fall of power or (if we are thinking of Brutus) the vulnerability of idealism or some such thing.

To the reply that these are mere truisms, we can counter: Yes, but the truisms are presented in such a way that they take on life and become a part of us rather than remain things of which we say, "I've heard it said, and I guess it's so." Surely we are in no danger of equating the play with the theme that we sense underlies it. If, for example, we say (as Ionesco himself said of his play) that *Rhinoceros* is "an attack on collective hysteria and the epidemics that lurk beneath the surface of reason," we do not believe that our statement of the theme is the equivalent of the play itself. We recognize that the play presents the theme with such detail that our statement is only a wedge to help us enter into the play, so that we may more fully appropriate it.

A brief illustration may be helpful here. A critic examining Ibsen's achievements begins by trying to see what some of the plays are in fact about.

> We must not waste more than a paragraph on such fiddle-faddle as the notion that *Ghosts* is a play about venereal disease or that *A Doll's House* is a play about women's rights. On these terms, *King Lear* is a play about housing for the elderly and *Hamlet* is a stage-debate over the reality of spooks. Venereal disease and its consequences are represented onstage in *Ghosts;* so, to all intents and purposes, is incest; but the theme of the play is inherited guilt, and the sexual pathology of the Alving family is an engine in the hands of that theme. *A Doll's House* represents a woman imbued with the idea of becoming a person, but it proposes nothing categorical about women becoming people; in fact, its real theme has nothing to do with the sexes. It is the irrepressible conflict of two different personalities which have founded themselves on two radically different estimates of reality.
>
> Robert M. Adams, "Ibsen on the Contrary," in *Modern Drama,* ed. Anthony Caputi (New York, 1966), p. 345

Such a formulation can be most useful; a grasp of the theme helps us see what the plot is really all about, what the plot suggests in its universal meaning or applicability.

A few words about the preceding quotation may be appropriate here. Notice that Adams's paragraph moves from a vigorous colloquial opening through some familiar examples, including a brief comparison with plays by another dramatist, to a fairly formal close. The disparity in tone between opening and closing is not distressing because even in the opening we sense the writer's mastery of his material, and we sympathize with his impatience. Adams's next paragraph, not given here, extends his suggestion that the plays are not about nineteenth-century problems: he argues that under the bourgeois décor, under the frock coat and the bustle, we detect two kinds of people—little people and great people. His third paragraph elaborates this point by suggesting that, allowing for variations, the dichotomy consists of satyrs and saints, and he provides the details necessary to make this dichotomy convincing. Among Ibsen's little people, or satyrs, are Parson Manders, Peter Stockmann, Hjalmar Ekdal, and Torvald Helmer; among the great people, or saints, are Mrs. Alving, Thomas Stockmann, Gregers Werle, and Nora Helmer. In short, Adams's argument about Ibsen's themes advances steadily and is convincingly illustrated with concrete references.

Some critics (influenced by Aristotle's statement that a drama is an imitation of an action) use **action** in a sense equivalent to theme. In this sense, the action is the underlying happening—the inner happening—for example, "the enlightenment of someone" or "the coming of unhappiness" or "the finding of the self by self-surrender." One might say that the theme of *Macbeth,* for example, is embodied in some words that Macbeth himself utters: "Blood will have blood." Of course, this is not to say that these words and no other words embody the theme or the action. Francis Fergusson suggests that another expression in *Macbeth,* to the effect that Macbeth "outran the pauser, reason," describes the action of the play:

> To "outrun" reason suggests an impossible stunt, like lifting oneself by one's own bootstraps. It also suggests a competition or race, like those of nightmare, which cannot be won. As for the word "reason," Shakespeare associates it with nature and nature's order, in the individual soul, in society, and in the cosmos. To outrun reason is thus to violate nature itself, to lose the bearings of common sense and of custom, and to move into a spiritual realm bounded by the irrational darkness of Hell one way, and the superrational grace of faith the other way. As the play develops before us, all the modes of this absurd, or evil, or supernatural, action are attempted, the last being Malcolm's and Macduff's acts of faith.

The Human Image in Dramatic Literature (New York, 1957), p. 118

Critics like Fergusson, who are influenced by Aristotle's *Poetics,* assume that the dramatist conceives of an action and then imitates it or sets it forth by means of first a plot and characters and then by means of language, gesture, and perhaps spectacle and music. When the Greek comic dramatist Menander told a friend he had finished his play and now had only to write it, he must have meant that he had the action or the theme firmly in mind and had worked out the plot and the requisite characters. All that remained was to set down the words.

Plot

Plot is variously defined sometimes as equivalent to "story" (in this sense a synopsis of *Julius Caesar* has the same plot as *Julius Caesar*) but more often, and more usefully, as the dramatist's particular arrangement of the story. Thus, because Shakespeare's *Julius Caesar* begins with a scene dramatizing an encounter between plebeians and tribunes, its plot is different from that of a play on Julius Caesar in which such a scene (not necessary to the story) is omitted. Richard G. Moulton, discussing the early part of Shakespeare's plot in *Julius Caesar,* examines the relationship between the first two scenes.

> ... The opening scene strikes appropriately the key-note of the whole action. In it we see the tribunes of the people—officers whose whole *raison d'être* is to be the mouthpiece of the commonalty—restraining their own clients from the noisy honors they are disposed to pay Caesar. To the justification in our eyes of a conspiracy against Caesar, there could not be a better starting-point than this hint that the popular worship of Caesar, which has made him what he is, is itself reaching its reaction-point. Such a suggestion moreover makes the whole play one complete *wave* of popular fickleness from crest to crest.
>
> The second is the scene upon which the dramatist mainly relies for the *crescendo* in the justification of the conspirators. It is a long scene, elaborately contrived so as to keep the conspirators and their cause before us at their very best, and the victim at his very worst.

Shakespeare as a Dramatic Artist (Oxford, 1893), pp. 188–189

Moulton's discussion of the plot continues at length. One may argue that he presents too favorable a view of the conspirators (when he says we see the conspirators at their best, he seems to overlook their fawning), but that is not our concern here; here we have been talking about the process of examining juxtaposed scenes, a process Moulton's words illustrate well.

Handbooks on the drama often suggest that a plot (arrangement of happenings) should have a **rising action,** a **climax,** and a **falling action.** This sort of plot may be diagramed as a pyramid: The tension rises through complications or **crises** to a climax, at which point the climax is the apex, and the tension allegedly slackens as we witness the **dénouement** (unknotting). Shakespeare sometimes used a pyramidal structure, placing his climax neatly in the middle of what seems to us to be the third of five acts. Roughly the first half of *Romeo and Juliet,* for example, shows Romeo winning Juliet; but when in

3.1 he kills her cousin Tybalt, Romeo sets in motion (it is often said) the second half of the play, the losing of Juliet and of his own life. Similarly, in *Julius Caesar* Brutus rises in the first half of the play, reaching his height in 3.1 with the death of Caesar; but later in this scene he gives Marc Antony permission to speak at Caesar's funeral, and thus he sets in motion his own fall, which occupies the second half of the play. In *Macbeth*, the protagonist attains his height in 3.1 ("Thou hast it now: King"), but he soon perceives that he is going downhill:

> I am in blood
> Stepped in so far, that, should I wade no more,
> Returning were as tedious as go o'er.

In *Hamlet,* the protagonist proves to his own satisfaction Claudius's guilt in 3.2, by the play within the play, but almost immediately he begins to worsen his position by failing to kill Claudius when he is an easy target (3.3) and by contaminating himself with the murder of Polonius (3.4).

No law demands such a structure, and a hunt for the pyramid usually causes the hunter to overlook all the crises but the middle one. William Butler Yeats once suggestively diagramed a good plot not as a pyramid but as a line moving diagonally upward, punctuated by several crises. And it has been said that in Beckett's *Waiting for Godot,* "nothing happens, twice." Perhaps it is sufficient to say that a good plot has its moments of tension, but that the location of these will vary with the play. They are the product of **conflict,** but it should be noted that not all conflict produces tension; there is conflict but little tension in a ball game when the home team is ahead 10–0 and the visiting pitcher comes to bat in the ninth inning with two out and none on base.

Regardless of how a plot is diagramed, the **exposition** is the part that tells the audience what it has to know about the past, the **antecedent action.** Two gossiping servants who tell each other that after a year away in Paris the young master is coming home tomorrow with a new wife are giving the audience the exposition. The exposition in Shakespeare's *Tempest* is almost ruthlessly direct: Prospero tells his naive daughter, "I should inform thee farther," and for about 150 lines he proceeds to tell her why she is on an almost uninhabited island. Prospero's harangue is punctuated by his daughter's professions of attention; but the Elizabethans (and the Greeks) sometimes tossed out all pretense at dialogue and began with a **prologue,** like the one spoken by the Chorus at the opening of *Romeo and Juliet:*

> Two households, both alike in dignity
> In fair Verona, where we lay our scene,
>
> From ancient grudge break to new mutiny,
> Where civil blood makes civil hands unclean.
> From forth the fatal loins of these two foes
> A pair of star-crossed lovers take their life....

But the exposition may also extend far into the play, being given in small, explosive revelations.

Exposition has been discussed as though it consists simply of informing the audience about events, but exposition can do much more. It can give us an understanding of the characters who themselves are talking about other characters, it can evoke a mood, and it can generate tension. When we summarize the opening act and treat it as "mere exposition," we are probably losing what is in fact dramatic in it. Moulton, in his analysis of the first two scenes in *Julius Caesar,* does not make the mistake of thinking that the first scenes exist merely to tell the audience certain facts.

In fact, exposition usually includes **foreshadowing.** Details given in the exposition, which we may at first take as mere background, often turn out to be highly relevant to later developments. For instance, in the very short first scene of *Macbeth* the Witches introduce the name of Macbeth, but in such words as "fair is foul" and "when the battle's lost and won" they also give glimpses of what will happen: Macbeth will become foul, and though he will seem to win (he becomes king), he will lose the most important battle. Similarly, during the exposition in the second scene we learn that Macbeth has loyally defeated Cawdor, who betrayed King Duncan, and Macbeth has been given Cawdor's title. Later we will find that, like Cawdor, Macbeth betrays Duncan; that is, in giving us the background about Cawdor, the exposition is also telling us (though we don't know it when we first see or read the play) something about what will happen to Macbeth.

In writing about an aspect of plot, you may want to consider one of the following topics:

1. Is the plot improbable? If so, is the play, therefore, weak?
2. Does a scene that might at first glance seem unimportant or even irrelevant serve an important function?
3. If certain actions that could be shown onstage take place offstage, what is the reason? In *Macbeth,* for instance, why do you suppose the murder of Duncan takes place offstage, whereas Banquo and Macduff's family are murdered onstage? Why, then, might Shakespeare have preferred not to show us the murder of Duncan? What has he gained? (A good way to approach this sort of question is to think of what your own reaction would be if the action were shown onstage.)
4. If the play has several conflicts—for example, between pairs of lovers or between parents and their children and also between the parents themselves—how are these conflicts related? Are they parallel? Or contrasting?
5. Does the arrangement of scenes have a structure? For instance, do the scenes depict a rise and then a fall?
6. Does the plot seem satisfactorily concluded? Any loose threads? If so, is the apparent lack of a complete resolution a weakness in the play?

An analysis of plot, then, will consider the arrangement of the episodes and the effect of juxtapositions, as well as the overall story. A useful essay may be written on the function of one scene. Such an essay may point out, for example, that the long, comparatively slow scene (4.3) in *Macbeth,* in which Malcolm, Macduff, an English doctor, and Ross converse near the palace of the King of England, is not so much a leisurely digression as may at first be thought. After reading it closely, you may decide that it has several functions. For example, it serves to indicate the following:

1. The forces that will eventually overthrow Macbeth are gathering.
2. Even good men must tell lies during Macbeth's reign.
3. Macbeth has the vile qualities that the virtuous Malcolm pretends to have.
4. Macbeth has failed—as the King of England has not—to be a source of health to the realm.

It doubtless will take an effort to come to these or other conclusions, but once you have come to such ideas (probably by means of brainstorming and listing), the construction of an essay on the function of a scene is usually fairly simple: An introductory paragraph announces the general topic and thesis—an apparently unnecessary scene will be shown to be functional—and the rest of the essay demonstrates the functions, usually in climactic order if some of the functions are more important than others.

How might you organize such an essay? If you think all of the functions are equally important, perhaps you will organize the material from the most obvious to the least obvious, thereby keeping the reader's attention to the end. If on the other hand, you believe that although justifications for the scene can be imagined, the scene is nevertheless unsuccessful, say so; announce your view early, consider the alleged functions one by one, and explain your reasons for finding them unconvincing as you take up each point.

Sometimes an analysis of the plot will examine the relationships between the several stories in a play: *A Midsummer Night's Dream* has supernatural lovers, mature royal lovers, young Athenian lovers, a bumpkin who briefly becomes the lover of the fairy queen, and a play (put on by the bumpkins) about legendary lovers. How these are held together and how they help define each other and the total play are matters that concern anyone looking at the plot of *A Midsummer Night's Dream.* Richard Moulton suggests that Shakespeare's subplots "have the effect of assisting the main stories, smoothing away their difficulties and making their prominent points yet more prominent." Moulton demonstrates his thesis at some length, but a very brief extract from his discussion of the Jessica–Lorenzo story in *The Merchant of Venice* may be enough to suggest the method. The main story concerns Shylock and his rivals, Antonio, Bassanio, and Portia. Shylock's daughter, Jessica, is not needed for the narrative purpose of the main story. Why, then, did Shakespeare include her?

(*Remember:* When something puzzles you, you have an essay topic at hand.)
Part of Moulton's answer runs thus:

> A Shylock painted without a tender side at all would be repulsive ... and yet it
> appears how this tenderness has grown hard and rotten with the general debase-
> ment of his soul by avarice, until, in his ravings over his loss, his ducats and his
> daughter are ranked as equally dear.
>
> > I would my daughter were dead at my foot, and the jewels in her ear!
> > Would she were hearsed at my foot, and the ducats in her coffin!
>
> For all this we feel that he is hardly used in losing her. Paternal feeling may take
> a gross form, but it is paternal feeling none the less, and cannot be denied our
> sympathy; bereavement is a common ground upon which not only high and
> low, but even the pure and the outcast, are drawn together. Thus Jessica at
> home makes us hate Shylock; with Jessica lost we cannot help pitying him.
>
> *Shakespeare as a Dramatic Artist,* p. 79

Conventions

Artists and their audience have some tacit—even unconscious—agree-
ments. When we watch a motion picture and see an image dissolve and then
reappear, we understand that some time has passed. Such a device, unrealistic
but widely accepted, is a **convention.** In the theater, we sometimes see on the
stage a room, realistic in all details except that it lacks a fourth wall; were that
wall in place, we would see it and not the interior of the room. We do not regret the missing wall, and, indeed, we are scarcely aware that we have entered
into an agreement to pretend that this strange room is an ordinary room with
the usual number of walls. Sometimes the characters in a play speak verse, although outside the theater no human beings speak verse for more than a few
moments. Again we accept the device because it allows the author to make a
play, and we want a play. In *Hamlet* the characters are understood to be
speaking Danish, in *Julius Caesar* Latin, in *A Midsummer Night's Dream*
Greek, yet they all speak English for our benefit.

Two other conventions are especially common in older drama: the **soliloquy** and the **aside.** In the former, although a solitary character speaks his or
her thoughts aloud, we do not judge him or her to be a lunatic; in the latter,
a character speaks in the presence of others but is understood not to be heard
by them, or to be heard only by those to whom he or she directs those words.

The soliloquy and the aside strike us as artificial—and they are. But they
so strike us only because they are no longer customary. Because we are accus-
tomed to it, we are not bothered by the artificiality of music accompanying dialogue in a motion picture. The conventions of the modern theater are equally artificial but are so customary that we do not notice them. The
Elizabethans, who saw a play acted without a break, would probably find
strange our assumption that, when we return to the auditorium after a ten-

minute intermission, the ensuing action may be supposed to follow immediately the action before the intermission.

Costumes, Gestures, and Settings

The language of a play, broadly conceived, includes the costumes that the characters wear, the gestures that the characters make, and the settings in which the characters move. As Ezra Pound says, "The medium of drama is not words, but persons moving about on a stage using words."

Let's begin with **costume**, specifically with Nora Helmer's changes of costume in Ibsen's *A Doll's House*. In the first act, Nora wears ordinary clothing, but in the middle of the second act she puts on "a long, many-colored shawl" when she frantically rehearses her tarantella. The shawl is supposed to be appropriate to the Italian dance, but surely its multitude of colors also helps express Nora's conflicting emotions, her near hysteria, expressed, too, in the fact that "her hair comes loose and falls down over her shoulders," but "She doesn't notice." The shawl and her disheveled hair, then, *speak* to us as clearly as the dialogue does.

In the middle of the third act, after the party and just before the showdown, Nora appears in her "Italian costume," and her husband, Torvald, wears "evening dress" under an open black cloak. She is dressed for a masquerade (her whole life has been a masquerade, it turns out), and Torvald's formal suit and black cloak help express the stiffness and the blight that have forced her to present a false front throughout their years of marriage. A little later, after Nora sees that she never really has known her husband for the selfish creature he is, she leaves the stage, and when she returns she is "in an everyday dress." The pretense is over. She is no longer Torvald's "doll." When she finally leaves the stage—leaving the house—she "Wraps her shawl around her." This is not the "many-colored shawl" she used in rehearsing the dance, but the "big, black shawl" she wears when she returns from the dance. The blackness of this shawl helps express the death of her old way of life; Nora is now aware that life is not child's play.

Ibsen did not invent the use of costumes as dramatic language; it goes back to the beginnings of drama, and one has only to think of Hamlet's "inky cloak" or of Lear tearing off his clothing or of the fresh clothing in which Lear is garbed after his madness in order to see how eloquently costumes can speak. To this may be added the matter of disguises—for example, Edgar's disguise in *King Lear*—which are removed near the end of plays, when the truth is finally revealed and the characters can be fully themselves. In short, the removal of disguises *says* something.

Gestures, too, are a part of the language of drama. Helmer "playfully pulls [Nora's] ear," showing his affection—and his domineering condescension; Nora claps her hands, Mrs. Linde (an old friend of Nora) "tries to read but seems unable to concentrate," and so forth. All such gestures clearly and naturally convey states of mind. One of the most delightful and revealing gestures in the play occurs when, in the third act, Helmer demonstrates to Mrs. Linde the ugliness of knitting ("Look here: arms pressed close to the sides") and the elegance of embroidering ("... with your right [hand] you move the needle—like this—in an easy, elongated arc"). None of his absurd remarks throughout the play is quite so revealing of his absurdity as is this silly demonstration.

Some gestures or stage directions that imply gestures are a bit more complex. For example, when Nora "walks cautiously over to the door to the study and listens," this direction conveys Nora's fear that her husband may detect her foibles—or even her crime. We read this stage direction almost at the start of the play, when we do not yet know who is who or what is what, but we do know from this gesture alone that Nora is not at ease even in her own home. When Mrs. Linde sees her former lover, Krogstad, she "starts, looks, turns away toward the window," a natural enough reaction but one that indicates her desire to escape from this confining box-set. Similarly, when Nora "wildly" dances during her rehearsal in the second act, the action indicates the terrible agitation in her mind. One other, quieter example: In Act III, when the dying Dr. Rank for the last time visits Nora in order to gain comfort, she lights his cigar, and a moment later Rank replies—these are his last words—"And thanks for the light." Thus, we not only hear words about a cigar, but we *see* an act of friendship, a flash of light in this oppressive household.

Gesture may be interpreted even more broadly: the mere fact that a character enters, leaves, or does not enter may be highly significant. John Russell Brown comments on the actions and the absence of certain words that in *Hamlet* convey the growing separation between King Claudius and his wife, Gertrude:

> Their first appearance together with a public celebration of marriage is a large and simple visual effect, and Gertrude's close concern for her son suggests a simple, and perhaps unremarkable modification.... But Claudius enters without Gertrude for his "Prayer Scene" (III.iii) and, for the first time, Gertrude enters without him for the Closet Scene (III.iv) and is left alone, again for the first time, when Polonius hides behind the arras. Thereafter earlier accord is revalued by an increasing separation, often poignantly silent, and unexpected. When Claudius calls Gertrude to leave with him after Hamlet has dragged off Polonius' body, she makes no reply; twice more he urges her and she is still silent. But he does not remonstrate or question; rather he speaks of his own immediate concerns and, far from supporting her with assurances, becomes more aware of his own fears:
>
> >O, come away!
> >My soul is full of discord and dismay.
>
> >(V.i.44–45)
>
> Emotion has been so heightened that it is remarkable that they leave together

without further words. The audience has been aware of a new distance between Gertrude and Claudius, of her immobility and silence, and of his self-concern, haste and insistence.

Shakespeare's Plays in Performance (New York, 1967), p. 139

Sometimes the dramatist helps us interpret the gestures; Shaw and O'Neill give notably full stage directions, but detailed stage directions before the middle of the nineteenth century are rare.

Drama of the nineteenth and early twentieth centuries (for example, the plays of Ibsen, Chekhov, and Odets) is often thought to be "realistic," but even a realistic playwright or stage designer selects his or her materials. A realistic **setting** (indication of the locale), then, can say a great deal, can serve as a symbol. Here is Ibsen on nonverbal devices:

> I can do quite a lot by manipulating the prosaic details of my plays so that they become theatrical metaphors and come to mean more than what they are; I have used costume in this way, lighting, scenery, landscape, weather; I have used trivial every-day things like inky fingers and candles; and I have used living figures as symbols of spiritual forces that act upon the hero. Perhaps these things could be brought into the context of a modern realistic play to help me to portray the modern hero and the tragic conflict which I now understand so well.

> Quoted by John Northam, "Ibsen's Search for the Hero," in *Ibsen,* ed. Rolf Fjelde (Englewood Cliffs, N.J., 1965), p. 99

In the setting of *Hedda Gabler,* for example, Ibsen uses two suggestive details as more than mere background: Early in the play Hedda is distressed by the sunlight that shines through the opened French doors, a detail that we later see helps reveal her fear of the processes of nature. More evident and more pervasive is her tendency, when she cannot cope with her present situation, to move to the inner room, at the rear of the stage, in which hangs a picture of her late father. And over and over again in Ibsen we find the realistic setting of a nineteenth-century drawing room, with its heavy draperies and its bulky furniture, helping convey his vision of a bourgeois world that oppresses the individual who struggles to affirm other values.

Twentieth-century dramatists are often explicit about the symbolic qualities of the setting. Here is an example from O'Neill's *Desire under the Elms.* Only a part of the initial stage direction is given.

> The house is in good condition but in need of paint. Its walls are a sickly grayish, the green of the shutters faded. Two enormous elms are on each side of the house. They bend their trailing branches down over the roof. They appear to protect and at the same time subdue. There is a sinister maternity in their aspect, a crushing, jealous absorption.... They are like exhausted women resting their sagging breasts and hands and hair on its roof....

A second example is part of Miller's description of the set in *Death of a Salesman:*

Before us is the Salesman's house. We are aware of towering, angular shapes behind it, surrounding it on all sides. Only the blue light of the sky falls upon the house and forestage; the surrounding area shows an angry glow of orange. As more light appears, we see a solid vault of apartment houses around the small, fragile-seeming home.

Material such as this cannot be skimmed. These directions and the settings they describe are symbols that help give the plays their meaning. Not surprisingly, O'Neill's play has Freudian overtones, Miller's (in a broad sense) Marxist overtones. O'Neill is concerned about passion, Miller (notice the "solid vault of apartment houses" that menaces the salesman's house) about social forces that warp the individual. An essay might examine in detail the degree to which the setting contributes to the theme of the play. Take, for example, O'Neill's setting. The maternal elms are the most important aspect, but an essayist might first point out that the "good condition" of the house suggests it was well built, presumably some years ago. The need of paint, however, suggests both present neglect and indifference to decoration, and, indeed, the play is partly concerned with a strong, miserly father who regards his sons as decadent. The house,"a sickly grayish," helps embody the suggestion of old strength but present decadence. One might continue through the stage directions, explaining the relevance of the details. Contrasts between successive settings can be especially important.

Because Shakespeare's plays were performed in broad daylight on a stage that (compared with Ibsen's, O'Neill's, and Miller's) made little use of scenery, he had to use language to manufacture his settings. But the attentive ear or the mind's eye responds to these settings, too. Early in *King Lear,* when Lear reigns, we hear that we are in a country "With plenteous rivers, and wide-skirted meads"; later, when Lear is stripped of his power, we are in a place where "For many miles about / There's scarce a bush."

In any case, a director must provide some sort of setting—even if only a bare stage—and this setting will be part of the play. A recent production of *Julius Caesar* used great cubes piled on top of each other as the background for the first half of the play, suggesting the pretensions and the littleness of the figures who strutted on the stage. In the second half of the play, when Rome is in the throes of a civil war, the cubes were gone; a shaggy black carpet, darkness at the rear of the stage, and a great net hanging above the actors suggested that they were wretched little creatures groping in blindness. In a review of a production, you will almost surely want to pay some attention to the function of the setting.

Characterization and Motivation

Characterization, or personality, is defined most obviously, as in fiction (see p. 69), by what the characters do (a stage direction tells us that "Hedda paces up and down, clenching her fists"), by what they say (she asks her husband to draw the curtains), by what others say about them, and by the setting in which they move.

The characters are also defined in part by other characters whom they in some degree resemble. Hamlet, Laertes, and Fortinbras have each lost their fathers, but Hamlet spares the praying King Claudius, whereas Laertes, seeking vengeance on Hamlet for murdering Laertes's father, says he would cut Hamlet's throat in church; Hamlet meditates about the nature of action, but Fortinbras leads the Norwegians in a military campaign and ultimately acquires Denmark. Here is Kenneth Muir commenting briefly on the way Laertes helps us see Hamlet more precisely. (Notice how Muir first offers a generalization, then supports it with details, and finally, drawing a conclusion from the details he has just presented, offers an even more important generalization that effectively closes his paragraph.)

> In spite of Hamlet's description of him as "a very noble youth," there is a coarseness of fibre in Laertes which is revealed throughout the play. He has the stock responses of a man of his time and position. He gives his sister copy-book advice; he goes to Paris (we are bound to suspect) to tread the primrose path; and after his father's death and again at his sister's grave he shows by the ostentation and "bravery of his grief" that he pretends more than he really feels. He has no difficulty in raising a successful rebellion against Claudius, which suggests that the more popular prince could have done the same. Laertes, indeed, acts more or less in the way that many critics profess to think Hamlet ought to act; and his function in the play is to show precisely the opposite. Although Hamlet himself may envy Laertes' capacity for ruthless action we ought surely to prefer Hamlet's craven scruples.
>
> *Shakespeare: The Great Tragedies* (London, 1961), pp. 12–13

Muir has not exhausted the topic in this paragraph. If you are familiar with *Hamlet* you may want to think about writing an entire essay comparing Hamlet with Laertes.

Other plays provide examples of such **foils,** or characters who set one another off. Macbeth and Banquo both hear prophecies, but they act and react differently; Brutus is one kind of assassin, Cassius another, and Casca still another. In *Waiting for Godot,* the two tramps Didi and Gogo are contrasted with Pozzo and his slave Lucky, the former two suggesting (roughly) the contemplative life, the latter two the practical or active (and, it turns out, mistaken) life.

Any analysis of a character, then, will probably have to take into account, in some degree, the other characters that help show what he or she is, that help set forth his or her motivation (grounds for action, inner drives, goals). In Ibsen's *Doll's House,* Dr. Rank plays a part in helping define Nora:

> This is not Rank's play, it is Nora's. Rank is a minor character—but he plays a vital dramatic role. His function is to act as the physical embodiment, visible on

the stage, of Nora's moral situation as she sees it. Nora is almost hysterical with terror at the thought of her situation—almost, but it is part of her character that with great heroism she keeps her fears secret to herself; and it is because of her reticence that Rank is dramatically necessary, to symbolize the horror she will not talk about. Nora feels, and we feel, the full awfulness of Rank's illness, and she transfers to herself the same feeling about the moral corruption which she imagines herself to carry. Nora sees herself, and we see her seeing herself (with our judgment), as suffering from a moral disease as mortal, as irremediable as Rank's disease, a disease that creeps on to a fatal climax. This is the foe that Nora is fighting so courageously.

> John Northam, "Ibsen's Search for the Hero," p. 103

WRITING A REVIEW OF A PRODUCTION

Your instructor may ask you to write a review of a local production. A review requires analytic skill, but it is not identical with an analysis. First, a reviewer normally assumes that the reader is unfamiliar with the production being reviewed and also with the play if the play is not a classic. Thus, the first paragraph usually provides a helpful introduction along these lines:

> Marsha Norman's new play, *'night, Mother,* a tragedy with only two actors and one set, shows us a woman's preparation for suicide. Jessie has concluded that she no longer wishes to live, and so she tries to put her affairs into order, which chiefly means preparing her rather uncomprehending mother to get along without her.

Inevitably some retelling of the plot is necessary if the play is new, and a summary of a sentence or two is acceptable even for a familiar play. The review will, however, chiefly be concerned with

describing,

analyzing, and

evaluating.

If the play is new, much of the evaluation may center on the play itself, but if the play is a classic, the evaluation probably will chiefly be devoted to the acting, the set, and the direction. Other points:

1. **Save the playbill;** it will give you the names of the actors, and perhaps a brief biography of the author, a synopsis of the plot, and a photograph of the set, all of which may be helpful.
2. **Draft your review as soon as possible,** while the performance is still fresh in your mind. If you can't draft it immediately after seeing the play, at least jot down some notes about the setting and the staging, the acting, and the audience's response.

3. **If possible, read the play**—ideally, before the performance and again after it.
4. **In your first draft, don't worry about limitations of space;** write as long a review as you can, putting down everything that comes to mind. Later you can cut it to the required length, retaining only the chief points and the necessary supporting details, but in your first draft try to produce a fairly full record of the performance and your response to it, so that a day or two later, when you revise, you won't have to trust a fading memory for details.

A Sample Review: "An Effective *Macbeth*"

If you read reviews of plays in *Time*, *Newsweek,* or a newspaper, you will soon develop a sense of what reviews normally do. The following example, an undergraduate's review of a production of *Macbeth*, is typical except in one respect: as has been mentioned, reviews of new plays customarily include a few sentences summarizing the plot and classifying the play (a tragedy, a farce, a rock musical, or whatever), perhaps briefly putting it into the context of the author's other works, but because *Macbeth* is so widely known, the reviewer has chosen not to insult her readers by telling them that *Macbeth* is a tragedy by Shakespeare.

PRELIMINARY JOTTINGS

During the two intermissions and immediately after the end of the performance, the reviewer made a few jottings, which the next day she rewrote thus:

```
Compare with last year's Midsummer Night's Dream
Set: barren;
     pipe framework at rear. Duncan exits on it. Useful?
witches: powerful, not funny
  stage: battlefield? barren land?
    costume: earth-colored rags
     they seduce -- even caress -- Mac.
Macbeth
  witches caress him?
     strong; also gentle (with Lady M)
Lady Macb.
     sexy in speech about unsexing her
     too attractive? Prob. ok
Banquo's ghost: naturalistic; covered with blood
Duncan: terrible; worst actor except for Lady Macduff's boy
costumes: leather, metal; only Duncan in robes
pipe framework used for D, and murder of Lady Macduff
forest: branches unrealistic; stylized? or cheesy?
```

THE FINISHED VERSION

The published review appears below, accompanied by some marginal notes commenting on its strengths.

Title conveys informa-
tion about thesis.

Opening paragraph is
informative, letting the
reader know the review-
er's overall attitude.

Reviewer promptly turns
to a major issue.

An Effective <u>Macbeth</u>

<u>Macbeth</u> at the University Theater is a thoughtful and occasionally exciting produc-tion, partly because the director, Mark Urice, has trusted Shakespeare and has not imposed a gimmick on the play. The characters do not wear cowboy costumes as they did in last year's production of <u>A Midsummer Night's</u> <u>Dream.</u>

Probably the chief problem confronting a director of <u>Macbeth</u> is how to present the witches so that they are powerful supernatural forces and not silly things that look as though they came from a Halloween party. Urice gives us ugly but not absurdly grotesque witches, and he introduces them most effectively. The stage seems to be a bombed-out battlefield littered with rocks and great chunks of earth, but some of these begin to stir -- the earth seems to come alive -- and the clods move, unfold, and become the witches, dressed in brown and dark gray rags. The sug-gestion is that the witches are a part of na-ture, elemental forces that can hardly be es-caped. This effect is increased by the moans and creaking noises that they make, all of which could be comic but which in this produc-tion are impressive.

First sentence of this paragraph provides an effective transition.

The witches' power over Macbeth is further emphasized by their actions. When the witches first meet Macbeth, they encircle him, touch him, caress him, even embrace him, and he seems helpless, almost their plaything. More-over, in the scene in which he imagines that he sees a dagger, the director has arranged for one of the witches to appear, stand near Macbeth, and guide his hand toward the invisible dagger. This is, of course, not in the text, but the interpretation is reasonable rather than intrusive. Finally, near the end of the play, just before Macduff kills Macbeth, a witch appears and laughs at Macbeth as Macduff explains that he was not "born of woman." There is no doubt that throughout the tragedy Macbeth has been a puppet of the witches.

Paragraph begins with a broad assertion and then offers supporting details.

Stephen Beers (Macbeth) and Tina Peters (Lady Macbeth) are excellent. Beers is sufficiently brawny to be convincing as a battle-field hero, but he also speaks the lines sensitively, and so the audience feels that in addition to being a hero he is a man of insight and imagination, and even a man of gentleness. One can believe Lady Macbeth when she says that she fears he is "too full of the milk of human kindness" to murder Duncan. Lady Macbeth is especially effective in the scene in which she asks the spirits to "unsex her." During this speech she is reclining on a bed and as she delivers the lines she becomes increasingly sexual in her bodily motions, de-

Reference to a particular source.

riving excitement from her own stimulating
words. Her attachment to Macbeth is strongly
sexual, and so too is his attraction to her.
The scene when she persuades him to kill Duncan ends with them passionately embracing. The
strong attraction of each for the other, so
evident in the early part of the play, disappears after the murder, when Macbeth keeps his
distance from Lady Macbeth and does not allow
her to touch him. The acting of the other per-
formers is effective, except for Duncan (John
Berens), who recites the lines mechanically
and seems not to take much account of their
meaning.

Description, but also analysis.

The set consists of a barren plot at the
rear on which stands a spidery framework of
piping, of the sort used by construction com-
panies, supporting a catwalk. This framework

Concrete details.

fits with the costumes (lots of armor,
leather, heavy boots), suggesting a sort of
elemental, primitive, and somewhat sadistic
world. The catwalk, though effectively used
when Macbeth goes off to murder Duncan (whose
room is presumably upstairs and offstage) is
not much used in later scenes. For the most
part it is an interesting piece of scenery but
it is not otherwise helpful. For instance,

Concrete details to support evaluation.

there is no reason why the scene with
Macduff's wife and children is staged on it.
The costumes are not in any way Scottish -- no
plaids -- but in several scenes the sound of a
bagpipe is heard, adding another weird or
primitive tone to the production.

Summary   This <u>Macbeth</u> appeals to the eye, the ear,
                  and the mind. The director has given us a uni-
                  fied production that makes sense and that is
                  faithful to the spirit of Shakespeare's play.

The marginal notes call attention to certain qualities in the review, but three additional points should be made:

1. The reviewer's feelings and evaluations are clearly expressed, not in such expressions as "furthermore I feel," and "it is also my opinion," but in such expressions as "a thoughtful and occasionally exciting production," "excellent," and "appeals to the eye, the ear, and the mind."
2. The evaluations are supported by details. For instance, the evaluation that the witches are effectively presented is supported by a brief description of their appearance.
3. The reviewer is courteous, even when (as in the discussion of the cat-walk, in the next-to-last paragraph) she is talking about aspects of the production she doesn't care for.

SUMMING UP: GETTING IDEAS FOR WRITING ABOUT DRAMA

The following questions may help you formulate ideas for an essay on a play.

PLOT AND CONFLICT

1. Does the exposition introduce elements that will be ironically ful-filled? During the exposition do you perceive things differently from the way the characters perceive them?
2. Are certain happenings or situations recurrent? If so, what significance do you attach to them?
3. If more than one plot, do the plots seem to be related? Is one plot clearly the main plot, and another plot a sort of subplot, a minor variation on the theme?
4. Do any scenes strike you as irrelevant?
5. Are certain scenes so strongly foreshadowed that you anticipated them? If so, did the happenings in these scenes merely fulfill your expectations, or did they also surprise you?
6. What kinds of conflict are presented? One character against another,

one group against anther, one part of a personality against another part in the same person?

7. How is the conflict resolved? By an unambiguous triumph of one side, or by a triumph that is also in some degree a loss for the triumphant side? Do you find the resolution satisfying, or unsettling, or what? Why?

CHARACTER

1. A dramatic character is not likely to be thoroughly realistic, a copy of someone we might know. Still, we may ask if the character is consistent and coherent. We may also ask if the character is complex, or a rather simple representative of some human type?

2. How is the character defined? Consider what the character says and does and what others say about him or her and do to him or her. Also consider other characters who more or less resemble the character in question, because the similarities—and the differences—may be significant.

3. How trustworthy are the characters when they characterize themselves? When they characterize others?

4. Do characters change as the play goes on, or do we simply know them better at the end?

5. What do you make of the minor characters? Are they merely necessary to the plot, or are they foils to other characters? Or do they serve some other functions?

6. If a character is tragic, does the tragedy seem to proceed from a moral flaw, from an intellectual error, from the malice of others, from sheer chance, or from some combination of these?

7. What are the character's goals? To what degree do you sympathize with them? If a character is comic, do you laugh *with* or *at* the character?

8. Do you think the characters are adequately motivated?

9. Is a given character so meditative that you feel he or she is engaged less in a dialogue with others than in a dialogue with the self? If so, do you feel that this character is in large degree a spokesperson for the author, commenting not only on the world of the play but also on the outside world?

NONVERBAL LANGUAGE

1. If the playwright does not provide full stage directions, try to imagine for a least one scene what gestures and tones might accompany each speech. (The first scene is usually a good one to try your hand at.)

2. What do you make of the setting? Does it help reveal character? Do changes of scene strike you as symbolic? If so, symbolic of what?

THE PLAY ON FILM

1. If the play has been turned into a film, what has been added? What has been omitted? Why?

2. Has the film medium been used to advantage—for example, in focusing attention through close-ups or reaction shots (shots showing not the speaker but a person reacting to the speaker)? Or do some of the inventions—for example, outdoor scenes that were not possible in the play—seem mere busywork, distracting from the urgency or the conflict or the unity of the play?

7

Writing about Poetry

THE SPEAKER AND THE POET

The **speaker** or **voice** or **mask** or **persona** (Latin for "mask") that speaks a poem is not usually identical with the poet who writes it. The author assumes a role, or counterfeits the speech of a person in a particular situation. Robert Browning, for instance, in "My Last Duchess" (1842) invented a Renaissance duke who, in his palace, talks about his first wife and his art collection with an emissary from a count who is negotiating to offer his daughter in marriage to the duke.

In reading a poem, then, the first and most important question to ask yourself is this: Who is speaking? If an audience and a setting are suggested, keep them in mind, too, although these are not always indicated in a poem. For instance, Emily Dickinson's "Wild Nights" (1861) is the utterance of an impassioned lover, but we need not assume that the beloved is actually in the presence of the lover. In fact, since the second line says, "Were I with thee," the reader must assume that the person addressed is *not* present. The poem apparently represents a state of mind—a sort of talking to oneself—rather than an address to another person.

Wild Nights—Wild Nights
Emily Dickinson (1830–1886)

Wild Nights—Wild Nights,
Were I with Thee
Wild Nights should be
Our luxury!   4

Futile—the Winds
To a Heart in port—
Done with the Compass—
Done with the Chart!   8

Rowing in Eden
—Ah, the Sea!
Might I but moor—Tonight—
In Thee.   12

Clearly, the speaker is someone passionately in love. The following questions invite you to look more closely at how the speaker of "Wild Nights" is characterized.

QUESTIONS TO STIMULATE IDEAS ABOUT
"WILD NIGHTS—WILD NIGHTS"

This chapter, near the end, will list many questions that you may ask yourself in order to get ideas for writing about any poem. Here, however, are a few questions about this particular poem, to help you to think about it.

1. How does this poem communicate the speaker's state of mind? For example, in the first stanza (lines 1–4), what—beyond the meaning of the words—is communicated by the repetition of "Wild Nights"? In the last stanza (lines 9–12), what is the tone of "Ah, the Sea!"? ("Tone" means something like emotional coloring, as for instance when one speaks of a "businesslike tone," a "bitter tone," or an "eager tone.")

2. Paraphrase (put into your own words) the second stanza. What does this stanza communicate about the speaker's love for the beloved? Compare your paraphrase and the original. What does the form of the original sentences (the *omission*, for instance, of the verbs of lines 5 and 6 and of the subject in lines 7 and 8) communicate?

3. Paraphrase the last stanza. How does "Ah, the Sea!" fit into your paraphrase? If you had trouble fitting it in, do you think the poem would be better off without it? If not, why not?

The voice speaking a poem, however, often does have the ring of the author's own voice, and to make a distinction between speaker and author may at times seem perverse. In fact, some poetry (especially contemporary American poetry) is highly autobiographical. Still, even in autobiographical poems it may be convenient to distinguish between author and speaker. The speaker of a given poem is, let's say, Sylvia Plath in her role as parent, or Sylvia Plath in her role as daughter, not simply Sylvia Plath the poet.

The Language of Poetry: Diction and Tone

How is a voice or mask or persona created? From the whole of language, the author consciously or unconsciously selects certain words and grammatical constructions; this selection constitutes the persona's diction. It is, then, partly by the diction that we come to know the speaker of a poem. Just as in life there is a difference between people who speak of a *belly-button,* a *navel,* and an *umbilicus,* so in poetry there is a difference between speakers who use one word rather than another. Of course, it is also possible that all three of these words are part of a given speaker's vocabulary, but the speaker's choice among the three would depend on the situation; that is, in addressing a child, the speaker would probably use the word *belly-button;* in addressing an adult other than a family member or close friend, the speaker might be more likely to use *navel,* and if the speaker is a physician addressing an audience of physicians, he or she might be most likely to use *umbilicus.* This is only to say that the dramatic situation in which one finds oneself helps define oneself, helps establish the particular role that one is playing.

Some words are used in virtually all poems: *I, see, and,* and the like. Still, the grammatical constructions in which they appear may help define the speaker. In Dickinson's "Wild Nights," for instance, such expressions as "Were I with Thee" and "Might I" indicate an educated speaker.

Speakers have attitudes toward themselves, their subjects, and their audiences, and, consciously or unconsciously, they choose their words, pitch, and modulation accordingly; all these add up to their tone. In written literature, tone must be detected without the aid of the ear, although it's a good idea to read poetry aloud, trying to find the appropriate tone of voice; that is, the reader must understand by the selection and sequence of words the way the words are meant to be heard—playfully, angrily, confidentially, ironically, or whatever. The reader must catch what Frost calls "the speaking tone of voice somehow entangled in the words and fastened to the page for the ear of the imagination."

Writing about the Speaker: Robert Frost's "The Telephone"

Robert Frost once said that

> everything written is as good as it is dramatic…. [A poem is] heard as sung or spoken by a person in a scene—in character, in a setting. By whom, where and when is the question. By the dreamer of a better world out in a storm in autumn; by a lover under a window at night.

Suppose, in reading a poem Frost published in 1916, we try to establish "by whom, where and when" it is spoken. We may not be able to answer all three questions in great detail, but let's see what the poem suggests. As you read it, you'll notice—alerted by the quotation marks—that the poem has *two* speakers; the poem is a tiny drama. Thus, the closing quotation marks at the end of line 9 signal to us that the first speech is finished.

The Telephone
Robert Frost (1874–1963)

"When I was just as far as I could walk
From here today
There was an hour
All still
When leaning with my head against a flower   5
I heard you talk.
Don't say I didn't, for I heard you say—
You spoke from that flower on the window sill—
Do you remember what it was you said?"

"First tell me what it was you thought you heard."   10

"Having found the flower and driven a bee away,
I leaned my head,
And holding by the stalk,
I listened and I thought I caught the word—
What was it? Did you call me by my name?   15
Or did you say—
Someone said 'Come'—I heard it as I bowed."

"I may have thought as much, but not aloud."

"Well, so I came."

Suppose we ask: Who are these two speakers? What is their relationship? What's going on between them? Where are they? Probably these questions cannot be answered with absolute certainty, but some answers are more probable than others. For instance, line 8 ("You spoke from that flower on the window sill") tells us that the speakers are in a room, probably of their home—rather than, say, in a railroad station—but we can't say whether they live in a farmhouse or in a house in a village, town, or city, or in an apartment.

Let's put the questions (even if they may turn out to be unanswerable) into a more specific form.

QUESTIONS

1. One speaker speaks lines 1–9, 11–17, and 19. The other speaks lines 10 and 18. Can you tell the gender of each speaker? For sure, probably, or not at all? On what do you base your answer?
2. Try to visualize this miniature drama. In line 7 the first speaker says, "Don't say I didn't ...." What happens—what do you see in your mind's eye—after line 6 that causes the speaker to say this?
3. Why do you suppose the speaker of lines 10 and 18 says so little? How would you characterize the tone of these two lines? What sort of relationship do you think exists between the two speakers?
4. How would you characterize the tone of lines 11–17? Of the last line of the poem?

If you haven't jotted down your responses, consider doing so before reading what follows.

Journal Entries

Given questions somewhat like these, students were asked whether they could identify the speakers by sex, to speculate on their relationship, and then to add whatever they wished to say. One student recorded the following thoughts:

> These two people care about each other -- maybe husband and wife, or lovers -- and a man is doing most of the talking, though I can't prove it. He has walked as far as possible -- that is, as far as possible and still get back on the same day -- and he seemed to hear the other person call him. He claims that she spoke to him "from that flower on the window sill," and that's why I think the second person is a woman. She's at home, near the window. Somehow I even imagine she was at the window near the kitchen sink, maybe working while he was out on this long walk.
>
> Then she speaks one line; she won't say if she did or didn't speak. She is very cautious or suspicious: "First tell me what it was you thought you heard." Maybe she doesn't want to say something and then have her husband embarrass her by saying, "No, that's not what I thought." Or maybe she just doesn't feel like talking. Then he claims that he heard her speaking through a flower, as though the flower was a telephone, just as though it was hooked up to the flower on the window sill. But at first he won't say what he supposedly heard, or "thought" he heard. Instead, he

says that maybe it was someone else: "<u>Someone</u> said 'Come.'"
Is he teasing her? Pretending that she may have a rival?

Then she speaks -- again just one line, saying, "I may
have thought as much, but not aloud." She won't admit that
she <u>did</u> think this thought. And then the man says, "Well, so
I came." Just like that; short and sweet. No more fancy talk
about flowers as telephones. He somehow (through telepathy?)
got the message, and so here he is. He seems like a sensitive guy, playful (the stuff about the flowers as
telephones) but also he knows when to stop kidding around.

Another student also identified the couple as a man and woman and
thought that this dialogue occurs after a quarrel:

As the poem goes on, we learn that the man wants to be with
the woman, but it starts by telling us that he walked as far
away from her as he could. He doesn't say why, but I think
from the way the woman speaks later in the poem, they had a
fight and he walked out. Then, when he stopped to rest, he
thought he heard her voice. He really means that he was
thinking of her and he was hoping she was thinking of him.
So he returns, and he tells her he heard her calling him,
but he pretends he heard her call him through a flower on
their window sill. He can't admit that <u>he</u> was thinking about
her. This seems very realistic to me; when someone feels a
bit ashamed, it's sometimes hard to admit that you were
wrong, and you want the other person to tell you that things
are OK anyhow. And judging from line 7, when he says "Don't
say I didn't," it seems that she is going to interrupt him
by denying it. She is still angry, or maybe she doesn't want
to make up too quickly. But he wants to pretend that <u>she</u>
called him back. So when he says, "Do you remember what it
was you said?" she won't admit that she <u>was</u> thinking of him,
and she says, "First tell me what it was you thought you
heard." She's testing him a little. So he goes on, with the
business about flowers as telephones, and he says "someone"
called him. He understands that she doesn't want to be
pushed into forgiving him, so he backs off. Then she is
willing to admit that she did think about him, but still she
doesn't quite admit it. She is too proud to say openly that
she wants him back but she does say, "I <u>may</u> have thought as
much ...." And then, since they both have preserved their
dignity and also have admitted that they care about the other, he can say, "Well, so I came."

FURTHER THOUGHTS ABOUT "THE TELEPHONE"

1. In a paragraph or two or three, *evaluate* one of these two entries recorded by students. Do you think the comments are weak, plausible, or convincing, and *why* do you think so? Can you offer additional supporting evidence, or counter-evidence?

2. Two small questions: In a sentence or two, offer a suggestion why in line 11 Frost wrote, "and driven a bee away." After all, the bee plays no role in the poem. Second, in line 17 Frost has the speaker say, "I heard it as I bowed." Of course, "bowed" rhymes with "aloud," but let's assume that the need for a rhyme did not dictate the choice of this word. Do you think "I heard it as I bowed" is better than, say, "heard it as I waited" or "I heard it as I listened"? Why?

PARAPHRASE

Our interest in the shifting tones of the voice that speaks the words should not cause us to neglect the words themselves, the gist of the idea expressed. Sometimes a line may be obscure—for instance, because a word is no longer current or is current only in a region. The Irish poet William Butler Yeats (1865–1939) begins one poem with

The friends that have it I do wrong …

Because the idiom "to have it" (meaning "to believe that," "to think that") is unfamiliar to many readers today, a discussion of the poem might include a paraphrase—a rewording, a translation into more familiar language, such as

The friends who think that I am doing the wrong thing …

Another brief example: in a poem by Emily Dickinson (1830–1886) the following line appears:

The sun engrossed the East….

Engrossed here has (perhaps among other meanings) a special commercial meaning, "to acquire most or all of a commodity; to monopolize a market," and so a paraphrase of the line might go thus:

The sun took over all of the east.

The point of a paraphrase is to help you or your reader understand at least the surface meaning, and the act of paraphrasing will usually help you understand at least some of the implicit meaning. Furthermore, a paraphrase makes you see that the poet's words—if the poem is a good one—are exactly right, better than the words we might substitute. It becomes clear that the thing said in the poem—not only the rough "idea" expressed but the precise tone with which it is expressed—is a sharply defined experience.

FIGURATIVE LANGUAGE

Robert Frost has said, "Poetry provides the one permissible way of saying one thing and meaning another." This, of course, is an exaggeration, but it shrewdly suggests the importance of figurative language—saying one thing in terms of something else. Words have their literal meanings, but they can also be used so that something other than the literal meaning is implied. "My love is a rose" is, literally, nonsense, for a person is not a five-petaled, many-stamened plant with a spiny stem. But the suggestions of rose (at least for Robert Burns, the Scottish poet who compared his beloved to a rose in the line, "My Luve is like a red, red rose") include "delicate beauty," "soft," and "perfumed," and, thus, the word *rose* can be meaningfully applied—figuratively rather than literally—to "my love." The girl is fragrant; her skin is perhaps like a rose in texture and (in some measure) color; she will not keep her beauty long. The poet has communicated his perception very precisely.

People who write about poetry have found it convenient to name the various kinds of figurative language. Just as the student of geology employs such special terms as *kames* and *eskers,* the student of literature employs special terms to name things as accurately as possible. The following paragraphs discuss the most common terms.

In a **simile,** items from different classes are explicitly compared by a connective such as *like, as,* or *than,* or by a verb such as *appears* or *seems.* (If the objects compared are from the same class, for example, "Tokyo is like Los Angeles," no simile is present.)

> Float like a butterfly, sting like a bee.
>> —Muhammad Ali

> It is a beauteous evening, calm and free.
> The holy time is quiet as a Nun,
> Breathless with adoration.
>> —William Wordsworth

> All of our thoughts will be fairer than doves.
>> —Elizabeth Bishop

> Seems he a dove? His feathers are but borrowed.
>> —Shakespeare

A **metaphor** asserts the identity, without a connective such as *like* or a verb such as *appears,* of terms that are literally incompatible.

Umbrellas clothe the beach in every hue.
—Elizabeth Bishop

The
whirlwind fife-and-drum of the storm bends the salt
marsh grass
—Marianne Moore

In the following poem, Keats's excitement on reading Chapman's sixteenth-century translation of the Greek poet Homer is communicated first through a metaphor and then through a simile.

On First Looking into Chapman's Homer
John Keats (1795–1821)

Much have I traveled in the realms of gold,	
And many goodly states and kingdoms seen;	
Round many western islands have I been	
Which bards in fealty° to Apollo hold.	*loyalty* 4
Oft of one wide expanse had I been told,	
That deep-browed Homer ruled as his demesne:°	*property*
Yet did I never breathe its pure serene	
Till I heard Chapman speak out loud and bold:	8
Then felt I like some watcher of the skies	
When a new planet swims into his ken;	
Or like stout Cortez when with eagle eyes	
He stared at the Pacific—and all his men	12
Looked at each other with a wild surmise—	
Silent, upon a peak in Darien.°	*in Central America*

We might pause for a moment to take a closer look at Keats's poem. If you write an essay on the figurative language in this sonnet, you will probably discuss the figure involved in asserting that reading is a sort of traveling (it brings us to unfamiliar worlds) and especially that reading brings us to realms of gold. Presumably, the experience of reading is valuable. "Realms of gold" not only continues and modifies the idea of reading as travel, but in its evocation of El Dorado (an imaginary country in South America, thought to be rich in gold and, therefore, the object of search by Spanish explorers of the Renaissance) it introduces a suggestion of the Renaissance appropriate to a poem about a Renaissance translation of Homer. The figure of traveling is amplified in the next few lines, which assert that the "goodly states and kingdoms" and "western islands" are ruled by poets who owe allegiance to a higher authority, Apollo.

The beginning of the second sentence (line 5) enlarges this already spacious area with its reference to "one wise expanse," and the ruler of this area (unlike the other rulers) is given the dignity of being named. He is Homer, "deep-browed," "deep" suggesting not only his high or perhaps furrowed forehead but the profundity of the thoughts behind the forehead. The speaker continues the idea of books as remote places, but now he also seems to think of this place as more than a rich area; instead of merely saying that until he read Chapman's translation he had not "seen" it (as in line 2) or "been" there (line 3), he says he never breathed its air; that is, the preciousness is not material but ethereal, not gold but something far more exhilarating and essential.

This reference to air leads easily to the next dominant image, that of the explorer of the illimitable skies (so vast is Homer's world) rather than of the land and sea. But the explorer of the skies is conceived as watching an *oceanic* sky. In hindsight we can see that the link was perhaps forged earlier in line 7, with "serene" (a vast expanse of air *or* water); in any case, there is an unforgettable rightness in the description of the suddenly discovered planet as something that seems to "swim" into one's ken.

After this climactic discovery we return to the Renaissance Spanish explorers (though, in fact, Balboa, and not Cortez, was the discoverer of the Pacific) by means of a simile that compares the speaker's rapture with Cortez's as he gazed at the expanse before him. The writer of an essay on the figurative language in a poem should, in short, try to call attention to the aptness (or ineptness) of the figures and to the connecting threads that make a meaningful pattern.

Two types of metaphor deserve special mention. In **synecdoche** the whole is replaced by the part, or the part by the whole. For example, "bread," in "Give us this day our daily bread," replaces all sorts of food. In **metonymy** something is named that replaces something closely related to it. For example, James Shirley names certain objects, using them to replace social classes to which they are related:

> Scepter and crown must tumble down
> And in the dust be equal made
> With the poor crooked scythe and spade.

The attribution of human feelings or characteristics to abstractions or to inanimate objects is called **personification.**

> Memory,
> that exquisite blunderer.
> —Amy Clampitt

There's Wrath who has learnt every trick of guerilla warfare,
The shamming dead, the night-raid, the feinted retreat.
> —W. H. Auden

Hope, thou bold taster of delight.
> —Richard Crashaw

Crashaw's personification, "Hope, thou bold taster of delight," is also an example of the figure called **apostrophe,** an address to a person or thing not literally listening. Wordsworth begins a sonnet by apostrophizing Milton:

Milton, thou shouldst be living at this hour,

and Ginsberg apostrophizes "gusts of wet air":

Fall on the ground, O great Wetness.

What conclusions can we draw about figurative language?

First, figurative language, with its literally incompatible terms, forces the reader to attend to the connotations (suggestions, associations) rather than to the denotations (dictionary definitions) of one of the terms.

Second, although figurative language is said to differ from ordinary discourse, it is found in ordinary discourse, as well as in literature. "It rained cats and dogs," "War is hell," "Don't be a pig," "Mr. Know-all," and other tired figures are part of our daily utterances. But through repeated use, these, and most of the figures we use, have lost whatever impact they once had and are only a shade removed from expressions that, though once figurative, have become literal: the *eye* of a needle, a *branch* office, the *face* of a clock.

Third, good figurative language is usually concrete, condensed, and interesting. The concreteness lends precision and vividness; when Keats writes that he felt "like some watcher of the skies / When a new planet swims into his ken," he more sharply characterizes his feelings than if he had said, "I felt excited." His simile isolates for us a precise kind of excitement, and the metaphoric "swims" vividly brings up the oceanic aspect of the sky. The effect of the second of these three qualities, condensation, can be seen by attempting to paraphrase some of the figures. A paraphrase will commonly use more words than the original, and it will have less impact—as the gradual coming of night usually has less impact on us than a sudden darkening of the sky, or as a prolonged push has less impact than a sudden blow. The third quality, interest, is largely dependent on the previous two; the successful figure often makes us open our eyes wider and take notice. Keats's "deep-browed Homer" arouses our interest in Homer as "thoughtful Homer" or "meditative Homer" does not. Similarly, when W. B. Yeats says:

An aged man is but a paltry thing,
A tattered coat upon a stick, unless
Soul clap its hands and sing, and louder sing
For every tatter in its mortal dress,

the metaphoric identification of an old man with a scarecrow jolts us out of all our usual unthinking attitudes about old men as kind, happy folk who are content to have passed from youth into age.

Preparing to Write about Figurative Language

As you prepare to write about figurative language, consider

1. the areas from which the images are drawn (for instance, religion, exploration, science, commerce, nature);
2. the kinds of images (for instance, similes, metaphors, overstatements, understatements);
3. any shifts from one type of imagery to another (for instance, from similes to metaphors, or from abundant figures of speech to literal speech) and the effects that the shifts arouse in you; and
4. the location of the images (perhaps they are concentrated at the beginning of the poem or in the middle or at the end) and if parts of the poem are richer in images than other parts, consider their effect on you.

If you underline or highlight images in your text or in a copy of the poem that you have written or typed, you'll probably be able to see patterns, and you can indicate the connections by drawing arrows or perhaps by making lists of related images. Thinking about these patterns, you will find ideas arising about some of the ways in which the poem makes its effect. With a little luck you will be able to formulate a tentative thesis for your essay, though as you continue to work—say, as you write a first draft—you will probably find yourself modifying the thesis in the light of additional thoughts that come to you while you are putting words onto paper.

IMAGERY AND SYMBOLISM

When we read *rose*, we may more or less call to mind a picture of a rose, or perhaps we are reminded of the odor or texture of a rose. Whatever in a poem appeals to any of our senses (including sensations of heat as well as of sight, smell, taste, touch, sound) is an image. In short, images are the sensory content of a work, whether literal or figurative. When a poet says "My rose" and is speaking about a rose, we have no figure of speech—though we still have an image. If, however, "My rose" is a shortened form of "My love is a rose," some would say that he or she is using a metaphor; but others would say that because the first term is omitted ("My love is"), the rose is a **symbol**. A poem about the transience of a rose might compel the reader to feel that the transience of female beauty is the larger theme even though it is never explicitly stated.

Some symbols are **conventional symbols**—people have agreed to accept them as standing for something other than their literal meanings: A poem about the cross would probably be about Christianity; similarly, the rose has long been a symbol for love. In Virginia Woolf's novel *Mrs. Dalloway,* the husband communicates his love by proffering this conventional symbol: "He was holding out flowers—roses, red and white roses. (But he could not bring himself to say he loved her; not in so many words.)" Objects that are not conventional symbols, however, may also give rise to rich, multiple, indefinable associations. The following poem uses the traditional symbol of the rose, but in a nontraditional way.

The Sick Rose
William Blake (1757–1827)

O rose, thou art sick!
The invisible worm
That flies in the night,
In the howling storm,

Has found out thy bed
Of crimson joy,
And his dark secret love
Does thy life destroy.

A reader might perhaps argue that the worm is invisible (line 2) merely because it is hidden within the rose, but an "invisible worm / That flies in the night" is more than a long, slender, soft-bodied, creeping animal; and a rose that has, or is, a "bed / Of crimson joy" is more than a gardener's rose. Blake's worm and rose suggest things beyond themselves—a stranger, more vibrant world than the world we are usually aware of. They are, in short, symbolic, though readers will doubtless differ in their interpretations. Perhaps we find ourselves half thinking, for example, that the worm is male, the rose female, and that the poem is about the violation of virginity. Or that the poem is about the destruction of beauty: Woman's beauty, rooted in joy, is destroyed by a power that feeds on her. But these interpretations are not fully satisfying: The poem presents a worm and a rose, and yet it is not merely about a worm and a rose. These objects resonate, stimulating our thoughts toward something else, but the something else is elusive. This is not to say, however, that symbols mean whatever any reader says they mean. A reader could scarcely support an interpretation arguing that the poem is about the need to love all aspects of nature. All interpretations are not equally valid; it's the writer's job to offer a reasonably persuasive interpretation.

   A symbol, then, is an image so loaded with significance that it is not simply literal, and it does not simply stand for something else; it is both itself *and* something else that it richly suggests, a kind of manifestation of something too complex or too elusive to be otherwise revealed. Blake's poem is about a blighted rose and at the same time about much more. In a symbol, as Thomas Carlyle wrote, "the Infinite is made to blend with the Finite, to stand visible, and as it were, attainable there."

STRUCTURE

The arrangement of the parts, the organization of the entire poem, is its **structure.** Sometimes a poem is divided into blocks of, say, four lines each, but even if the poem is printed as a solid block, it probably has some principle of organization—for example, from sorrow in the first two lines to joy in the next two, or from a question in the first three lines to an answer in the last line.

Consider this short poem by an English poet of the seventeenth century.

Upon Julia's Clothes
Robert Herrick (1591–1674)

Whenas in silk my Julia goes,
Then, then (methinks) how sweetly flows
That liquefaction of her clothes.

Next, when I cast mine eyes, and see
That brave° vibration, each way free,   *splendid*
O, how that glittering taketh me.

Annotating and Thinking about a Poem

One student began thinking about this poem by copying it, double-spaced, and by making the following notes on his copy.

Upon Julia's Clothes

Whenas in silk my Julia goes, — *cool tone?*

3 Then, then (methinks) how sweetly flows

That liquefaction of her clothes.

"Then, then" — more excited? almost at a loss for words?

$3\begin{cases}\text{\underline{Next}, when I cast mine eyes, and see} \\ \text{That brave vibration, each way \underline{free},} \\ \text{O, how that glittering taketh me.}\end{cases}$

free to do what?
free from what?

emotional?

The student got further ideas by thinking about several of the questions that, at the end of this chapter, we suggest you ask yourself while rereading a poem. Among the questions are these:

> Does the poem proceed in a straightforward way, or at some point or points does the speaker reverse course, altering his or her tone or perception?
>
> What is the effect on you of the form?

With such questions in mind, the student was stimulated to see if Herrick's poem has some sort of reversal or change and, if so, how it is related to the structure. After rereading the poem several times, thinking about it in the light of these questions and perhaps others that came to mind, he produced the following notes:

```
Two stanzas, each of three lines, with the same structure
Basic structure of 1st stanza: When X (one line), then Y
     (two lines)
Basic structure of second stanza: Next (one line), then Z
     (two lines)
```

When he marked the text after reading the poem a few times, he noticed that the last line—an exclamation of delight ("O, how that glittering taketh me")—is much more personal than the rest of the poem. A little further thought enabled him to refine this last perception:

```
Although the pattern of stanzas is repeated, the somewhat
analytic, detached tone of the beginning ("Whenas," "Then,"
"Next") changes to an open, enthusiastic confession of de-
light in what the poet sees.
```

Further thinking led to this:

```
Although the title is "Upon Julia's Clothes," and the first
five lines describe Julia's silken dress, the poem finally
is not only about Julia's clothing but about the effect of
Julia (moving in silk that liquefies or seems to become a
liquid) on the poet.
```

This is a nice observation, but when the student looked again at the poem the next day and started to write about it, he found that he was able to refine his observation.

Even at the beginning, the speaker is not entirely detached,
for he speaks of "<u>my</u> Julia."

In writing about Herrick's "Upon Julia's Clothes," the student tells us the thoughts did not come quickly or neatly. After two or three thoughts, he started to write. Only after drafting a paragraph and rereading the poem did he notice that the personal element appears not only in the last line ("taketh *me*") but even in the first line ("*my* Julia"). In short, for almost all of us, the only way to get to a good final essay is to read, to think, to jot down ideas, to write a draft, and to revise and revise again. Having gone through such processes, the student came up with the following excellent essay.

The Student's Finished Essay: "Herrick's Julia, Julia's Herrick"

By the way, the student did not hit on the final version of his title ("Herrick's Julia, Julia's Herrick") until shortly before he typed his final version. His preliminary title was

Structure and Personality in
Herrick's "Upon Julia's Clothing"

That's a bit heavy-handed but at least it is focused, as opposed to such an uninformative title as "On a Poem." He soon revised his tentative title to

Julia, Julia's Clothing, and Julia's Poet

That's quite a good title: It is neat, and it is appropriate, since it moves (as the poem and the essay do) from Julia and her clothing to the poet. Of course, it doesn't tell the reader exactly what the essay will be about, but it does stimulate the reader's interest. The essayist's final title, however, is even better:

Herrick's Julia, Julia's Herrick

Again, it is neat (the balanced structure, and structure is part of the student's topic), and it moves (as the poem itself moves) from Julia to the poet.

Herrick's Julia, Julia's Herrick

Robert Herrick's "Upon Julia's Clothes" begins as a description of Julia's clothing and ends as an expression of the poet's response not just to Julia's clothing but to Julia herself. Despite the apparently objective or detached tone of the first stanza and the first two lines of the second stanza, the poem finally conveys a strong sense of the speaker's excitement.

The first stanza seems to say, "Whenas" X (one line), "Then" Y (two lines). The second stanza repeats this basic structure of one line of assertion and two lines describing the consequence: "Next" (one line), "then" (two lines). But the logic or coolness of "Whenas," "Then," and "Next," and of such rather scientific language as "liquefaction" (a more technical-sounding word than "melting") and "vibration" is undercut by the breathlessness or excitement of "Then, then" (that is very different from a simple "Then"). It is also worth mentioning that although there is a personal rather than a fully detached note even in the first line, in "my Julia," this expression scarcely reveals much feeling. In fact, it reveals a touch of male chauvinism, a suggestion that the woman is a possession of the speaker's. Not until the last line does the speaker reveal that, far from Julia being his possession, he is possessed by Julia: "O, how that glittering taketh me." If he begins coolly, objectively, and somewhat complacently, and uses a structure that suggests a somewhat detached mind, in the exclamatory "O" he neverthe-less at last confesses (to our delight) that he is enraptured by Julia.

Other things, of course, might be said about this poem. For instance, the writer says nothing about the changes in the meter and their possible value in the poem. Nor does he say anything about the sounds of any of the words (he might have commented on the long vowels in "sweetly flows" and shown how the effect would have been different if instead of "sweetly flows" Herrick had written "swiftly flits"), but such topics might be material for another essay. Furthermore, another reader might have found the poem less charming—even offensive in its exclusive concern with Julia's appearance. Still, this essay is, in itself, an interesting and perceptive discussion of the way the poet used a repeated structure to set forth a miniature drama in which observation is, at the end, replaced by emotion.

Kinds of Structure

REPETITIVE

Although every poem has its own structure, if we stand back from a giv-en poem we may see that the structure is one of three common sorts: repeti-tive, narrative, or logical. **Repetitive structure** is especially common in lyrics that are sung, where a single state of mind is repeated from stanza to stanza so that the stanzas are pretty much interchangeable. As we read through "Auld Lang Syne," for instance, we get reaffirmation rather than progression. Here is a passage from Whitman's "By Blue Ontario's Shore" that similarly has a repetitive structure:

> I will confront these shows of the day and night,
> I will know if I am to be less than they,
> I will see if I am not as majestic as they,
> I will see if I am not as subtle and real as they,
> I will see if I am to be less generous than they.

NARRATIVE

In a poem with a **narrative structure** (we are not talking about "narra-tive poems," poems that tell a story, such as *The Odyssey* or *The Rime of the Ancient Mariner,* but about a kind of lyric poem) there is a sense of advance. Blake's "The Sick Rose" (p. 154) is an example. What comes later in the po-em could not come earlier. The poem seems to get somewhere, to settle down to an end. A lyric in which the speaker at first grieves and then derives some comfort from the thought that at least he was once in love similarly has a nar-rative structure. Here is a short poem with a narrative structure.

A slumber did my spirit seal
William Wordsworth (1770–1850)

A slumber did my spirit seal;
I had no human fears:
She seemed a thing that could not feel
The touch of earthly years.

No motion has she now, no force;
She neither hears nor sees;
Rolled round in earth's diurnal° course,   *daily*
With rocks, and stones, and trees.

In the first stanza "did" and "seemed" establish the time as the past; in the second stanza "now" establishes the time as the present. In the blank space between the stanzas the woman has died. If we were required to summarize the stanzas very briefly, we might for the first stanza come up with, "I thought she could not die," and for the second, "She is dead." But the poem is not so much about the woman's life and death as about the speaker's response to her life and death.

If this poem is a sort of narrative of the speaker's change in perceptions, exactly what are the perceptions? Is the idea, as some readers have argued, "I thought she seemed immortal, but now I am appalled that she is reduced to mere earthly matter"? Or is it, as other readers have argued, "I knew a woman who seemed more than earthly; now I see, pantheistically, that in her death she is part of the grandness of nature"? According to the first of these views, there is a chilling irony in the fact that the woman who in the first stanza seemed exempt from "The touch of earthly years" is, in the second stanza, laid in earth, with no motion of her own. She is as inert as the "rocks, and stones, and trees." In this view, the poem moves from a romantic state of mind to a report of facts, and the facts imply an abrupt understanding of the brutality of death. But according to the second view, the woman participates (with natural objects) in the grand motion of "earth's diurnal course." In further support of this second view it can be argued that Wordsworth is known to have held pantheistic beliefs and that the Latinism, *diurnal*—the longest word and the only unusual word in the poem—adds dignity, especially in a line noted for melodiousness: "*R*olled *r*ound in ea*r*th's diu*r*nal cou*r*se." Perhaps one can even push this view further and say that the second stanza does not offer a sharp contrast to the first but deepens it by revealing a mature and satisfying view of the woman's true immortality, an immortality perceived only naively in the first stanza.

Possibly the poem is of indeterminate meaning, and the disagreement cannot be settled, but you might spend a moment thinking about which of these views you prefer, and why. Or do you accept all of them? Or do you hold an entirely different view?

LOGICAL

The third kind of structure commonly found is **logical structure.** The speaker argues a case and comes to some sort of conclusion. Probably the most famous example of a poem that moves to a resolution through an argument is Andrew Marvell's "To His Coy Mistress." The speaker begins, "Had we but world enough, and time" (that is, "if"), and for twenty lines he sets forth what he might do. At the twenty-first line he says, "But," and he indicates that the preceding twenty lines, in the subjunctive, are not a description of a real condition. The real condition (as he sees it) is that Time oppresses us, and he sets this idea forth in lines 21–32. In line 33 he begins his conclusion,

"Now therefore," clinching it in line 45 with "Thus." Here is another example of a poem with a logical structure.

The Flea
John Donne (1573–1631)

Mark but this flea, and mark in this
How little that which thou deniest me is:
It sucked me first, and now sucks thee,
And in this flea our two bloods mingled be.
Thou knowest that this cannot be said   5
A sin, nor shame, nor loss of maidenhead;
    Yet this enjoys before it woo,
    And pampered swells with one blood made of two,
    And this, alas, is more than we would do.

O stay! Three lives in one flea spare,   10
Where we almost, yea, more than married are;
This flea is you and I, and this
Our marriage bed and marriage temple is.
Though parents grudge, and you, we're met
And cloistered in these living walls of jet.   15
    Though use° make you apt to kill me,   *custom*
    Let not to that, self-murder added be,
    And sacrilege, three sins in killing three.

Cruel and sudden! Hast thou since
Purpled thy nail in blood of innocence?   20
Wherein could this flea guilty be,
Except in that drop which it sucked from thee?
Yet thou triumph'st and saist that thou
Find'st not thyself, nor me, the weaker now.
    'Tis true. Then learn how false fears be;   25
    Just so much honor, when thou yield'st to me,
    Will waste, as this flea's death took life from thee.

The speaker is a lover who begins by assuring his mistress that sexual intercourse is of no more serious consequence than a flea bite. Between the first and second stanzas the woman has apparently threatened to kill the flea, moving the lover to exclaim in line 10, "O stay! Three lives in one flea spare." In this second stanza he reverses his argument, now insisting on the importance of the flea, arguing that since it has bitten both man and woman it holds some of their lives, as well as its own. Unpersuaded of its importance, the woman kills the flea between the second and third stanzas; and the speaker uses her action to reinforce his initial position when he says, beginning in line 25, that the death of the flea has no serious consequences and her yielding to him will have no worse consequences.

Verbal Irony

Among the commonest devices in poems with logical structure (although this device is employed elsewhere, too) is **verbal irony.** The speaker's words mean more or less the opposite of what they seem to say. Sometimes it takes the form of **understatement,** as when Andrew Marvell's speaker remarks with cautious wryness, "The grave's a fine and private place, / But none, I think, do there embrace," or when Sylvia Plath sees an intended suicide as "the big strip tease"; sometimes it takes the form of **overstatement,** or **hyperbole,** as when Donne's speaker says that in the flea he and the lady are "more than married." Speaking broadly, intensely emotional contemporary poems, such as those of Plath, often use irony to undercut—and thus make acceptable—the emotion.

Paradox

Another common device in poems with a logical structure is **paradox:** the assertion of an apparent contradiction, as in "This flea is you and I." But again it must be emphasized that irony and paradox are not limited to poems with a logical structure. In "Auld Lang Syne," for instance, there is the paradox that the remembrance of joy evokes a kind of sadness, and there is understatement in "we've wandered mony a weary fitt," which stands (roughly) for something much bigger, such as "we have had many painful experiences."

EXPLICATION

In Chapter 3, which included a discussion of Langston Hughes's "Harlem," we saw that an explication is a line-by-line commentary on what is going on in a text. (*Explication* literally means "unfolding," or "spreading out.") Although your explication will for the most part move steadily from the beginning to the end of the selection, try to avoid writing along these lines (or, one might say, along this one line): "In line one ..., In the second line ..., In the third line ...,"; that is, don't hesitate to write such things as

> The poem begins ... In the next line ... The speaker immediately adds ... She then introduces ... The next stanza begins by saying ...

And of course you may discuss the second line before the first if that seems the best way of handing the passage.

An explication is not concerned with the writer's life or times, and it is not a paraphrase (a rewording)—though it may include paraphrase if a passage in the original seems unclear perhaps because of an unusual word or an unfamiliar expression. On the whole, however, an explication goes beyond paraphrase, seeking to make explicit what the reader perceives as implicit in the work. To this end it calls attention, as it proceeds, to the implications of words (for instance, to their tone), the function of rhymes (for instance, how they may connect ideas, as in *throne* and *alone*), the development of contrasts, and any other contributions to the meaning.

A Sample Explication of Yeats's "The Balloon of the Mind"

Take this short poem (published in 1917) by the Irish poet William Butler Yeats (1865–1939). The "balloon" in the poem is a dirigible, a blimp.

The Balloon of the Mind
William Butler Yeats

Hands, do what you're bid:
Bring the balloon of the mind
That bellies and drags in the wind
Into its narrow shed.

ANNOTATIONS AND JOURNAL ENTRIES

A student began thinking about the poem by copying it, double-spaced. Then she jotted down her first thoughts.

sounds abrupt

Hands, do what you're bid:

Bring the balloon of the mind

That bellies and drags in the wind

Into its narrow shed.

balloon imagined by the mind? Or a mind like a balloon?

no real rhymes? line seems to drag — it's so long!

Later she wrote some notes in a journal.

I'm still puzzled about the meaning of the words, "The balloon of the mind." Does "balloon of the mind" mean a balloon that belongs to the mind, sort of like "a disease of the heart"? If so, it means a balloon that the mind has, a balloon that the mind possesses, I guess by imagining it. Or does it mean that the mind is like a balloon, as when you say "he's a pig of a man," meaning he is like a pig, he is a pig? Can it mean both? What's a balloon that the mind imagines? Something like dreams of fame, wealth? Castles in Spain?

Is Yeats saying that the "hands" have to work hard to make dreams a reality? Maybe. But maybe the idea really is that the mind is like a balloon -- hard to keep under control, floating around. Very hard to keep the mind on the job. If the mind is like a balloon, it's hard to get it into the hangar (shed).

"Bellies." Is there such a verb? In this poem it seems to mean something like "puffs out" or "flops around in the wind." Just checked The American Heritage Dictionary, and it says "belly" can be a verb, "to swell out," "to bulge." Well, you learn something every day.

A later entry:

OK; I think the poem is about a writer trying to keep his balloon-like mind under control, trying to keep it working at the job of writing something, maybe writing something with the "clarity, unity, and coherence" I keep hearing about in this course.

Here is the student's final version of the explication.

Yeats's "Balloon of the Mind" is about writing poetry, specifically about the difficulty of getting one's floating thoughts down in lines on the page. The first line, a short, stern, heavily stressed command to the speaker's hands, perhaps implies by its severe or impatient tone that these hands will be disobedient or inept or careless if not watched closely: the poor bumbling body so often fails to achieve the goals of the mind. The bluntness of the command in the first line is emphasized by the fact that all the

subsequent lines have more syllables. Furthermore, the first
line is a grammatically complete sentence, whereas the
thought of line 2 spills over into the next lines, implying
the difficulty of fitting ideas into confining spaces, that
is, of getting one's thoughts into order, especially into a
coherent poem.

Lines 2 and 3 amplify the metaphor already stated in the
title (the product of the mind is an airy but unwieldy balloon) and they also contain a second command, "Bring." Alliteration ties this command "Bring" to the earlier "bid";
it also ties both of these verbs to their object, "balloon"
and to the verb that most effectively describes the balloon,
"bellies." In comparison with the abrupt first line of the
poem, lines 2 and 3 themselves seem almost swollen, bellying
and dragging, an effect aided by using adjacent unstressed
syllables ("of the," "[bell]ies and," "in the") and by using
an eye rhyme ("mind" and "wind") rather than an exact rhyme.
And then comes the short last line: almost before we could
expect it, the cumbersome balloon -- here the idea that is to
be packed into the stanza -- is successfully lodged in its
"narrow shed." Aside from the relatively colorless "into,"
the only words of more than one syllable in the poem are
"balloon," "bellies," and "narrow," and all three emphasize
the difficulty of the task. But after "narrow" -- the word
itself almost looks long and narrow, in this context like a
hangar -- we get the simplicity of the monosyllable "shed."
The difficult job is done, the thought is safely packed
away, the poem is completed -- but again with an off rhyme
("bid" and "shed"), for neatness can go only so far when
hands and mind and a balloon are involved.

Note: The reader of an explication needs to see the text, and because the ex-
plicated text is usually short, it is advisable to quote it all. (Remember, your

imagined audience probably consists of your classmates; even if they have already read the work you are explicating, they have not memorized it, and so you helpfully remind them of the work by quoting it.) You may quote the entire text at the outset, or you may quote the first unit (for example a stanza), then explicate that unit, and then quote the next unit, and so on. And if the poem or passage of prose is longer than, say, six lines, it is advisable to number each line at the right for easy reference.

RHYTHM AND VERSIFICATION: A GLOSSARY FOR REFERENCE

Rhythm

Rhythm (most simply, in English poetry, stresses at regular intervals) has a power of its own. A highly pronounced rhythm is common in such forms of poetry as charms, college yells, and lullabies; all of them are aimed at inducing a special effect magically. It is not surprising that *carmen,* the Latin word for poem or song, is also the Latin word for charm and the word from which our word *charm* is derived.

In much poetry, rhythm is only half heard, but its presence is suggested by the way poetry is printed. Prose (from Latin *prorsus,* "forward," "straight on") keeps running across the paper until the right-hand margin is reached; then, merely because the paper has given out, the writer or printer starts again at the left, with a small letter. But verse (Latin *versus,* "a turning") often ends well short of the right-hand margin. The next line begins at the left—usually with a capital—not because paper has run out but because the rhythmic pattern begins again. Lines of poetry are continually reminding us that they have a pattern.

Note that a mechanical, unvarying rhythm may be good to put the baby to sleep, but it can be deadly to readers who want to stay awake. Poets vary their rhythm according to their purposes; they ought not to be so regular that they are (in W. H. Auden's words) "accentual pests." In competent hands, rhythm contributes to meaning; it says something. Ezra Pound has a relevant comment: "Rhythm *must* have meaning. It can't be merely a careless dash off, with no grip and no real hold to the words and sense, a tumty tum tumty tum tum ta."

Consider this description of Hell from John Milton's *Paradise Lost* (stressed syllables are marked by ´; unstressed syllables by ˅):

> ´ ´ ´ ´ ´ ´ ˅ ´ ˅ ´
> Rocks, caves, lakes, fens, bogs, dens, and shades of death.

The normal line in *Paradise Lost* is written in iambic feet—alternate unstressed and stressed syllables—but in this line Milton immediately follows one heavy stress with another, helping communicate the "meaning"—the oppressive monotony of Hell. As a second example, consider the function of the rhythm in two lines by Alexander Pope:

˘ ′ ˘ ′ ˘ ′ ′ ′ ˘ ′
When Ajax strives some rock's vast weight to throw,

˘ ′ ′ ′ ˘ ˘ ˘ ′ ′ ′
The line too labors, and the words move slow.

The stressed syllables do not merely alternate with the unstressed ones; rather, the great weight of the rock is suggested by three consecutive stressed words, "rock's vast weight," and the great effort involved in moving it is suggested by another three consecutive stresses, "line too labors," and by yet another three, "words move slow." Note, also, the abundant pauses within the lines. In the first line, for example, unless one's speech is slovenly, one must pause at least slightly after "Ajax," "strives," "rock's," "vast," "weight," and "throw." The grating sounds in "Ajax" and "rock's" do their work, too, and so do the explosive *t*'s. When Pope wishes to suggest lightness, he reverses his procedure, and he groups *un*stressed syllables:

Not so, when swift Camilla scours the plain,

′ ˘ ˘ ′ ˘ ′ ˘ ′ ˘ ˘ ˘ ′
Flies o'er th' unbending corn, and skims along the main.

This last line has twelve syllables and is, thus, longer than the line about Ajax, but the addition of *along* helps communicate lightness and swiftness because in this line (it can be argued) neither syllable of *along* is strongly stressed. If *along* is omitted, the line still makes grammatical sense and becomes more regular, but it also becomes less imitative of lightness.

The very regularity of a line may be meaningful, too. Shakespeare begins a sonnet thus:

˘ ′ ˘ ′ ˘ ′ ˘ ′ ˘ ′
When I do count the clock that tells the time.

This line about a mechanism runs with appropriate regularity. (It is worth noting, too, that "*c*ount the *c*lock" and "*t*ells the *t*ime" emphasize the regularity by the repetition of sounds and syntax.) But notice what Shakespeare does in the middle of the next line:

˘ ′ ˘ ′ ′ ′ ˘ ′ ˘ ′
And see the brave day sunk in hideous night.

The technical vocabulary of **prosody** (the study of the principles of verse structure, including meter, rhyme and other sound effects, and stanzaic patterns) is large. An understanding of these terms will not turn anyone into a poet, but it will enable you to write about some aspects of poetry more efficiently. The following are the chief terms of prosody.

Meter

Most poetry written in English has a pattern of stressed (accented) sounds, and this pattern is the **meter** (from the Greek word for "measure"). Strictly speaking, we really should not talk of "unstressed" or "unaccented" syllables, since to utter a syllable—however lightly—is to give it some stress. It is really a matter of *relative* stress, but the fact is that "unstressed" or "unaccented" are parts of the established terminology of versification.

In a line of poetry, the **foot** is the basic unit of measurement. It is on rare occasions a single stressed syllable; generally a foot consists of two or three syllables, one of which is stressed. The repetition of feet, then, produces a pattern of stresses throughout the poem.

Two cautions:

1. A poem will seldom contain only one kind of foot throughout; significant variations usually occur, but one kind of foot is dominant.

2. In reading a poem, one chiefly pays attention to the sense, not to a presupposed metrical pattern. By paying attention to the sense, one often finds (reading aloud is a great help) that the stress falls on a word that according to the metrical pattern would be unstressed. Or a word that according to the pattern would be stressed may be seen to be unstressed. Furthermore, by reading for sense one finds that not all stresses are equally heavy; some are almost as light as unstressed syllables, and some have a **hovering stress**; that is, the stress is equally distributed over two adjacent syllables. To repeat: One reads for sense, allowing the syntax to help indicate the stresses.

Metrical Feet. The most common feet in English poetry are the six listed below.

Iamb (adjective: **iambic**): one unstressed syllable followed by one stressed syllable. The iamb, said to be the most common pattern in English speech, is surely the most common in English poetry. The following example has four iambic feet:

```
    ˘  /    ˘  /   ˘  /     ˘   /
My heart  is like  a sing  -ing bird.
```
> —Christina Rossetti

Trochee (**trochaic**): one stressed syllable followed by one unstressed.

```
 /   ˘   / ˘ / ˘   /   ˘   / ˘  / ˘
We were very tired, we were very merry
```
> —Edna St. Vincent Millay

Anapest (**anapestic**): two unstressed syllables followed by one stressed.

```
   ˘   ˘   /    ˘  ˘  /   ˘  ˘  /   ˘  ˘  /
There are man  -y who say  that a dog  has his day.
```
> —Dylan Thomas

Dactyl (dactylic): one stressed syllable followed by two unstressed. This trisyllabic foot, like the anapest, is common in light verse or verse suggesting joy, but its use is not limited to such material, as Longfellow's *Evangeline* shows. Thomas Hood's sentimental "The Bridge of Sighs" begins:

/ ˘ ˘ / ˘ ˘
Take her up tenderly.

Spondee (spondaic): two stressed syllables; most often used as a substitute for an iamb or trochee.

/ / ˘ / ˘ / ˘ /
Smart lad, to slip betimes away.

—A. E. Housman

Pyrrhic: two unstressed syllables; it is often not considered a legitimate foot in English.

Metrical Lines. A metrical line consists of one or more feet and is named for the number of feet in it. The following names are used:

monometer: one foot
dimeter: two feet
trimeter: three feet
tetrameter: four feet
pentameter: five feet
hexameter: six feet
heptameter: seven feet

A line is scanned for the kind and number of feet in it, and the **scansion** tells you if it is, say, anapestic trimeter (three anapests):

˘ ˘ / ˘ ˘ / ˘ ˘ /
As I came to the edge of the woods.

—Robert Frost

Or, in another example, iambic pentameter:

˘ / ˘ / ˘ / ˘ / ˘ /
The summer thunder, like a wooden bell

—Louise Bogan

A line ending with a stress has a **masculine ending;** a line ending with an extra unstressed syllable has a **feminine ending.** The **caesura** (usually indicated by the symbol / /) is a slight pause within the line. It need not be indicated by punctuation (notice the fourth and fifth lines in the following quotation), and it does not affect the metrical count:

Awake, my St. John! / / leave all meaner things
To low ambition, / / and the pride of kings.
Let us / / (since Life can little more supply
Than just to look about us / / and to die) 4
Expatiate free / / o'er all this scene of Man;
A mighty maze! / / but not without a plan;

A wild, / / where weeds and flowers promiscuous shoot;
Or garden, / / tempting with forbidden fruit.   8
          —Alexander Pope

The varying position of the caesura helps give Pope's lines an informality that plays against the formality of the pairs of rhyming lines.

    An **end-stopped line** concludes with a distinct syntactical pause, but a **run-on line** has its sense carried over into the next line without syntactical pause. (The running-on of a line is called **enjambment.**) In the following passage, only the first is a run-on line:

Yet if we look more closely we shall find
Most have the seeds of judgment in their mind:
Nature affords at least a glimmering light;
The lines, though touched but faintly, are drawn right.
          —Alexander Pope

    Meter produces **rhythm,** recurrences at equal intervals, but rhythm (from a Greek word meaning "flow") is usually applied to larger units than feet. Often it depends most obviously on pauses. Thus, a poem with run-on lines will have a different rhythm from a poem with end-stopped lines even though both are in the same meter. And prose, though it is unmetrical, may have rhythm, too.

    In addition to being affected by syntactical pause, rhythm is affected by pauses attributable to consonant clusters and to the length of words. Polysyllabic words establish a different rhythm from monosyllabic words, even in metrically identical lines. One may say, then, that rhythm is altered by shifts in meter, syntax, and the length and ease of pronunciation. Even with no such shift, even if a line is repeated verbatim, a reader may sense a change in rhythm. The rhythm of the final line of a poem, for example, may well differ from that of the line before even though in other respects the lines are identical, as in Frost's "Stopping by Woods on a Snowy Evening," which concludes by repeating "And miles to go before I sleep." One may simply sense that this final line ought to be spoken, say, more slowly and with more stress on "miles."

Patterns of Sound

    Though rhythm is basic to poetry, rhyme—the repetition of the identical or similar stressed sound or sounds—is not. Rhyme is, presumably, pleasant in itself; it suggests order; and it also may be related to meaning, for it brings two words sharply together, often implying a relationship, as in the now trite *dove* and *love* or in the more imaginative *throne* and *alone.*

    Perfect or **exact rhyme:** Differing consonant sounds are followed by identical stressed vowel sounds, and the following sounds, if any, are identical (*foe—toe; meet—fleet; buffer—rougher*). Notice that perfect rhyme involves identity of sound, not of spelling. *Fix* and *sticks*, like *buffer* and *rougher*, are perfect rhymes.

Half-rhyme (or off-rhyme): Only the final consonant sounds of the words are identical; the stressed vowel sounds, as well as the initial consonant sounds, if any, differ (*soul—oil; mirth—forth; trolley—bully*).

Eye-rhyme: The sounds do not in fact rhyme, but the words look as though they would rhyme (*cough—bough*).

Masculine rhyme: The final syllables are stressed and, after their differing initial consonant sounds, are identical in sound (*stark—mark; support—retort*).

Feminine rhyme (or double rhyme): Stressed rhyming syllables are followed by identical unstressed syllables (*revival—arrival; flatter—batter*). **Triple rhyme** is a kind of feminine rhyme in which identical stressed vowel sounds are followed by two identical unstressed syllables (*machinery—scenery; tenderly—slenderly*).

End rhyme (or terminal rhyme): The rhyming words occur at the ends of the lines.

Internal rhyme: At least one of the rhyming words occurs within the line (Oscar Wilde's "Each narrow *cell* in which we *dwell*").

Alliteration: sometimes defined as the repetition of initial sounds ("*All* the *a*wful *a*uguries" or "*B*ring me my *b*ow of *b*urning gold"), and sometimes as the prominent repetition of a consonant ("after li*f*e's *f*it*f*ul *f*ever").

Assonance: the repetition, in words of proximity, of identical vowel sounds preceded and followed by differing consonant sounds. Whereas *tide* and *hide* are rhymes, *tide* and *mine* are assonantal.

Consonance: the repetition of identical consonant sounds and differing vowel sounds in words in proximity (*fail—feel; rough—roof; pitter—patter*). Sometimes, consonance is more loosely defined merely as the repetition of a consonant (*fail—peel*).

Onomatopoeia: the use of words that imitate sounds, such as *hiss* and *buzz*. A common mistaken tendency is to see onomatopoeia everywhere—for example, in *thunder* and *horror*. Many words sometimes thought to be onomatopoeic are not clearly imitative of the thing they refer to; they merely contain some sounds that, when we know what the word means, seem to have some resemblance to the thing they denote. Tennyson's lines from "Come down, O maid" are usually cited as an example of onomatopoeia:

> The moan of doves in immemorial elms
> And murmuring of innumerable bees.

Stanzaic Patterns

Lines of poetry are commonly arranged into a rhythmical unit called a stanza (from an Italian word meaning "room" or "stopping-place"). Usually, all the stanzas in a poem have the same rhyme pattern. A stanza is sometimes called a **verse,** though *verse* may also mean a single line of poetry. (In discussing stanzas, rhymes are indicated by identical letters. Thus, *abab* indicates that the first and third lines rhyme with each other, while the second and fourth lines are linked by a different rhyme. An unrhymed line is denoted by *x*.) Common stanzaic forms in English poetry are the following:

Couplet: a stanza of two lines, usually, but not necessarily, with end-rhymes. *Couplet* is also used for a pair of rhyming lines. The **octosyllabic couplet** is iambic or trochaic tetrameter:

> Had we but world enough, and time,
> This coyness, lady, were no crime.
>
> —Andrew Marvell

Heroic couplet: a rhyming couplet of iambic pentameter, often "closed," that is, containing a complete thought, with a fairly heavy pause at the end of the first line and a still heavier one at the end of the second. Commonly, a parallel or an *antithesis* (contrast) is found within a line or between the two lines. It is called heroic because in England, especially in the eighteenth century, it was much used for heroic (epic) poems.

> Some foreign writers, some our own despise;
> The ancients only, or the moderns, prize.
>
> —Alexander Pope

Triplet (or **tercet**): a three-line stanza, usually with one rhyme.

> Whenas in silks my Julia goes
> Then, then (methinks) how sweetly flows
> That liquefaction of her clothes.
>
> —Robert Herrick

Quatrain: a four-line stanza, rhymed or unrhymed. The **heroic** (or **elegiac**) **quatrain** is iambic pentameter, rhyming *abab;* that is, the first and third lines rhyme (so they are designated *a*), and the second and fourth lines rhyme (so they are designated *b*).

Sonnet: a fourteen-line poem, predominantly in iambic pentameter. The rhyme is usually according to one of the two following schemes. **The Italian** (or **Petrarchan**) **sonnet** has two divisions: the first eight lines (rhyming *a b b a a b b a*) are the **octave;** the last six (rhyming *c d c d c d,* or a variant) are the **sestet.** Keats's "On First Looking into Chapman's Homer" (p. 150) is an Italian sonnet. The second kind of sonnet, the **English** (or **Shakespearean**) **sonnet,** is arranged usually into three quatrains and a couplet, rhyming *a b a b c d c d e f e f g g.* Many sonnets have a marked correspondence between the rhyme scheme and the development of the thought. Thus, an Italian sonnet may state a generalization in the octave and a specific example in the sestet. Or an English sonnet may give three examples—one in each quatrain—and draw a conclusion in the couplet.

Blank Verse and Free Verse

A good deal of English poetry is unrhymed, much of it in **blank verse,** that is, unrhymed iambic pentameter. Introduced into English poetry by Surrey in the middle of the sixteenth century, late in the century it became the standard medium (especially in the hands of Marlowe and Shakespeare) of English drama. A passage of blank verse that has a rhetorical unity is sometimes called a **verse paragraph.**

The second kind of unrhymed poetry fairly common in English, especially in the twentieth century, is **free verse** (or *vers libre*): rhythmical lines varying in length, adhering to no fixed metrical pattern, and usually unrhymed. The pattern is often largely based on repetition and parallel grammatical structure. Here is a sample of free verse.

When I heard the learn'd astronomer
Walt Whitman (1819–1892)

When I heard the learn'd astronomer,
When the proofs, the figures, were ranged in columns before me,
When I was shown the charts and diagrams, to add, divide, and measure
    them.
When I sitting heard the astronomer where he lectured with much
    applause in the lecture-room.
How soon unaccountable I became tired and sick,   5
Till rising and gliding out I wander'd off by myself,
In the mystical moist night-air, and from time to time,
Look'd up in perfect silence at the stars.

What can be said about the rhythmic structure of this poem? Rhymes are absent, and the lines vary greatly in the number of syllables, ranging from nine (the first line) to twenty-three (the fourth line), but when we read the poem we sense a rhythmic structure. The first four lines obviously hang together, each beginning with "When"; indeed, three of these four lines begin "When I." We may notice, too, that each of these four lines has more syllables than its predecessor (the numbers are nine, fourteen, eighteen, and twenty-three); this increase in length, like the initial repetition, is a kind of pattern.

In the fifth line, however, which speaks of fatigue and surfeit, there is a shrinkage to fourteen syllables, offering an enormous relief from the previous swollen line with its twenty-three syllables. The second half of the poem—the pattern established by "When" in the first four lines is dropped, and in effect we get a new stanza, also of four lines—does not relentlessly diminish the number of syllables in each succeeding line, but it *almost* does so: fourteen, fourteen, thirteen, ten.

The second half of Whitman's poem, thus, has a pattern, too, and this pattern is more or less the reverse of the first half of the poem. We may notice, too, that the last line (in which the poet, now released from the oppressive lecture hall, is in communion with nature) is very close to an iambic pentameter line; that is, the poem concludes with a metrical form said to be the most natural in English.

The effect of naturalness or ease in this final line, moreover, is increased by the absence of repetitions (e.g., not only of "When I," but even of such syntactic repetitions as "charts and diagrams," "tired and sick," "rising and gliding") that characterize most of the previous lines. Of course, this final effect of naturalness is part of a carefully constructed pattern in which rhythmic structure is part of meaning. Though at first glance free verse may appear unrestrained, as T. S. Eliot (a practitioner) said, "No *vers* is *libre* for the man who wants to do a good job"—or for the woman who wants to do a good job.

In recent years poets who write what earlier would have been called "free verse" have characterized their writing as **open form.** Such poets as Charles Olson, Robert Duncan, and Denise Levertov reject the "closed form" of the traditional, highly patterned poem, preferring instead a form that seems spontaneous or exploratory. To some readers the unit seems to be the phrase or the line rather than the group of lines, but Denise Levertov insists that the true writer of open-form poetry must have a "form sense"; she compares such a writer to "a sort of helicopter scout flying over the field of the poem, taking aerial photos and reporting on the state of the forest and its creatures—or over the sea to watch for the schools of herring and direct the fishing fleet toward them."* And, Levertov again, "Form is never more than a *revelation* of content."

SAMPLE ESSAY ON METRICS: "SOUND AND SENSE IN HOUSMAN'S 'EIGHT O'CLOCK' "

Once you have decided to write about some aspect of versification, write your own copy of the poem, double-spaced or even triple-spaced, providing plenty of space to mark the stresses, indicate pauses, and annotate in any other way that strikes you. At this stage, it's probably best to use pencil for your scansion, since on rereading the poem you may revise some of your views, and you can simply erase and revise.

---

*"Some Notes on Organic Form," reprinted in *The Poetics of the New American Poetry,* ed. Donald M. Allen and Warren Tallman (New York, 1973), pp. 316–317.

Here is an excellent analysis by a student. Notice that she quotes the poem and indicates the metrical pattern and that she proceeds chiefly by explaining the effect of the variations or departures from the norm in the order in which they occur.

Notice, too, that although it is usually a good idea to announce your thesis early—that is, in the first paragraph—this writer does *not* say, "This paper will show that Housman effectively uses rhythm to support his ideas" or some such thing. It's sufficient that the writer announces her topic in the title and again, in slightly different words, in the first sentence (the paper will "analyze the effects of sounds and rhythms in Housman's 'Eight O'Clock'"). We know where we will be going, and we read with perhaps even a bit of suspense, looking to see what the analysis will produce.

Sound and Sense in Housman's "Eight O'Clock"

Before trying to analyze the effects of sounds and rhythms in Housman's "Eight O'Clock," it will be useful to quote the poem and to indicate which syllables are stressed and which are unstressed. It must be understood, however, that the following scansion is relatively crude, because it falsely suggests that all stressed syllables (marked ∕) are equally stressed, but of course they are not: in reading the poem aloud, one would stress some of them relatively heavily, and one would stress others only a trifle more than the unstressed syllables. It should be understood, too, that in the discussion that follows the poem some other possible scansions will be proposed.

He stood, | and heard | the steeple

  Sprinkle | the quar | ters on | the mor | ning town.

One, two, | three, four, | to mar | ket-place | and people

  It tossed | them down.

Strapped, noosed, | nighing | his hour.

  He stood | and coun | ted them | and cursed | his luck;

And then | the clock | colléc | ted in | the tower

Its strength, | and struck.

As the first line of the second stanza makes especially clear, the poem is about a hanging at eight o'clock, according to the title. Housman could have written about the man's thoughts on the justice or injustice of his fate, or about the reasons for the execution, but he did not. Except for the second line of the second stanza—"He stood and counted them and cursed his luck"—he seems to tell us little about the man's thoughts. But the poem is not merely a narrative of an event; the sound effects in the poem help to convey an idea as well as a story.

The first line establishes an iambic pattern. The second line begins with a trochee ("Sprinkle"), not an iamb, and later in the line possibly "on" should not be stressed even though I marked it with a stress and made it part of an iambic foot, but still the line is mainly iambic. The poem so far is a fairly jingling description of someone hearing the church clock chiming at each quarter of the hour. Certainly, even though the second line begins with a stress, there is nothing threatening in "Sprinkle," a word in which we almost hear a tinkle.

But the second half of the first stanza surprises us, and maybe even jolts us. In "One, two, three, four" we get four consecutive heavy stresses. These stresses are especially emphatic because there is a pause, indicated by a comma, after each of them. Time is not just passing to the chimes of a clock: this is a countdown, and we sense that it may lead to something significant. Moreover, the third line, which is longer than the two previous lines, does not end with a pause. This long line (eleven syllables) runs on into the

next line, almost as though once the countdown has begun
there is no stopping it. But then we do stop suddenly, because the last line of the stanza has only four syllables—far
fewer than we would have expected. In other words, this line
stops unexpectedly because it has only two feet. The first
line had three feet, and the second and third lines had five
feet. Furthermore, this short, final line of the stanza ends
with a heavy stress in contrast to the previous line, which
ends with an unstressed syllable, "péople." As we will see,
the sudden stopping at the end is a sort of preview of a
life cut short. Perhaps it is also a preview of a man dropping through a trapdoor and then suddenly stopping when the
slack in the hangman's rope has been taken up.

In the first line of the second stanza the situation is
made clear, and it is also made emphatic by three consecutive stresses: "Strápped, nooséd, nighing his hóur." The
pauses before each of these stresses make the words
especially emphatic. And though I have marked the first two
words of the next line "He stóod," possibly "He" should be
stressed too. In any case even if "He" is not heavily
stressed, it is certainly stressed more than the other unstressed syllables, "and," "-ed" (in "counted"), and "his."
Similarly in the third line of the stanza an effective reading might even stress the first word as well as the second,
thus: "Ánd thén." And although normal speech would stress
only the second syllable in "collécted," in this poem the
word appears after "clock," and so one must pause after the
k sound in "clock" (one simply can't say "clock collected"
without pausing briefly between the two words), and the effect is to put more than usual stress on the first syllable,
almost turning it into "collécted." And so this line really
can reasonably be scanned like this:

And then the clock collected in the tower.

And again the third line of the stanza runs over into the fourth, propelling us onward. The final line surely begins with a stress, even though "Its" is not a word usually stressed, and so in the final line we begin with two strong stresses, "Its strength." This line, like the last line of the first stanza, is unusually short, and it too ends with a heavy stress. The total effect, then, of the last two lines of this stanza is of a clock striking, not just sprinkling music but forcefully and emphatically and decisively strik-ing. The pause after "strength" is almost like the suspense-ful pause of a man collecting his strength before he strikes a blow, and that is what the clock does:

And then the clock collected in the tower.

Its strength, and struck.

If "clock collected" has in its <u>k</u> sounds a sort of ticktock effect, the clock at the end shows its force, for when it strikes the hour, the man dies.

I said near the beginning of this essay that Housman did not write about the man's thought about the justice or in-justice of the sentence, and I think this is more or less true, but if we take into account the sound effects in the poem we can see that in part the poem <u>is</u> about the man's thoughts: he sees himself as the victim not only of his "luck" but of this machine, this ticking, unstoppable con-traption that strikes not only the hours but a man's life.

SUMMING UP: GETTING IDEAS FOR WRITING ABOUT POETRY

If you are going to write about a fairly short poem (say, under thirty lines), it's not a bad idea to copy out the poem, writing or typing it double-spaced. By writing it out, you will be forced to notice details, down to the punctuation. After you have copied the poem, proofread it carefully against the original. Catching an error—even the addition or omission of a comma—may help you notice a detail in the original that you might otherwise have overlooked. Now that you have the poem with ample space between the lines, you have a worksheet with room for jottings.

A good essay is based on a genuine response to a poem; a response may be stimulated in part by first reading the poem aloud and then considering the following questions.

FIRST RESPONSE

1. What was your response to the poem on first reading? Did some parts especially please or displease you or puzzle you? After some study—perhaps checking the meanings of some of the words in a dictionary and reading the poem several times—did you modify your initial response?

SPEAKER AND TONE

1. Who is the speaker? (Consider age, sex, personality, frame of mind, and tone of voice.) Is the speaker defined fairly precisely (for instance, an older woman speaking to a child), or is the speaker simply a voice meditating? (Jot down your first impressions, and then reread the poem and make further jottings, if necessary.)
2. Do you think the speaker is fully aware of what he or she is saying, or does the speaker show his or her personality and values unconsciously. What is your attitude toward this speaker?
3. Is the speaker narrating or reflecting on an earlier experience or attitude? If so, does he or she convey a sense of new awareness—for instance, of regret for innocence lost?

AUDIENCE

1. To whom is the speaker speaking? What is the situation (including time and place)? (In some poems the audience is strongly implied; others, especially those in which the speaker is meditating, may have no audience.)

STRUCTURE AND FORM

1. Does the poem proceed in a straightforward way, or at some point or points does the speaker reverse course, altering his or her tone or perception? If a shift occurs, what do you make of it?
2. Is the poem organized into sections? If so, what are these sections—stanzas, for instance—and how does each section (characterized, perhaps, by a certain tone of voice or a group of rhymes) grow out of what precedes it?
3. What is the effect on you of the form—say, quatrains (stanzas of four lines) or blank verse (unrhymed lines of ten syllables)? If the sense

overflows the form, running without pause from (for example) one quatrain into the next, what effect does it have on you?

CENTER OF INTEREST AND THEME

1. What is the poem about? Is the interest chiefly in a distinctive character, or in meditation? That is, is the poem chiefly psychological or chiefly philosophical?
2. Is the theme stated explicitly or implicitly? How might you state the theme in a sentence?

DICTION

1. Do certain words have rich and relevant associations that relate to other words and help define the speaker and the theme, or both?
2. What is the role of figurative language, if any? Does it help define the speaker or the theme?
3. What do you think is to be taken figuratively or symbolically, and what literally?

SOUND EFFECTS

1. What is the role of sound effects, including repetitions of sound and of entire words and shifts in versification?
2. If off-rhymes occur (for instance, "dizzy" and "easy" or "home" and "come"), what effect do they have on you? Do they, for instance, add a note of tentativeness or uncertainty?
3. If unexpected stresses or pauses occur, what do they communicate about the speaker's experience? How do they affect you?

8

Writing about Film

This chapter offers some comments about the nature of film, some definitions of indispensable technical terms, a few suggestions about topics, a sample essay by a student, and a list of questions that you may want to ask yourself as you begin to think about writing on a film.

FILM AS A MEDIUM

Perhaps one's first thought is that a film (excluding cartoons, documentaries, newsreels, and so on) is rather like a play: a story is presented by means of actors. The film, of course, regularly uses some techniques not possible in the playhouse, such as close-ups and rapid changes of scene, but even these techniques can usually be approximated in the playhouse—for example, by means of lighting. It may seem, then, that one can experience a film as though it were a photographic record of a play. And, indeed, some films are nothing more than film records of plays.

There are, however, crucial distinctions between film and drama. First, though drama uses such visual matters as gestures, tableaux effects, and scenery, the plays that we value most highly are *literature:* the word dominates, the visual component is subordinate. One need not be a film fanatic who believes that the invention of the sound track was an impediment to film in order to realize that a film is more a matter of pictures than of words. The camera usually roves, giving us crowded streets, empty skies, rainy nights, or close-ups of filled ashtrays and chipped coffee cups. A critic has aptly said that in Ingmar Bergman's *Smiles of a Summer Night* "the almost unbearably ornate crystal goblets, by their aspect and their positioning in the image, convey the oppressive luxuriousness of the diners' lives in purely and uniquely filmic terms." In the words of the Swiss director Eric Rohmer, "the cinema is the description of man and his surroundings."*

Some of the greatest sequences in cinema, such as the battle scene in Orson Welles's *Falstaff* (also titled *Chimes at Midnight*) or parts of the search for Anna in Michelangelo Antonioni's *L'Avventura,* have no dialogue but concentrate on purely visual matters. In *L'Avventura* a group of rich and bored Italians goes on a yachting excursion and visits a volcanic island off the coast of Sicily, where one member of the party—Anna—disappears. Anna's fiancé, Sandro, and Anna's best friend, Claudia, search for her, but during the search they find that they are attracted to each other and they become lovers; Claudia later discovers that Sandro is unfaithful to her—but she and Sandro both were unfaithful to Anna, and the implication is that Claudia and Sandro will (in their way) remain weary partners. During the film's two hours, long sequences occur when, in a conventional sense, little "happens"—for example, there are shots of the sea, or of a character far from the camera, walking on the island during bad weather. Of course, in this film the setting itself is an important part of the story, the barren and crumbling island being symbolic of the decadent people who walk on it and symbolic also of the vast inhospitable universe in which these figures—rendered small by their distance from the camera—aimlessly move. The long silences (episodes without dialogue or background music) are as important as what is said, and what is seen is more important than what is said.

In short, the speaker in a film does not usually dominate. In a play the speaker normally holds the spectator's attention, but in a film when a character speaks, the camera often gives us a **reaction shot,** focusing not on the speaker but on the face or gestures of a character who is affected by the speech, thus giving the spectator a visual interpretation of the words. In Truffaut's *400 Blows,* for example, we hear a reform school official verbally assault a boy, but we see the uncomfortable boy, not the official. Even when the camera does focus on the speaker, it is likely to offer an interpretation. An extreme example is a scene from *Brief Encounter:* A gossip is talking, and the camera gives us a close-up of her jabbering mouth which monstrously fills the screen.

This distance between film and drama can be put in another way: A film is more like a novel than a play, the action being presented not directly by ac-

---

*Films made for television, however, in contrast to the films under discussion, are, for the most part, fairly close to drama. Outdoor scenes, except for car chases and crashes, are relatively few. These television films show people talking and moving on a stage, but the films convey relatively little sense of a large world. This is not surprising; television technology is still primitive, and (unlike film) television cannot clearly portray a distant object (for example a horseman on the skyline), nor can it sharply portray fine detail even of an object close to the camera. Perhaps one should add here, however, that in the middle 1960s some directors, especially Jean-Luc Godard, rejected the idea that cinema is primarily a visual medium. Godard's characters sit around (they scarcely seem to *act*) talking about politics and their emotions.

tors but by a camera, which, like a novelist's point of view, comments on the story while telling it. A novelist may, like a dramatist, convey information about a character through dialogue and gesture but may also simply tell us about the character's state of mind. Similarly, a film maker may use the camera to inform us about unspoken thought. In Murnau's *Last Laugh,* when the hotel doorman reads a note firing him, the camera blurs; when he gets drunk, the camera spins so that the room seems to revolve. Somewhat similarly, Antonioni's *Red Desert* occasionally uses out-of-focus shots to convey Giuliana's view of the world; when she is more at ease—for example, with her husband— the shots are in proper focus. In Bertolucci's *Conformist* a shot of a chase through the woods is filmed with a hand-held camera whose shaky images convey to us the agitated emotions of the chase. At the end of *Bonnie and Clyde,* when Clyde is riddled with bullets, because his collapse is shot in slow motion he seems endowed not only with unusual grace but also with almost superhuman powers of endurance.

Even the choice of film stock is part of the comment. A highly sensitive or "fast" film needs less light to catch an image than a "slow" film does, but it is usually grainier. Perhaps because black-and-white newsreels often use fast film, a grainy quality may suggest authenticity or realism. Moreover, fast film can be processed to show less subtle gradations from black to white than slow film does, and this high contrast makes it especially suitable for the harsh, unromantic *Battle of Algiers.* Different film stocks may be used within a single motion picture. In *Wild Strawberries,* for instance, Bergman uses high-contrast stock for the nightmare sequence, though elsewhere in the film the contrasts are subtle. Color film has its own methods of tone and texture control.

The medium, as everyone knows, is part of the message; Sir Laurence Olivier made Shakespeare's *Henry V* in color but *Hamlet* in black and white because these media say different things. Peter Brook's film of *King Lear* is also in black and white, with an emphasis on an icy whiteness that catches the play's spirit of old age and desolation; a *Lear* in color probably would have an opulence that would work against the lovelessness and desolation of much of the play. John Houseman said that he produced *Julius Caesar* in black and white because he wanted "intensity" rather than "grandeur" and because black and white evoked newsreels of Hitler and thus helped establish the connection between Shakespeare's play and relatively recent politics. Peter Ustinov said that he made *Billy Budd* in black and white because he wanted it to seem real; and Richard Brooks's *In Cold Blood,* also in black and white, tried to look like a documentary. Similarly, although by 1971 most fiction films were being made in color, Peter Bogdanovich made *The Last Picture Show* in black and white, partly to convey a sense of the unexciting life of a small town in America in the 1950s and partly to evoke the films of the fifties. When a film is made in color, however, the colors may be symbolic (or at least suggestive) as well as realistic. In *A Clockwork Orange,* for example, hot colors (oranges and reds) conveying vitality and aggressiveness in the first half of the film are displaced in the second half by cool colors (blues and greens) when the emphasis turns to "clockwork,"—to mechanization.

The kind of lens used also helps determine what the viewer sees. In *The Graduate* Benjamin runs toward the camera (he is trying to reach a church before his girl marries another man), but he seems to make no progress because a telephoto lens was used and thus his size does not increase as it normally would. The lens, that is, helps communicate his desperate sense of frustration. Conversely, a wide-angle lens makes a character approach the camera with menacing rapidity; he quickly looms into the foreground. Of course, a film maker, though resembling a novelist in offering pervasive indirect comment, is not a novelist any more than he or she is a playwright or director of a play; the medium has its own techniques, and the film maker works with them, not with the novel's or the drama's. The wife who came out of the movie theater saying to her husband "What a disappointment; it was exactly like the book" knew what a film ought to be.

FILM TECHNIQUES

At this point it may be well to suspend generalizations temporarily and to look more methodically at some techniques of film making. What follows is a brief grammar and dictionary of film, naming and explaining the cinematic devices that help film makers embody their vision in a work of art. An essay on film will probably discuss some of these devices, but there is no merit in mechanically trotting them all out.

Shots

A shot is what is recorded between the time a camera starts and the time it stops, that is, between the director's call for "action" and the call to "cut." Perhaps the average shot is about 10 seconds (very rarely a fraction of a second, and usually not more than 15 or so seconds). The average film is about an hour and a half, with about 600 shots, but Hitchcock's *Birds* uses 1360 shots. Three common shots are (1) a **long shot** or **establishing shot,** showing the main object at a considerable distance from the camera and thus presenting it in relation to its general surroundings (for example, captured soldiers, seen across a prison yard, entering the yard); (2) a **medium shot,** showing the object in relation to its immediate surroundings (a couple of soldiers, from the knees up, with the yard's wall behind them); (3) a **close-up,** showing only the main object, or, more often, only a part of it (a soldier's face or his bleeding feet).

In the outside world we can narrow our vision to the detail that interests us by moving our head and by focusing our eyes, ignoring what is not of immediate interest. The close-up is the movie director's chief way of directing our vision and of emphasizing a detail. (Another way is to focus sharply on the significant image, leaving the rest of the image in soft focus.) The close-up, a way of getting emphasis, has been heavily used in recent years, not always successfully. As Dwight Macdonald said of *Midnight Cowboy* and *Getting Straight,* "a movie told in close-ups is like a comic book, or like a novel composed in punchy one-sentence paragraphs and set throughout in large caps. How refreshing is a long or middle shot, a glimpse of the real world, so lovely and so *far away,* in the midst of those interminable processions of [a] hairy ogre face."

Two excellent film versions of Shakespeare's *Henry V* nicely show the different effects that long shots and close-ups can produce. Sir Laurence Olivier's version (1944) used abundant long shots and, on the whole, conveyed a highly pictorial sweeping epic version of the war in which Henry was engaged. Made during World War II, the film was a patriotic effort to inspire the English by showing the heroism of combat. On the other hand, Kenneth Branagh's version, made in 1989, used lots of close-ups of soldiers with mud-splattered faces, emphasizing the grittiness of war. Olivier brought out the splendor and romance, Branagh the labor and pain of war.

While taking a shot, the camera can move: It can swing to the right or left while its base remains fixed (a **pan shot**), up or down while fixed on its axis (a **tilt shot**), forward or backward (a **traveling shot**), or in and out and up and down fastened to a crane (a **crane shot**). The **zoom lens,** introduced in the 1950s and widespread by the middle 1960s, enables the camera to change its focus fluidly so that it can approach a detail—as a traveling shot does—while remaining fixed in place. Much will depend on the angle (high or low) from which the shots are made. If the camera is high (a **high-angle shot**), looking down on figures, it usually will dwarf them, perhaps even reduce them to crawling insects, making them vulnerable, pitiful, or contemptible. The higher the angle, the more likely it is to suggest a God's-eye view of entrapped people. If the camera is low (a **low-angle shot**), close to the ground and looking up, thereby showing figures against the sky, it probably will give them added dignity. In Murnau's *Last Laugh,* we first get low-angle shots of the self-confident doorman, communicating his grand view of himself; later, when he loses his strength and is reduced to working as a lavatory attendant, we see him from above, and he seems dwarfed. But these are not invariable principles. A shot in *Citizen Kane,* for example, shows Kane from above, but it does not dwarf him; rather, it shows him dominating his wife and then in effect obliterating her by casting a shadow over her. Similarly, a low-angle shot does not always add dignity: Films in which children play important parts often have lots of low-angle shots showing adults as menacing giants; and in *Dr. Strangelove* Stanley Kubrick regularly photographed Colonel Jack D. Ripper from low angles, thus emphasizing the colonel's power. In *Citizen Kane,* Kane is often photographed from floor level, similarly emphasizing his power, but some low-angle shots late in the film, showing him in his cavernous mansion, help convey his loneliness. In short, by its distance from the subject, its height from the ground, and its angle of elevation, the camera comments on or interprets what happens. It seems to record reality, but it offers its own version. It is only a slight exaggeration to say that the camera always lies, that is, gives a personal vision of reality.

Slow motion and **fast motion** also offer comments. In Branagh's *Henry V,* for example, as in Orson Welles's *Falstaff,* part of a battle is filmed in slow motion, thus emphasizing the weariness of the soldiers. On the other hand, a fast motion shot of factory workers or of vacationers betting in Las Vegas will—probably comically—emphasize their frantic activity.

Sequences

A group of related scenes—such as the three scenes of soldiers mentioned earlier—is a **sequence,** though a sequence is more likely to have thirty scenes than three. A sequence corresponds roughly to a chapter in a novel, the shots being sentences and the scenes being paragraphs. Within a sequence may be an **intercut,** a switch to another action that, for example, provides an ironic comment on the main action of the sequence. If intercuts are so abundant in a sequence that, in effect, two or more sequences are going at once (for example, shots of the villain about to ravish the heroine, alternating with shots of the hero riding to her rescue), we have **parallel editing** (also called a **cross-cut**). In the example just given, probably the tempo would increase, the shots being progressively shorter as we get to the rescue. Though often a sequence will have an early establishing shot, it need not. Sometimes an establishing shot is especially effective if delayed, as in Dreyer's *Day of Wrath,* in which scenes of a witch tied to the top rungs of a ladder lead to a long shot of the context: The witch has been tied to the top of a tall ladder near a great heap of burning faggots. Still at a distance, the next shot shows the soldiers tilting the ladder up into the air and onto the pyre.

Transitions

Within a sequence, the transitions normally are made by **straight cuts**—a strip of film is spliced to another, resulting in an instantaneous transfer from one shot to the next. Usually, an audience is scarcely (if at all) conscious of transitions from, say, a long shot of a character to a medium shot of him, or from a close-up of a speaker to a close-up of his auditor. But sometimes the director wants the audience to be fully aware of the change, as an author may emphasize a change by beginning a new paragraph or, even more sharply, by beginning a new chapter. Two older, and now rather unfashionable, relatively conspicuous transitions are sometimes still used, usually between sequences rather than within a sequence. These are the **dissolve** (the shot dissolves while a new shot appears to emerge from beneath it, there being a moment when we get a superimposition of both scenes), and the **fade** (in the **fade-out** the screen grows darker until black; in the **fade-in** the screen grows lighter until the new scene is fully visible). In effect the camera is saying "Let us now leave X and turn to Y," or "Two weeks later." In *2001* a prehistoric apelike creature discovers that it can use a bone as a tool, and it destroys a skeleton with it. Then it throws the bone triumphantly into the air, where the bone dissolves into a spaceship of the year 2001. The point is that the spaceship is the latest of our weapons and that progress is linked with destructiveness. Two older methods, even less in favor today than the dissolve and the fade but used in many excellent old films and in some modern films that seek an archaic effect, are the **wipe** (a sort of windshield wiper crosses the screen, wiping off the first scene and revealing the next), and the **iris** (in an **iris-in,** the new scene first appears in the center of the previous scene and then this circle expands until it fills the screen; an **iris-out** shows the new scene first appearing along the perimeter and then the circle closes in on the previous scene). Chaplin more than once ended a scene with an iris-out of the tramp walking jauntily toward the horizon. François Truffaut used iris shots in *The Wild Child,* suggesting by the encircling darkness the boy's isolation from most of the world surrounding him as he concentrated on a single object before him. In Kurosawa's *High and Low* a wipe is used with no archaic effect: An industrialist, trying to decide whether to pay an enormous ransom to free a child, has been told to toss the money from a train; the scene showing him arriving at his decision in his luxurious home is wiped off by a train that rushes across the screen. He has decided to pay.

Editing

All of the transitions discussed a moment ago are examples of editing techniques. A film, no less than a poem or a play or a picture or a palace, is something made, and it is not made by simply exposing some footage. Shots—often taken at widely separated times and places—must be appropriately joined. For example, we see a man look off to the right, and then we get a shot of what he is looking at and then a shot of his reaction. Until the shots are assembled, we don't have a film—we merely have the footage. V. I. Pudovkin put it this way: "The film is not *shot,* but built, built up from the separate strips of celluloid that are its raw material." This building-up is the process of **editing.** In *Film Technique* Pudovkin gives some examples of editing:

1. In the simplest kind of editing, the film tells a story from the best viewpoints, that is, sometimes from long shots, sometimes from medium shots, sometimes from close-ups.

2. Simultaneous actions, occurring in different places, can be narrated by cutting back and forth from one to the other.

3. Relationships can be conveyed by contrast (shots of starvation cut in with shots of gluttony), by symbolism (in Pudovkin's *Mother,* shots of an ice floe melting are cut into shots of a procession of workers, thereby suggesting that the workers' movement is a natural force coming to new life), and by *leit-motif* (that is, repetition of the same shot to emphasize a recurring theme).

More than a story can be told, of course; something of the appropriate emotion can be communicated by juxtaposing, say, a medium-long shot of a group of impassively advancing soldiers against a close-up of a single terrified victim. Similarly, emotion can be communicated by the duration of the shots (quick shots suggest haste; prolonged shots suggest slowness) and by the lighting (progressively darker shots can suggest melancholy; progressively lighter shots can suggest hope or joy). An extremely obvious but effective example occurs in Charlie Chaplin's *Modern Times* (1936), a satire on industrialism. We see a mass of workers hurrying to their jobs, and a moment later we see a herd of sheep on the move, this shot providing a bitter comic comment on the previous shot.

The Russian theorists of film called this process of building by quick cuts **montage.** The theory held that shots, when placed together, add up to more than the sum of the parts. Montage, for them, was what made a film a work of art and not a mere replica of reality. American writers commonly use the term merely to denote quick cutting, and French writers use it merely in the sense of cutting.*

All this talk about ingenious shots and their arrangement, then, assumes that the camera is a sort of pen, carefully setting forth images and thus at every point guiding the perceiver. The director (through the actors, camera technicians, cutters, and a host of others) makes an artifact, rather as a novelist makes a book or a sculptor makes a statue, and this artifact is a sort of elaborate contraption that manipulates the spectators by telling them at every second exactly how they ought to feel. But since, say, the 1950s, a reaction has occurred against such artistry, a feeling that although the elaborate editing of, say, Eisenstein and the other Russians is an esthetic triumph, it is also a moral failure because by its insistent tricky commentary it seems to deny the inherent worth of the event in itself as it happens. Moreover, just as the nineteenth-century narrator in the novel, who continually guided the reader ("Do not fear, gentle reader, for even at this moment plans were being laid …") was in the twentieth-century novel sloughed off, forcing the readers in large measure

---

*You don't have to be in Hollywood or in Russia or France to write a script. You may find it challenging and entertaining to recall either some incident you were involved in or a scene from a novel and then to recast it as a script, indicating shots, camera angles, lighting, and sound track.

to deduce the story for themselves, so too some contemporary film makers emphasize improvisation, fully aware that the film thus made will not at every point guide or dominate the viewer. Rather, the viewers of such a film become something of creators themselves, making the work of art by sorting out the relevant from the irrelevant images. Norman Mailer, in an essay on his film *Maidstone,* calls attention to the fact that in making this sort of film the camera, expecting an interesting bit of acting, may zoom in on what later turns out to be dull, but the scene is not deleted or shot again. The dull parts, the mistakes, are kept, and what was missed is not reenacted. In *Maidstone,* Mailer says, "When significant movement was captured, it was now doubly significant because one could not take it for granted. Watching film became an act of interpretation and restoration for what was missed."

THEME

It is time now to point out an obvious fact: Mastery of technique, though necessary to good film making, will not in itself make a good film. A good film is not a bag of cinematic devices but the embodiment, through cinematic devices, of a vision, an underlying theme. What is this theme or vision? It is a film maker's perception of some aspect of existence that he or she thinks is worthy of our interest. Normally, this perception involves characters and a plot. Though recent American films, relying heavily on color, rock music in stereophonic sound, quick cutting, and the wide screen, have tended to emphasize the emotional experience and deemphasize narrative, still most of the best cinema is concerned with what people do, that is, with character and plot. Character is what people are, plot is what happens, but the line between character and plot fades, for what people are is in large measure what they do, and what is done is in large measure the result of what people are.

Character and plot, then, finally are inseparable; in a good film, everything hangs together. Harold Lloyd said that he had idea men who suggested numerous bits of comic business, and then he chose "the ones that [he] thought would be most appropriate to the particular film we were doing." The operative words are "most appropriate." A very funny bit of business might not be appropriate—might somehow not seem to fit—in a particular film because it was not in harmony with the underlying theme or vision or idea, the "clothes rack" (Lloyd's term) on which the funny bits (the clothes) were hung. In *The Freshman,* Lloyd said, the underlying idea or theme was the student's enormous desire for popularity, and everything in the film had to further this theme. Consider the comments of the late Truffaut on the themes of *The 400 Blows* and *Jules and Jim,* and on the disastrous lack of a theme in *Shoot the Piano Player:*

In *400 Blows,* I was guided by the desire to portray a child as honestly as possible, and to invest his actions with a moral significance. Similarly with *Jules and Jim,* my desire to keep the film from seeming either pornographic, indelicate, or conventional guided me. The trouble with *Shoot the Piano Player* was that I was able to do anything—that the subject itself didn't impose its own form .... As it stands, there are some nice bits in the film, but it can't be said: this is the best work on this particular theme. There isn't any theme.

(It does not follow, of course, that the artist is fully aware of the theme from the start. Antonioni mentions that "it often happens that I experience fragmentary feelings before the experiences themselves take hold." But if they do not finally take hold, the film will probably arouse the sort of response that Truffaut mentions in his comments on *Shoot the Piano Player*.)

And so we come back to the idea of a vision or, in a less exalted word, a theme. Some critics, we recall, have argued that the concept of theme is meaningless: A film is only a detailed presentation of certain imaginary people in imaginary situations, not a statement about an aspect of life. Susan Sontag, in a challenging essay in *Against Interpretation,* argues that our tendency to seek a meaning in what we perceive is a manifestation of a desire to control the work of art by reducing its rich particulars to manageable categories. But Sontag's view itself is reductive. If we read in a newspaper about a marriage or a business failure or a baseball game, we take it only as a particular happening of some interest, and we do not assume that it implies much if anything beyond itself. It tells of something that has happened, but it does not tell what ought to happen or what usually happens; that is, it does not imply anything about the ways of people in general. When, however, we read a novel, or see on the stage or screen a happening, we inevitably feel—if only because we are asked to give the event an hour or more of our attention—that it is offered to us as noteworthy, an example not of what *happened* (it didn't happen; it's fictional) but an example of what *happens.* The characters in the fictional work are (like the characters in newspaper items) individuals, not mere abstractions, but (unlike those in newspaper items) they are significant individuals, in some measure revealing to us a whole class of people or a way of life. An artist gives us a representation that can be thought about.

Sometimes we sense that a film has an arguable thesis. Stanley Kubrick, for example, has said that *A Clockwork Orange* "warns against the new psychedelic fascism—the eye-popping, multimedia, quadrasonic, drug-oriented conditioning of human beings by other human beings—which many believe will usher in the forfeiture of human citizenship and the beginning of zombiedom." A film maker, however, need not argue a thesis that is subject to verification (for example, that the older generation seeks to repress the younger generation); it is enough if he or she sees in the human experience something worth our contemplation (for example, the conflict between generations) and embodies it on film. A theme can usually be named by an abstract noun or phrase (the quest for happiness, the difficulty of achieving self-knowledge, the fragility of love) and though we recognize that any such formula is not the whole life, it is nonetheless important. Adequately embodied in a film (or in any other kind of art) this exploration of experience alters our experience of life, including our experience of ourselves. Let Truffaut have the last word on this topic:

> I also believe that every film must contain some degree of "planned violence" upon its audience. In a good film, people must be made to see something that they don't want to see: they must be made to approve of someone of whom they had disapproved, they must be forced to look where they had refused to look.

GETTING READY TO WRITE

Mastery of terminology does not make anyone a perceptive film critic, but it helps writers communicate their perceptions to their readers. Probably an essay on a film will not be primarily about the use of establishing shots or of wipes or of any such matters, but rather it will be about some of the reasons why a particular film pleases or displeases, succeeds or fails, seems significant or insignificant, and in discussing these large matters it is sometimes necessary (or at least economical) to use the commonest technical terms. Large matters are often determined in part by such seemingly small matters as the distance of the camera from its subject or the way in which transitions are made, and one may as well use the conventional terms. But it is also true that a film maker's technique and technology alone cannot make a first-rate film. An idea, a personal vision, a theme (see pp. 189–191) must be embodied in all that is flashed on the screen.

Writing an essay about a new film—one not yet available for study on the VCR—presents difficulties not encountered in writing about stories, plays, and poems. Because we experience film in a darkened room, we cannot easily take notes, and because the film may be shown only once, we cannot always take another look at passages that puzzle us. But some brief notes can be taken even in the dark; it is best to amplify them as soon as light is available, while one still knows what the scrawls mean. If you can see the film more than once, do so; and, of course, if the script has been published, study it. Draft your paper as soon as possible after your first viewing, and then see the film again. You can sometimes check hazy memories of certain scenes and techniques with fellow viewers. But even with multiple viewings and the aid of friends, it is almost impossible to get the details right; it is best for the writer to be humble and for the reader to be tolerant.

A SAMPLE ESSAY ON VISUAL SYMBOLS: "A JAPANESE *MACBETH*"

Printed here is a student's essay on a film. Because it is on a version of *Macbeth*, it is in some degree a comparison between a film and a play, but it does not keep shifting back and forth and does not make the obvious point that many differences are found. Rather, it fairly quickly announces that it will be concerned with one kind of difference—the use of visual symbols that the camera can render effectively—and it then examines four such symbols.

Here is the skeleton of the essay, "A Japanese *Macbeth*," paragraph by paragraph:

> The Japanese film of *Macbeth* is not a film of a stage performance; it is a cinematic version.
>
> The film sometimes changes Shakespeare's plot, but this essay will be concerned only with the changes that are visual symbols: the fog, the castle, the forest, the horses.
>
> The fog, the castle, and the forest can be treated briefly. The fog shows nature blinding man; the castle shows man's brief attempt to impose his will on the natural landscape; the forest shows nature entrapping man.
>
> The nervous, active horses—which could not be actually shown on the Elizabethan stage—suggest man's fierce, destructive passions.
>
> The film, though literally false to the play, is artistically true.

This is a solid organization: The title, though not especially imaginative, at least catches our interest and gives a good idea of the general topic; the first paragraph introduces a significant point; and the second narrows it and announces precisely what the essay will cover. The third paragraph studies three of the four symbols announced in the second paragraph, and the fourth paragraph studies the fourth, more complicated symbol. The concluding paragraph in a way reaffirms the opening paragraph, but it does so now in the light of concrete evidence that has been offered. Organizing the essay is only part of the job. The writer of this essay has done more than work out an acceptable organization; she has some perceptions to offer, and she has found the right details and provided neat transitions so that the reader can move through the essay with pleasure.

A Japanese Macbeth

Essayist's general position, and implicit thesis, is clear from the start.   A Japanese movie-version of Macbeth sounds like a bad idea -- until one sees Kurosawa's film, Throne of Blood, in which Toshiro Mifune plays Washizu, the equivalent of Macbeth. It is a much more satisfying film than, say, Olivier's <u>Othello,</u> largely because it is not merely a filmed version of a play as it might be performed on a stage, but rather it is a freely re-created version that is designed for the camera. The very fact that it is in Japanese is probably a great help to Western-ers. If it were in English, we would be upset at the way some speeches are cut, but because it is in Japanese, we do not compare the words to Shakespeare's, and we concentrate on the visual aspects of the film.

As the paragraph pro-ceeds, it zooms in on the topic.

There are several differences in the plots of the two works. Among the alterations are such things as these: Shakespeare's three witches are reduced to one; Lady Washizu has a miscarriage; Washizu is killed by his own troops and not by Macduff. But this paper will discuss another sort of change, the introduc-tion of visual symbols, which the camera is adept at rendering, and which play an impor-tant part in the film. The four chief visual symbols are the fog, the castle, the forest, and the horses.

Essayist tells us exactly what will be covered in the rest of the essay.

The fog, the castle, and the forest, though highly effective, can be dealt with rather briefly. When the film begins we get a slow panoramic view of the ruined castle seen through the fog. The film ends with a similar panoramic view. These two scenes end with a dissolve, though almost all of the other scenes end abruptly with sharp cuts, and so

Transition (through repetition of part of previous sentence) and helpful forecast.

Analysis, not mere plot-telling.

the effect is that of lingering sorrow at the
transience of human creations, and awe at the
permanence of the mysterious natural world,
whose mist slowly drifts across what once was
a mighty castle built by a great chief. The
castle itself, when we come to see it in its
original condition, is not a particularly
graceful Japanese building. Rather, it is a
low, strong building, appropriate for an energetic warrior. The interior scenes show low,
oppressive ceilings, with great exposed beams
that almost seem to crush the people within
the rooms. It represents man's achievement in
the center of the misty tangled forest of the
mysterious world, but it also suggests, de-

Thoughtful interpreta-
tion.

spite its strength, how stifling that achievement is, in comparison with the floating mists
and endless woods. The woods, rainy and misty,
consist of curiously gnarled trees and vines,
and suggest a labyrinth that has entrapped
man, even though for a while man thinks he is
secure in his castle. Early in the film we see
Washizu riding through the woods, in and out
of mists, and behind a maze of twisted trees
that periodically hide him from our sight.

Further interpretation.

Maybe it is not too fanciful to suggest that
the branches through which we glimpse him
blindly riding in the fog are a sort of net
that entangles him. The trees and the mist are
the vast unfathomable universe; man can build
his castle, can make his plans, but he cannot
subdue nature for long. He cannot have his way

Essayist moves chrono-logically.

Summary leads, at the end of the paragraph, to interpretation.

The first half of this paragraph is a well-handled comparison.

A reminder of a point made earlier, but now developed at length.

forever; death will ultimately catch him, despite his strength. One later scene of the forest must be mentioned. Near the end of the film, when the forest moves (the soldiers are holding up leafy boughs to camouflage themselves), we get a spectacular shot; Shakespeare talks of the forest moving, but in the film we see it. Suddenly the forest seems to give a shudder and to be alive, crawling as though it is a vast horde of ants. Nature is seen to rise up against Washizu's crimes.

Shakespeare's stage could do very little about such an effect as the fog, though his poetry can call it to mind, and it could do even less about the forest. Kurosawa did not feel bound to the text of the play: he made a movie, and he took advantage of the camera's ability to present impressive and significant scenic effects. Similarly, he made much use of horses, which, though mentioned in Shakespeare's play, could not be shown on the Elizabethan stage. In fact, in Macbeth (III.iii.12–13) Shakespeare more or less apologizes for the absence of horses when one murderer explains to the other that when horsemen approach the palace it is customary for them to leave their horses and to walk the rest of the way. But the film gives us plenty of horses, not only at the start, when Washizu is galloping in the terrifying forest, but throughout the film, and they are used to suggest the terror of existence, and the evil

passions in Washizu's heart. Shakespeare provided a hint. After King Duncan is murdered,
Shakespeare tells us that Duncan's horses
"Turned wild in nature, broke their stalls,"
and even that they ate each other
(II.iv.16-18). In the film, when Washizu and
his wife plot the murder of their lord, we see
the panic-struck horses running around the
courtyard of the castle -- a sort of parallel
to the scene of Washizu chaotically riding in
and out of the fog near the beginning of the
movie. The horses in the courtyard apparently
have sensed man's villainous plots, or perhaps
they are visual equivalents of the fierce emotions in the minds of Washizu and his wife.
Later, when Washizu is planning to murder Miki
(the equivalent of Banquo), we see Miki's
white horse kicking at his attendants. Miki
saddles the horse, preparing to ride into the
hands of his assassins. Then Kurosawa cuts to
a long shot of the courtyard at night, where
Miki's attendants are nervously waiting for
him to return. Then we hear the sound of a
galloping horse, and suddenly the white horse
comes running in, riderless. Yet another use
of this motif is when we cut to a wild horse,
after Washizu's wife has said that she is
pregnant. In the film the wife has a miscarriage, and here again the horse is a visual
symbol of the disorder engendered within her
(the child would be the heir to the usurped
throne), as the other horses were symbols for

Thoughtful generalization.

the disorder in her mind and in Macbeth's. All of these cuts to the horses are abrupt, contributing to the sense of violence that the unrestrained horses themselves embody. Moreover, almost the only close-ups in the film are some shots of horses, seen from a low angle, emphasizing their powerful, oppressive brutality.

Conclusion is chiefly a restatement but the last sentence gives it an interesting twist.

Throne of Blood is not Shakespeare's Macbeth -- but even a filmed version of a staged version of the play would not be Shakespeare's Macbeth either, for the effect of a film is simply not identical with the effect of a play with live actors on the stage. But Throne of Blood is a fine translation of Macbeth into an approximate equivalent. Despite its lack of faithfulness to the literal text, it is in a higher way faithful. It is a work of art, like its original.

SUMMING UP: GETTING IDEAS FOR WRITING ABOUT FILM

These questions may help bring impressions out into the open and may with some reworking provide topics for essays.

1. If the film is adapted from fiction or drama, does it slavishly follow its original and neglect the potentialities of the camera? Or does it so revel in cinematic devices that it distorts the original work? (Of course, an adaptation need not go to either extreme. *An Occurrence at Owl Creek Bridge* is a close adaptation of Ambrose Bierce's story, and yet it is visually interesting.)
2. If the film is adapted from fiction or drama, does it do violence to the theme of the original? Is the film better than its source? Are the additions or omissions due to the medium or to a crude or faulty inter-

pretation of the original? Is the film *The Color Purple* more sensational or less than the book? In what ways can it be said that the film is different from the book?

3. Can film deal as effectively with inner action—mental processes—as with external, physical action? In a given film, how is the inner action conveyed?

4. Are shots and sequences adequately developed, or do they seem jerky? (A shot may be jerky by being extremely brief or at an odd angle; a sequence may be jerky by using discontinuous images or fast cuts. Sometimes, of course, jerkiness may be desirable.) If such cinematic techniques as wipes, dissolves, and slow motion are used, are they meaningful and effective?

5. Are the characters believable?

6. Are the actors appropriately cast? (Wasn't it a mistake to cast Robert Redford as Gatsby? Audrey Hepburn as Eliza Doolittle? Nureyev as Valentino?)

7. Does the sound track offer more than realistic dialogue? Is the music appropriate and functional? (Music may, among other things, imitate natural sounds, give a sense of locale or of ethnic group, suggest states of mind, provide ironic commentary, or—by repeated melodies—help establish connections.) Are volume, tempo, and pitch—whether of music or of such sounds as the wind blowing or cars moving—used to stimulate emotions?

8. All works of art are contrivances, of course, but (as a Roman saying puts it) the art is to conceal art. Does the film seem arty, a mere *tour de force,* or does it have the effect of inevitability, the effect of rightness, conveying a sense that a vision has been honestly expressed? Are characters or scenes clumsily dragged in? Are unusual effects significant? Does the whole add up to something? Do we get scenes or characters or techniques that at first hold us by their novelty but then have nothing further to offer?

9. Is the title significant? Are the newspaper or television advertisements appropriate?

Some final advice: Early in the essay it is usually desirable to sketch enough of the plot to give the readers an idea of what happens. (In the previous essay the student does not sketch the plot, but she says it is a version of *Macbeth* and thus gives the necessary information.) Do not try to recount everything that happens; it can't be done, and the attempt will frustrate you and bore your readers. Once you introduce the main characters and devote a few sentences to the plot, thus giving the readers a comfortable seat, get down to the job of convincing them that you have something interesting to say about the film—that the plot is trivial, or that the hero is not really cool but cruel, or that the plot and the characters are fine achievements but the camera work is sometimes needlessly tricksy, or that all is well.

Incidentally, a convenient way to give an actor's name in your essay is to put it in parentheses after the character's name or role, thus: "The detective (Humphrey Bogart) finds a clue ...." Then, as you go on to talk about the film, use the names of the characters or the roles, not the names of the actors, except of course when you are talking about the actors themselves, as in "Bogart is exactly right for the part."

Part Three

9

Style and Format

PRINCIPLES OF STYLE

Writing is hard work (Lewis Carroll's school in *Alice's Adventures in Wonderland* taught reeling and writhing), and there is no point fooling ourselves into believing that it is all a matter of inspiration. Evidence abounds that many of the poems, stories, plays, and essays that seem to flow so effortlessly as we read them were in fact the product of innumerable revisions. "Hard labor for life" was Conrad's view of his career as a writer. This labor for the most part is directed not to prettifying language but to improving one's thoughts and then getting the words that communicate these thoughts exactly.

The efforts are not guaranteed to pay off, but failure to expend effort is sure to result in writing that will strike the reader as confused. It won't do to comfort yourself with the thought that you have been misunderstood. You may know what you *meant to say,* but your reader is the judge of what indeed you *have said.*

Big books have been written on the elements of good writing, but the best way to learn to write is to generate ideas by such methods as annotating the text, listing, brainstorming, free writing, and making entries in a journal. Then, with some ideas at hand, you can write a first draft, which you will revise—perhaps in the light of comments by your peers—and later will revise yet again, and again. After you hand your essay in, your instructor will annotate it. Study the annotations an experienced reader puts on your essay. In revising the annotated passages, you will learn what your weaknesses are. After drafting your next essay, put it aside for a day or so; when you reread it, preferably aloud, you may find much that bothers you. If the argument does not flow, check to see whether your organization is reasonable and whether you have made adequate transitions. Do not hesitate to delete interesting but irrelevant material that obscures the argument. Make the necessary revisions again and again if time permits. Revision is indispensable if you wish to avoid (in Maugham's words) "the impression of writing with the stub of a blunt pencil."

Still, a few principles can be briefly set forth here. On Dr. Johnson's belief that we do not so much need to be taught as to be reminded, these principles are brief imperatives rather than detailed instructions. They will not suppress your particular voice. Rather, they will get rid of static, enabling your voice to come through effectively. You have something to say, but you can say it only after your throat is cleared of "Well, what I meant was," and "It's sort of, well, you know." Your readers do *not* know; they are reading in order *to* know. The paragraphs that follow are attempts to help you let your individuality speak clearly.

Get the Right Word

DENOTATION

Be sure the word you choose has the right explicit meaning, or **denotation.** Don't say "tragic" when you mean "pathetic," "sarcastic" when you mean "ironic," "free verse" when you mean "blank verse," "disinterested" when you mean "uninterested."

CONNOTATION

Be sure the word you choose has the right association or implication— that is, the right **connotation.** Here are three examples of words with the wrong connotations for their contexts: "The heroic spirit is not dead. It still *lurks* in the hearts of men." ("Lurks" suggests a furtiveness inappropriate to the heroic spirit. Something like "lives" or "dwells" is needed.) "Close study will *expose* the strength of Woolf's style." ("Reveal" would be better than "expose" here; "expose" suggests that some weakness will be brought to light, as in "Close study will expose the flimsiness of the motivation.") "Although Creon suffers, his suffering is not great enough to *relegate* him to the role of tragic hero." (In place of "relegate," we need something like "elevate" or "exalt.")

CONCRETENESS

Catch the richness, complexity, and uniqueness of things. Do not write "Here one sees his lack of emotion" if you really mean "Here one sees his indifference" or "his iciness" or "his impartiality" or whatever the exact condition is. Instead of "The clown's part in *Othello* is very small," write "The clown appears in only two scenes in *Othello*" or "The clown in *Othello* speaks only thirty lines." ("Very," as in "very small" or "very big," is almost never the right word. A role is rarely "very big"; it "dominates" or "overshadows" or "is second only to ....")

In addition to using the concrete word and the appropriate detail, use il-lustrative **examples.** Northrop Frye, writing about the perception of rhythm, illustrates his point:

> Ideally, our literary education should begin, not with prose, but with such things as "this little pig went to market"—with verse rhythm reinforced by physical as-sault. The infant who gets bounced on somebody's knee to the rhythm of "Ride a cock horse" does not need a footnote telling him that Banbury Cross is twenty miles northeast of Oxford. He does not need the information that "cross" and "horse" make (at least in the pronunciation he is most likely to hear) not a rhyme but an assonance…. All he needs is to get bounced.
>
> *The Well-tempered Critic* (Bloomington, Ind., 1963), p. 25

Frye does not say our literary education should begin with "simple rhymes" or with "verse popular with children." He says "with such things as 'this little pig went to market,'" and then he goes on to add "Ride a cock horse." We know exactly what he means. Notice, too, that we do not need a third example. Be detailed, but know when to stop.

LEVELS OF USAGE

Although the dividing lines cannot always be drawn easily, tradition recognizes three levels: formal, informal, and vulgar or popular, though some-times "popular" is used to designate a level between informal and vulgar. **For-mal writing**—at its highest or most formal—presumes considerable impor-tance in the writer, the audience, and the topic. A noted figure, say a respected literary critic, examining an influential book and addressing the world of thoughtful readers, may use a formal style, as Lionel Trilling does here in a criticism of V. L. Parrington's *Main Currents in American Literature:*

> To throw out Poe because he cannot be conveniently fitted into a theory of American culture, to speak of him as a biological sport and as a mind apart from the main current, to find his gloom to be merely personal and eccentric, "only the atrabilious wretchedness of a dipsomaniac," as Hawthorne's was "no more than the skeptical questioning of life by a nature that knew no fierce storms," to judge Melville's response to American life to be less noble than that of Bryant or of Greeley, to speak of Henry James as an escapist, as an artist similar to Whistler, a man characteristically afraid of stress—this is not merely to be mis-taken in aesthetic judgment; rather it is to examine without attention and from the point of view of a limited and essentially arrogant conception of reality the documents which are in some respects the most suggestive testimony to what America was and is, and of course to get no answer from them.
>
> *The Liberal Imagination* (New York, 1950), p. 21

Notice that in Trilling's sentence the structure is this: "To throw …, to speak …, to find …, to judge …, to speak …" and we still do not have an independent clause. Two-thirds of the way through, with "this is not merely to be mistaken," the previous words come into focus, but the meaning is still incomplete. To do such-and-such "is not merely to be mistaken," but what *is* it to be? At last we are told: "It is to examine without attention … and … to get no answer.…"

Consider also the beginning of the Gettysburg Address. Unless you are the president of the United States dedicating a national cemetery during a civil war, it is best not to speak of "Four score and seven years." "Eighty-seven" will have to do. Of course, formal English includes many simple words ("four," "and," "seven"), but it is notable for its use of relatively uncommon words, such as "score" and "hallow," and its long sentences, balanced or antithetical, which suspend their meaning until the end.

A formal sentence need not be long. Here is a fairly short formal sentence by W. H. Auden: "Owing to its superior power as a mnemonic, verse is superior to prose as a medium for didactic instruction." In another frame of mind Auden might have written something less formal, along these lines: "Because it stays more easily in the memory, verse is better than prose for teaching." This revision of Auden's sentence can be called **informal,** but it is high on the scale, the language of an educated person writing courteously to an audience he conceives of as his peers. It is the level of almost all serious writing about literature. A low, informal version might be: "Poetry sticks in your head better than prose; so if you want to teach something, poetry is better." This is the language any of us might use in our casual moments, but it is almost never the language used in writing about literature.

Remember, when you are writing, *you* are the teacher; you are trying to help someone see things as you see them, and it is unlikely that either solemnity or heartiness will help anyone else see anything your way. There is rarely a need to write that some of the best folk singers have been "incarcerated" or (at the other extreme) have been "thrown in the clink." "Imprisoned" or "put into prison" will probably do the job best. Nor will it do to "finagle" with an inappropriate expression by putting it in "quotes." As the previous sentence indicates, the apologetic quotation marks do not make such expressions acceptable, only more obvious and more offensive. The quotation marks tell the reader that the writer knows he or she is using the wrong word but is unwilling to find the right word. If for some reason a relatively low word such as *finagle* is the right one, use it and don't apologize with quotation marks (for instance, the use of "fiddle-faddle" without quotation marks on page 122).

In short, in "every phrase / And sentence that is right," as T. S. Eliot says in *Four Quartets,*

> every word is at home,
> Taking its place to support the others,
> The word neither diffident nor ostentatious,
> An easy commerce of the old and the new,
> The common word exact without vulgarity,

The formal word precise but not pedantic,
The complete consort dancing together.

REPETITION AND VARIATION

Although some repetitions—say, of words like *surely* or *it is noteworthy* —reveal a tic that ought to be cured by revision, don't be afraid to repeat a word if it is the best word. The following paragraph repeats "interesting," "paradox," "Salinger," "what makes," and "book"; notice also "feel" and "feeling":

> The reception given to *Franny and Zooey* in America has illustrated again the interesting paradox of Salinger's reputation there; great public enthusiasm, of the *Time* magazine and Best Seller List kind, accompanied by a repressive coolness in the critical journals. What makes this a paradox is that the book's themes are among the most ambitiously highbrow, and its craftsmanship most uncompromisingly virtuoso. What makes it an interesting one is that those who are most patronising about the book are those who most resemble its characters; people whose ideas and language in their best moments resemble Zooey's. But they feel they ought not to enjoy the book. There is a very strong feeling in American literary circles that Salinger and love of Salinger must be discouraged.
>
> Martin Green, *Re-appraisals* (New York, 1965), p. 197

Repetition, a device necessary for continuity and clarity, holds the paragraph together. Variations occur: "*Franny and Zooey*" becomes "the book," and then instead of "the book's" we get "its." Similarly, "those who" becomes "people," which in turn becomes "they." Such substitutions, which neither confuse nor distract, keep the paragraph from sounding like a broken phonograph record.

Pronouns are handy substitutes, and they ought to be used, but other substitutes need not always be sought. An ungrounded fear of repetition often produces a vice known as *elegant variation:* having mentioned *Franny and Zooey* an essayist next speaks of "the previously mentioned work," then of "the tale," and finally of "this work of our author." This vice is far worse than repetition; it strikes the reader as silly.

Pointless variation of this sort, however, is not to be confused with a variation that communicates additional useful information, such as "these two stories about the Glass family"; this variation is entirely legitimate, indeed necessary, for it furthers the discussion. But elegant variation can be worse than silly; it can be confusing, as in "My first *theme* dealt with plot, but this *essay* deals with character." The reader wonders if the writer means to suggest that an essay is different from a theme.

Notice in these lucid sentences by Helen Gardner the effective repetition of "end" and "beginning":

> *Othello* has this in common with the tragedy of fortune, that the end in no way blots out from the imagination the glory of the beginning. But the end here

does not merely by its darkness throw up into relief the brightness that was. On the contrary, beginning and end chime against each other. In both the value of life and love is affirmed.

The Noble Moor (Oxford, 1956), p. 203

The substitution of "conclusion" or "last scene" for the second "end" would be worse than pointless; it would destroy Gardner's point that there is *identity* or correspondence between beginning and end.

Do not repeat a word if it is being used in a different sense. Get a different word. Here are two examples of the fault: "This *theme* deals with the *theme* of the novel." (The first "theme" means "essay"; the second means "underlying idea," "motif.") "Caesar's *character* is complex. The comic *characters* too have some complexity." (The first "character" means "personality"; the second means "persons," "figures in the play.")

THE SOUND OF SENSE

Avoid awkward repetitions of sound, as in "The story is marked by a remarkable mystery," "The reason the season is Spring ...," "Circe certainly ...," "This is seen in the scene in which ...." These irrelevant echoes call undue attention to the words and thus get in the way of the points you are making. But word-play can be effective when it contributes to meaning. Gardner's statement that in the beginning and the end of *Othello* "the value of life and love is affirmed" makes effective use of the similarity in sound between "life" and "love." Her implication is that these two things that sound alike are indeed closely related, an idea that reinforces her contention that the beginning and the end of the play are in a way identical.

Write Effective Sentences

ECONOMY

Say everything relevant, but say it in the fewest words possible. The wordy sentence

There are a few vague parts in the story that give it a mysterious quality.

may be written more economically as

A few vague parts in the story give it a mysterious quality.

Nothing has been lost by deleting "There are" and "that." Even more economical is

A few vague parts add mystery to the story.

The original version says nothing that the second version does not say, and says nothing that the third version—9 words against 15—does not say. If you find the right nouns and verbs, you can often delete adjectives and adverbs. (Compare "a mysterious quality" with "mystery.") Another example of wordiness is: "Sophocles's tragic play *Antigone* is mistitled because Creon is the tragic hero, and the play should be named for him." These 20 words can be reduced, with no loss of meaning, to 9 words: "Sophocles's *Antigone* is mistitled; Creon is the tragic hero."

Something is wrong with a sentence if you can delete words and not sense the loss. A chapter in a recent book on contemporary theater begins:

> One of the principal and most persistent sources of error that tends to bedevil a considerable proportion of contemporary literary analysis is the assumption that the writer's creative process is a wholly conscious and purposive type of activity.

Well, there is something of interest here, but it comes along with a lot of hot air. Why that weaseling ("*tends* to bedevil," "a *considerable* proportion"), and why "type of activity" instead of "activity"? Those spluttering *p*'s ("principal and most persistent," "proportion," "process," "purposive") are a giveaway; the writer is letting off steam, not thinking. Pruned of the verbiage, what he says adds up to this:

> One of the chief errors bedeviling much contemporary criticism is the assumption that the writer's creative process is wholly conscious and purposive.

If he were to complain that this revision deprives him of his style, might we not fairly reply that what he calls his style is the display of insufficient thinking, a tangle of deadwood?

Cut out all the deadwood, but in cutting it out, do not cut out supporting detail. Supporting detail is wordiness only when the details are so numerous and obvious that they offend the reader's intelligence.

The **passive voice** (wherein the subject is the object of the action) is a common source of wordiness. Do not say "This story was written by Melville"; instead, say "Melville wrote this story." The revision is one-third shorter, and it says everything that the longer version says. Sometimes, of course, the passive voice, although less vigorous, may be preferable to the active voice. Changing "The novel was received in silence" to "Readers neglected the novel" makes the readers' response more active than it was. The passive catches the passivity of the response. Furthermore, the revision makes "readers" the subject, but the true subject is (as in the original) the novel.

PARALLELS

Use parallels to clarify relationships. Few of us are likely to compose such deathless parallels as "I came, I saw, I conquered" or "of the people, by the people, for the people," but we can see to it that coordinate expressions correspond in their grammatical form. A parallel such as "He liked to read and to write" (instead of "He liked reading and to write") makes its point neatly.

No such neatness appears in "Virginia Woolf wrote novels, delightful letters, and penetrating stories." The reader is left wondering what value the novels have. If one of the items has a modifier, usually all should have modifiers. Notice how the omission of "the noble" in the following sentence would leave a distracting gap: "If the wicked Shylock cannot enter the fairy story world of Belmont, neither can the noble Antony."

Other examples of parallels are: "Mendoza longs to be an Englishman and to marry the girl he loves" (*not* "Mendoza longs to be an Englishman and for the girl he loves"); "He talked about metaphors, similes, and symbols" (*not* "He talked about metaphors, similes, and about symbols"). If one wishes to emphasize the leisureliness of the talk, one might put it thus: "He talked about metaphors, about similes, and about symbols." The repetition of "about" in this version is not wordiness; because it emphasizes the leisureliness, it does some work in the sentence. Notice in the next example how Gardner's parallels ("in the," "in his," "in his," "in the") lend conviction:

> The significance of *Othello* is not to be found in the hero's nobility alone, in his capacity to know ecstasy, in his vision of the world, and in the terrible act to which he is driven by his anguish at the loss of that vision. It lies also in the fact that the vision was true.
>
> *The Noble Moor*, p. 205

SUBORDINATION

Make sure that the less important element is subordinate to the more important. In the following example the first clause, summarizing the writer's previous sentences, is a subordinate or dependent clause; the new material is made emphatic by being put into two independent clauses:

> As soon as the Irish Literary Theatre was assured of a nationalist backing, it started to dissociate itself from any political aim, and the long struggle with the public began.

The second and third clauses in this sentence, linked by "and," are coordinate—that is, of equal importance.

We have already discussed parallels ("I came, I saw, I conquered") and pointed out that parallel or coordinate elements should appear so in the sentence. The following line gives time and eternity equal treatment: "Time was against him; eternity was for him." The quotation is a **compound sentence**—composed of two or more clauses that can stand as independent sentences but that are connected with a coordinating conjunction such as *and, but, for, nor, yet,* and *if;* or with a correlative conjunction such as *not only … but also;* or with a conjunctive adverb such as *also* or *however;* or with a colon, a semicolon, or (rarely) a comma. But a **complex sentence** (an independent clause and one or more subordinate clauses) does not give equal treatment to each clause; whatever is outside the independent clause is subordinate, less important. Consider this sentence:

> Aided by Miss Horniman's money, Yeats dreamed of a poetic drama.

The writer puts Yeats's dream in the independent clause, subordinating the relatively unimportant Miss Horniman. (Notice, by the way, that emphasis by subordination often works along with emphasis by position. Here the independent clause comes *after* the subordinate clause; the writer appropriately put the more important material in the more emphatic position.)

Had the writer wished to give Miss Horniman more prominence, the passage might have run:

> Yeats dreamed of a poetic drama, and Miss Horniman subsidized that dream.

Here Miss Horniman at least stands in an independent clause, linked to the previous independent clause by "and." The two clauses, and the two people, are now of approximately equal importance.

If the writer had wanted to emphasize Miss Horniman and to deemphasize Yeats, he might have written:

> While Yeats dreamed of a poetic drama, Miss Horniman provided the money.

Here Yeats is reduced to the subordinate clause, and Miss Horniman is given the dignity of the only independent clause. (Again notice that the important point is also in the emphatic position, near the end of the sentence. A sentence is likely to sprawl if an independent clause comes first, followed by a long subordinate clause of lesser importance, such as the sentence you are now reading.)

In short, though simple sentences and compound sentences have their place, they make everything of equal importance. Since everything is not of equal importance, you must often write complex and compound-complex sentences, subordinating some things to other things.

Write Unified and Coherent Paragraphs

UNITY

A unified paragraph is a group of sentences (rarely a single sentence) on a single idea. The idea may have several twists or subdivisions, but all the parts—the sentences—should form a whole that can be summarized in one sentence. A paragraph is, to put the matter a little differently, one of the major points supporting your thesis. If your essay is some five hundred words long—about two double-spaced typewritten pages—you probably will not break it down into more than four or five parts or paragraphs. (But you *should* break your essay down into paragraphs, that is, coherent blocks that give the reader a rest between them. One page of typing is about as long as you can go before the reader needs a slight break.) A paper of five hundred words with a dozen paragraphs is probably faulty not because it has too many ideas but because it has too few *developed* ideas. A short paragraph—especially one consisting of a single sentence—is usually anemic; such a paragraph may be acceptable when it summarizes a highly detailed previous paragraph or group of paragraphs, or when it serves as a transition between two complicated paragraphs, but usually summaries and transitions can begin the next paragraph.

Each paragraph has a unifying idea, which may appear as a **topic sentence.** Most commonly, the topic sentence is the first sentence, forecasting what is to come in the rest of the paragraph; or it may be the second sentence, following a transitional sentence. Less commonly, it is the last sentence, summarizing the points that the paragraph's earlier sentences have made. Least commonly—but thoroughly acceptable—the topic sentence may appear nowhere in the paragraph, in which case the paragraph has a **topic idea**—an idea that holds the sentences together although it has not been explicitly stated. Whether explicit or implicit, an idea must unite the sentences of the paragraph. If your paragraph has only one or two sentences, the chances are that you have not adequately developed its idea. You probably have not provided sufficient details—perhaps including brief quotations—to support your topic sentence or your topic idea.

A paragraph can make several points, but the points must be related, and the nature of the relationship must be indicated so that the paragraph has a single unifying point. Here is a paragraph, unusually brief, that may seem to make two points but that, in fact, holds them together with a topic idea. The author is Edmund Wilson:

> James Joyce's *Ulysses* was an attempt to present directly the thoughts and feelings of a group of Dubliners through the whole course of a summer day. *Finnegans Wake* is a complementary attempt to render the dream fantasies and the half-unconscious sensations experienced by a single person in the course of a night's sleep.
>
> *The Wound and The Bow* (New York, 1947), p. 243

Wilson's topic idea is that *Finnegans Wake* complements *Ulysses.* Notice that the sentence about *Finnegans Wake* concludes the paragraph. Not surprisingly, Wilson's essay is about this book, and the structure of the paragraph allows him to get into his subject.

The next example may seem to have more than one subject (Richardson and Fielding were contemporaries; they were alike in some ways; they were different in others), but again the paragraph is unified by a topic idea (although Richardson and Fielding were contemporaries and were alike in some ways, they differed in important ways):

> The names of Richardson and Fielding are always coupled in any discussion of the novel, and with good reason. They were contemporaries, writing in the same cultural climate (*Tom Jones* was published in 1719, a year after *Clarissa*). Both had genius and both were widely recognized immediately. Yet they are ut-

terly different in their tastes and temperaments, and therefore in their visions of city and country, of men and women, and even of good and evil.

Elizabeth Drew, The Novel (New York, 1963), p. 59

This paragraph, like Edmund Wilson's, closes in on its subject.

The beginning and especially the end of a paragraph are usually the most emphatic parts. A beginning may offer a generalization that the rest of the paragraph supports. Or the early part may offer details, preparing for the generalization in the later part. Or the paragraph may move from cause to effect. Although no rule can cover all paragraphs (except that all must make a point in an orderly way), one can hardly go wrong in making the first sentence either a transition from the previous paragraph or a statement of the paragraph's topic. Here is a sentence that makes a transition and also states the topic: "Not only narrative poems but also meditative poems may have a kind of plot." This sentence gets the reader from plot in narrative poetry (which the writer has been talking about) to plot in meditative poetry (which the writer goes on to talk about).

COHERENCE

If a paragraph has not only unity but also a structure, then it has coherence, its parts fit together. Make sure that each sentence is properly related to the preceding and the following sentences. One way of gaining coherence is by means of transitions—words such as *furthermore, on the other hand,* and *but.* These words let the reader know how a sentence is related to the previous sentence.

Nothing is wrong with such obvious transitions as *moreover, however, but, for example, this tendency, in the next chapter,* and so on; but, of course, (1) these transitions should not start every sentence (they can be buried thus: "Zora Neal Hurston, moreover, ..."), and (2) they need not appear anywhere in the sentence. The point is not that transitions must be explicit, but that the argument must proceed clearly. The gist of a paragraph might run thus: "Speaking broadly, there were in the Renaissance two comic traditions.... The first ... The second ... The chief difference ... But both traditions ..."

Here is a paragraph by Elizabeth Drew, discussing one aspect of Dickens's *Great Expectations.* The structure is basically chronological, but notice, too, the effective use of a parallel as a linking device within the last sentence. (The links are italicized.)

> Some of the most poignant scenes in the book are the *opening ones,* which describe the atmosphere in which Pip grows up. *He is introduced* as "a small bundle of shivers" alone in the graveyard, *which is followed* by the terrifying intrusion of the world of active violence and fear as the convict seizes him. *Then we see* the household at the forge, where he is made to feel guilty and ashamed of

his very existence; the Christmas party at which he is baited and bullied by his elders; his treatment at the hands of the hypocritical Pumblechook; his introduction to Estella, who reveals to him that he is coarse and common. *Dickens knows*
that in children "there is nothing so finely perceived and so finely felt, as injustice," and looking back on his childhood, *Pip too knows* that truth: "Within myself, I had sustained, from my babyhood, a perpetual conflict with injustice."

The Novel, p. 197

INTRODUCTORY PARAGRAPHS

Beginning a long part of one of his long poems, Byron aptly wrote,
"Nothing so difficult as a beginning." Almost all writers—professionals as well
as amateurs—find that the beginning paragraphs in their drafts are false starts.
Don't worry too much about the opening paragraphs of your draft; you'll almost surely want to revise your opening later anyway, and when writing a first
draft you merely need something—almost anything may do— to get you going. Though on rereading you will probably find that the first paragraph or
two should be replaced, those opening words at least helped you break the
ice.

In your finished paper the opening cannot be mere throatclearing. It
should be interesting and informative. Don't paraphrase your title ("Sex in
1984") in your first sentence: "This theme will study the topic of sex in *1984.*"
The sentence contains no information about the topic here, at least none beyond what the title already gave, and no information about you, either—that
is, no sense of your response to the topic, such as might be present in, say, "In
George Orwell's *1984* the rulers put a lot of energy into producing antisexual
propaganda, but Orwell never convinces us of the plausibility of all of this activity."

Often you can make use of a quotation, either from the work or from a
critic. After all, if a short passage from the work caught your attention and set
you thinking and stimulated you to develop a thesis, it may well provide a
good beginning for your essay.

Here is a nice opening from a chapter on Norman Mailer, by Richard
Poirier: "Mailer is an unusually repetitious writer. Nearly all writers of any last-
ing interest are repetitious." The first sentence, simple though it is, catches
our attention; the second gives the first a richer meaning than we had attributed to it. Poirier then goes on to give examples of major writers who are
obsessed with certain topics, and he concludes the paragraph with a list of
Mailer's obsessions. Such an opening paragraph is a slight variant on a surefire
method: *You cannot go wrong in stating your thesis* in your opening paragraph,
moving from a rather broad view to a narrower one. If you look at the sample
essays in this book, you will see that most good opening paragraphs clearly indicate the writer's thesis. Here is an introductory paragraph, written by a student, on the ways in which Shakespeare manages in some degree to present
Macbeth sympathetically:

```
     Near the end of Macbeth, Malcolm speaks of Macbeth as a

"dead butcher" (5.8.69), and there is some -- perhaps much --

truth in this characterization. Macbeth is the hero of the

play, but he is also the villain. And yet to call him a vil-

lain is too simple. Despite the fact that he murders his

king, his friend Banquo, and even the utterly innocent Lady

Macduff and her children, he engages our sympathy, largely

because Shakespeare continually reminds us that Macbeth nev-

er (despite appearances) becomes a cold-blooded murderer.

Macbeth's violence is felt not only by his victims but by

Macbeth himself; his deeds torture him, plaguing his mind.

Despite all his villainy, he is a man with a conscience.
```

One other kind of introduction is tricky and should be used cautiously. Sometimes an introductory paragraph delicately misleads the audience; the second paragraph reverses the train of thought and leads into the main issue. Here is an example by Joseph Wood Krutch, from *"Modernism" in Modern Drama*. Only the first part of the second paragraph is given, but from it you can see what direction Krutch is taking.

> One evening in 1892, the first of Oscar Wilde's four successful comedies had in London its first performance. It is said that after the last curtain the audience rose to cheer—and it had good reason to do so. Not in several generations had a new play so sparkled with fresh and copious wit of a curiously original kind.
>
> By now the play itself, *Lady Windermere's Fan*, seems thin and faded. To be successfully revived as it was a few seasons ago in the United States, it has to be presented as "a period piece"—which means that the audience is invited to laugh at as well as with it....

> (Ithaca, N.Y., 1953), p. 43

Here is another example, this one containing the reversal at the end of the opening paragraph.

> Time and again I wanted to reach out and shake Peter Fonda and Dennis Hopper, the two motorcyclist heroes of *Easy Rider*, until they stopped their damned-fool pompous poeticizing on the subject of doing your own thing and being your own man. I dislike Fonda as an actor; he lacks humor, affects insufferable sensitivity and always seems to be fulfilling a solemn mission instead of playing a part. I didn't believe in these Honda hoboes as intuitive balladeers of the interstate highways, and I had no intention of accepting them as protagonists in a modern myth about the destruction of innocence. To my astonishment then the movie reached out and profoundly shook me.

> Joseph Morgenstern, "On the Road," *Newsweek*, July 21, 1969, p. 95

CONCLUDING PARAGRAPHS

With conclusions, as with introductions, try to say something interesting. It is not of the slightest interest to say "Thus we see ... [here the writer echoes the title and the first paragraph]." Some justification may be made for a summary at the end of a long paper because the reader may have half-forgotten some of the ideas presented 30 pages earlier, but a paper that can be held easily in the mind needs something different. In fact, if your paper is short—say two or three pages—you may not need to summarize or to draw a conclusion. Just make sure that your last sentence is a good one and that the reader does not expect anything further.

If you do feel that a concluding paragraph (as opposed to a final paragraph) is appropriate or necessary, make sure that you do not merely echo what you have already said. A good concluding paragraph may round out the previous discussion, normally with a few sentences that summarize (without the obviousness of "We may now summarize"), but it may also draw an inference that has not previously been expressed. To draw such an inference is not to introduce a new idea—a concluding paragraph is hardly the place for a new idea—but is to see the previous material in a fresh perspective. A good concluding paragraph closes the issue while enriching it. Notice how the two examples that follow wrap things up and at the same time, open out by suggesting a larger frame of reference.

The first example is the conclusion to Norman Friedman's "Point of View in Fiction." In this fairly long discussion of the development of a critical concept, Friedman catalogs various points of view and then spends several pages arguing that the choice of a point of view is crucial if certain effects are to be attained. The omniscient narrator of a novel who comments on all that happens, Friedman suggests, is a sort of free verse of fiction, and an author may willingly sacrifice this freedom for a narrower point of view if he or she wishes to make certain effects. Friedman concludes:

> All this is merely to say, in effect, that when an author surrenders in fiction, he does so in order to conquer; he gives up certain privileges and imposes certain limits in order the more effectively to render his story-illusion, which constitutes artistic truth in fiction. And it is in the service of this truth that he spends his creative life.

PMLA, 70 (1955), 1160–1184

Notice that Friedman devotes the early part of his paragraph to a summary of what has preceded, and then in the latter part he puts his argument in a new perspective.

A second example of a concluding paragraph that restates the old and looks toward the new comes from Richard B. Sewall's discussion of *The Scarlet Letter.*

> Henry James said that Hawthorne had "a cat-like faculty of seeing in the

dark"; but he never saw through the dark to radiant light. What light his vision reveals is like the fitful sunshine of Hester's and Dimmesdale's meeting in the forest—the tragic opposite of Emerson's triumphant gleaming sun that "shines also today."

The Vision of Tragedy (New Haven, 1959), p. 91

Again, don't feel that you must always offer a conclusion in your last paragraph. Especially if your paper is fairly short—let's say fewer than five pages—when you have finished your analysis or explication it may be enough to stop. If, for example, you have been demonstrating throughout your paper that in *Julius Caesar* Shakespeare condensed the time (compared to his historical source) and thus gave the happenings in the play an added sense of urgency, you scarcely need to reaffirm this point in your last paragraph. Probably it will be conclusion enough if you just offer your final evidence in a well-written sentence and then stop.

Write Emphatically

All that has been said about getting the right word, about effective sentences, and about paragraphs is related to the matter of **emphasis.** But we can add a few points here. The first rule (it will be modified in a moment) is: Be emphatic. But do not attempt to achieve emphasis, as Queen Victoria did, by a *style* consisting *chiefly* of *italics* and *exclamation* marks!!! Do not rely on such expressions as "very important," "definitely significant," and "really beautiful." The proper way to be emphatic is to find the right word, to use appropriate detail, to subordinate the lesser points, and to develop your ideas reasonably. The beginning and the end of a sentence (and of a paragraph) are emphatic positions; of these two positions, the end is usually the more emphatic. Here is a sentence that properly moves to an emphatic end:

Having been ill-treated by Hamlet and having lost her father, Ophelia goes mad.

If the halves are reversed, the sentence peters out:

Ophelia goes mad because she has been ill-treated by Hamlet and she has lost her father.

Still, even this version is better than the shapeless:

Having been ill-treated by Hamlet, Ophelia goes mad, partly too because she has lost her father.

The important point, that she goes mad, is dissipated by the lame addition of words about her father. In short, avoid anticlimaxes such as "Macbeth's deed is reprehensible and serious."

The usual advice, build to emphatic ends, needs modification. Don't write something that sounds like an advertisement for *The Blood of Dracula:*

"In her eyes DESIRE! In her veins—the blood of a MONSTER!!!" Be emphatic but courteous and sensible; do not shout.

One further caution: It is all very well to speak in a courteously low voice, but do not be so timid that you whisper assertions in a negative form. Think twice before you let something like this remain in your manuscript: "Gilman is not unsuccessful in her depiction of the pathos of madness." The writer seems reluctant to come out and say "Gilman succeeds in depicting the pathos of madness." If this statement needs qualification (for example, she succeeds only in such-and-such a part of the story), give the qualifications, but do not think that the weaseling "not unsuccessful" is adequate. It is not unlikely that the readers will not be pleased, which means that it is likely they will be displeased.

A Note on Authors' Names and Other Troublesome Matters

A good many rules, thinly disguised as pleasant suggestions, have been offered. The succeeding pages will offer more, but a few common difficulties don't lend themselves to discussion under any of the previous or the succeeding topics, and so they simply are grouped here.

1. If the author you are writing about is **male,** it is usually best to give his full name when you first mention him ("Most readers of Ken Kesey's *One Flew Over the Cuckoo's Nest* will remember ..."); but if he is so well known that his last name is a household word (for example, Dickens, Shakespeare, Thoreau), it is common to omit the first name even in the first reference. To say "In William Shakespeare's *Hamlet*" is almost to imply that the reader needs help in identifying Shakespeare. In subsequent references to a living male author, it is enough to give only his last name ("Moreover, Kesey ...") unless your sense of courtesy compels you to preface it with "Mr." No really comfortable convention exists; one feels a bit disrespectful in speaking of "Kesey," a bit stuffy in speaking of "Mr. Kesey," and very phony in speaking of "Ken." Never—not even in an attempt at whimsy—use "Mr." before the name of a dead author.

Things are even more uncomfortable in speaking of **females.** Male chauvinism is perhaps responsible for the convention of repeatedly using the full name for women ("Jane Austen," for the tenth time in the essay) or for repeatedly prefacing the last name with "Miss" or "Mrs." or "Ms." even though males may get no such courteous treatment. But these ostentatiously polite conventions are disappearing, and it is now customary to give women and men the same treatment.

2. Don't write "**e.g.**" when you mean "**i.e.**"—a common confusion; i.e. (Latin, *id est*), meaning "that is," should be distinguished from e.g. (*exempli gratia*), meaning "for example." Thus: "Modern poets, i.e., poets who wrote

after World War II ..." And: "Modern poets, e.g., Creeley and Sexton, unlike poets who wrote before World War II ..."

3. To indicate a **dash,** type two hyphens without hitting the space-bar before, between, or after them.

4. **Hyphenate "century" when it is used as an adjective.** "Nineteenth-century authors often held that ..." But: "Eliot, born in the nineteenth century, often held that ..." The principle is: Use a hyphen to join words that are used as a single adjective, for example, a "six-volume work," "an out-of-date theory," and so "a nineteenth-century author." Notice that the hyphen is neither preceded nor followed by a space.

REMARKS ABOUT MANUSCRIPT FORM

Basic Manuscript Form

Much of what follows is nothing more than common sense.

1. Use $8\frac{1}{2}'' \times 11''$ paper of good weight. Keep as lightweight a carbon copy as you wish or make a photocopy, but hand in a sturdy original.
2. If you write on a typewriter or a word processor, use a reasonably fresh ribbon, double-space, and type on one side of the page only. If you submit handwritten copy, use lined paper and write on one side of the page only in black or dark blue ink, on every other line. Most instructors do *not* want papers to be enclosed in any sort of binder. And most instructors want papers to be clipped together in the upper left corner; do not crimp or crease corners and expect them to hold together.
3. Leave an adequate margin—an inch or an inch and a half—at top, bottom, and sides.
4. Number the pages consecutively, using arabic numerals in the upper right-hand corner.
5. Put your name and class or course number in the upper right-hand corner of the first page. It is a good idea to put your name in the upper right corner of each page so that if page gets separated it can easily be restored to the proper essay.
6. Create your own title—one that reflects your topic or thesis. For example, a paper on Shirley Jackson's "The Lottery" should not be called "The Lottery" but might be called

```
Suspense in Shirley Jackson's "The Lottery"
```

or

```
Is "The Lottery" Rigged?
```

or

Jackson's "The Lottery" and Scapegoat Rituals

These titles do at least a little in the way of rousing a reader's interest.

7. Center the title of your essay below the top margin of the first page. Begin the first word of the title with a capital letter, and capitalize each subsequent word except articles (*a, an, the*), conjunctions (*and, but, if, when,* etc.), and prepositions (*in, on, with,* etc.), thus:

A Word on Behalf of Mrs. Walter Mitty

Notice that you do *not* enclose your title within quotation marks, and you do not underline it—though if it includes the title of a story, *that* is enclosed within quotation marks, as in the following example:

Illusion and Reality in Hawthorne's "Young Goodman Brown"

8. Begin the essay an inch or two below the title.
9. Your extensive revisions should have been made in your drafts, but minor last-minute revisions may be made—neatly —on the finished copy. Proofreading may catch some typographical errors, and you may notice some small weaknesses. You can make corrections with the following proofreader's symbols.

CORRECTIONS IN THE FINAL COPY

Changes in wording may be made by crossing through words and rewriting them:

The influence of Poe and Hawthorne ~~have~~ *has* greatly diminished.

Additions should be made above the line, with a caret below the line at the appropriate place:

The influence of Poe and Hawthorne has *greatly* diminished.

Transpositions of letters may be made thus:

The influence of Poe and Hawthorne has greatly diminished.

Deletions are indicated by a horizontal line through the word or words to be deleted. Delete a single letter by drawing a vertical or diagonal line through it; then indicate whether the letters on either side are to be closed up by drawing a connecting arc:

The influence of Poe and Hawthorne has greatly diminished.

Separation of words accidentally run together is indicated by a vertical line, *closure* by a curved line connecting the letters to be closed up:

The influence of Poe and Hawthorne has g reatly diminished.

Paragraphing may be indicated by the symbol ⁋ before the word that is to begin the new paragraph:

```
The influence of Poe and Hawthorne has greatly

diminished. ⁋ The influence of Borges has very largely re-

placed that of earlier writers of fantasy.
```

Quotations and Quotation Marks

First, a word about the *point* of using quotations. Don't use quotations to pad the length of a paper. Rather, give quotations from the work you are discussing so that your readers will see the material you are discussing and (especially in a research paper) so that your readers will know what some of the chief interpretations are and what your responses to them are.

Note: The next few paragraphs do *not* discuss how to include citations of pages, a topic discussed in the next chapter under the heading "How to Document: Footnotes and Internal Parenthetical Citations."

The Golden Rule: If you quote, *comment on* the quotation. Let the reader know what you make of it and why you quote it.

Additional principles:

1. **Identify the speaker or writer of the quotation** so that the reader is not left with a sense of uncertainty. Usually, in accordance with the principle of letting readers know where they are going, this identification precedes the quoted material, but occasionally it may follow the quotation, especially if it will provide something of a pleasant surprise. For instance, in a discussion of Flannery O'Connor's stories, you might quote a disparaging comment on one of the stories and then reveal that O'Connor herself was the speaker.

2. If the quotation is part of your own sentence, **be sure to fit the quotation grammatically and logically into your sentence.**

> *Incorrect:* Holden Caulfield tells us very little about "what my lousy childhood was like."
> *Correct:* Holden Caulfield tells us very little about what his "lousy childhood was like."

3. **Indicate any omissions or additions.** The quotation must be exact. Any material that you add—even one or two words—must be enclosed within square brackets, thus:

```
Hawthorne tells us that "owing doubtless to the depth of the

gloom at that particular spot [in the forest], neither the

travellers nor their steeds were visible."
```

If you wish to omit material from within a quotation, indicate the ellipsis by three spaced periods. If your sentence ends in an omission, add a closed-up period and then three spaced periods to indicate the omission. The following example is based on a quotation from the sentences immediately above this one:

```
The instructions say that "If you . . . omit material from
within a quotation, [you must] indicate the ellipsis. . . .
If your sentence ends in an omission, add a closed-up period
and then three spaced periods. . . .
```

Notice that although material preceded "If you," periods are not needed to indicate the omission because "If you" began a sentence in the original. Customarily, initial and terminal omissions are indicated only when they are part of the sentence you are quoting. Even such omissions need not be indicated when the quoted material is obviously incomplete—when, for instance, it is a word or phrase.

4. **Distinguish between short and long quotations,** and treat each appropriately. *Short quotations* (usually defined as fewer than five lines of typed prose or three lines of poetry) are enclosed within quotation marks and run into the text (rather than being set off, without quotation marks), as in the following example:

```
Hawthorne begins the story by telling us that "Young Goodman
Brown came forth at sunset into the street at Salem
village," thus at the outset connecting the village with
daylight. A few paragraphs later, when Hawthorne tells us
that the road Brown takes was "darkened by all of the
gloomiest trees of the forest," he begins to associate the
forest with darkness -- and a very little later with evil.
```

To set off a *long quotation* (more than four typed lines of prose or two lines of poetry), indent the entire quotation ten spaces from the left margin. Usually, a long quotation is introduced by a clause ending with a colon—for instance, "The following passage will make this point clear:" or "The closest we come to hearing an editorial voice is a long passage in the middle of the story:" or some such lead-in. After typing your lead-in, double-space, and then type the quotation, indented and double-spaced.

5. **Commas and periods go inside the quotation marks.**

```
Chopin tells us in the first sentence that "Mrs. Mallard was
```

afflicted with heart trouble," and in the last sentence the

doctors say that Mrs. Mallard "died of heart disease."

Exception: If the quotation is immediately followed by material in parentheses or in square brackets, close the quotation, then give the parenthetic or bracketed material, and then—after closing the parenthesis or bracket—put the comma or period.

Chopin tells us in the first sentence that "Mrs. Mallard was

afflicted with heart trouble" (17), and in the last sentence

the doctors say that Mrs. Mallard "died of heart disease"

(18).

Semicolons, colons, and dashes go outside the closing quotation marks.

Question marks and exclamation points go inside if they are part of the quotation, outside if they are your own.

In the following passage from a student's essay, notice the difference in the position of the question marks. The first is part of the quotation, so it is enclosed within the quotation marks. The second question mark, however, is the student's, so it comes after the closing quotation mark.

The older man says to Goodman Brown, "Sayest thou so?"

Doesn't a reader become uneasy when the man immediately

adds, "We are but a little way in the forest yet"?

QUOTATION MARKS OR UNDERLINING?

Use quotation marks around titles of short stories and other short works—that is, titles of chapters in books, essays, and poems that might not be published by themselves. Underline (to indicate italics) titles of books, periodicals, collections of essays, plays, and long poems such as *The Rime of the Ancient Mariner*.

10

Research Papers

WHAT RESEARCH IS NOT, AND
WHAT RESEARCH IS

Jeff, in a Mutt and Jeff cartoon, sells jars of honey. He includes in each jar a dead bee as proof that the product is genuine. Some writers—even some professionals—seem to think that a hiveful of dead quotations or footnotes is proof of research. But research requires much more than the citation of authorities. What it requires, briefly, is informed, *thoughtful* analysis.

Because a research paper requires its writer to collect and interpret evidence—usually including the opinions of earlier investigators—one sometimes hears that a research paper, unlike a critical essay, is not the expression of personal opinion. Such a view is unjust both to criticism and to research. A critical essay is not a mere expression of personal opinions; if it is any good, it offers evidence that supports the opinions and thus persuades the reader of their objective rightness. A research paper is in the final analysis largely personal because the author continuously uses his or her own judgment to evaluate the evidence, deciding what is relevant and convincing. A research paper is not the mere presentation of what a dozen scholars have already said about a topic; it is a thoughtful evaluation of the available evidence, and so it is, finally, an expression of what the author thinks the evidence adds up to.

Research can be a tedious and frustrating business; hours are spent reading books and articles that prove to be irrelevant, pieces of evidence contradict themselves, and time is always short.

Still, even though research is time-consuming, those who engage in it feel (at least sometimes) an exhilaration, a sense of triumph at having studied a problem thoroughly and arrived at conclusions that—for the moment, anyway—seem objective and irrefutable. Later, new evidence may turn up and require a new conclusion, but until that time one has built something that will endure wind and weather.

PRIMARY AND SECONDARY MATERIALS

The materials of literary research may be conveniently divided into two sorts, primary and secondary. The *primary materials* or sources are the real subject of study; the *secondary materials* are critical and historical accounts already written about these primary materials. For example, if you want to know whether Shakespeare's attitude toward Julius Caesar was highly traditional or highly original (or a little of each), you read the primary materials (*Julius Caesar* and other Elizabethan writings about Caesar); and, since research requires that you be informed about the present state of thought on your topic, you also read the secondary materials (post-Elizabethan essays, books on Shakespeare, and books on Elizabethan attitudes toward Caesar, or, more generally, on Elizabethan attitudes toward Rome and toward monarchs).

A second example: If you are concerned with Charlotte Perkins Gilman's representation of medical treatment for women in her story "The Yellow Wallpaper," Gilman's story and her autobiographical writings are primary material, and one might also consider primary material the medical discussions of the period, especially the writings of S. Weir Mitchell, a physician who treated Gilman. Articles and books about Gilman and about medicine in the late nineteenth century are secondary sources.

FROM TOPIC TO THESIS

Almost every literary work lends itself to research. As has already been mentioned, a study of Shakespeare's attitude toward Julius Caesar would lead to a study of other Elizabethan works and of modern critical works. Similarly, a study of the ghost of Caesar—does it have a real, objective existence, or is it merely a figment of Brutus's imagination?—could lead to a study of Shakespeare's other ghosts (for instance, those in *Hamlet* and *Macbeth*), and a study of Elizabethan attitudes toward ghosts. Or, to take an example from our own century, a reader of Edward Albee's *The Sandbox* might want to study the early, critical reception of the play. Did the reviewers like it? More precisely, did the reviewers in relatively highbrow journals evaluate it differently from those in popular magazines and newspapers? Or, what has Albee himself said about the play in the decades that have passed since he wrote it? Do his comments in essays and interviews indicate that he now sees the play as something different from what he saw when he wrote it? Or, to take yet another example of a work from the middle of our century, a reader might similarly study George Orwell's *1984,* looking at its critical reception, or Orwell's own view of it, or, say, at the sources of Orwell's inspiration. Let's look, for a few minutes, at this last topic.

Assume that you have read George Orwell's *1984* and that, in preparing to do some research on it, browsing through *The Collected Essays, Journalism, and Letters,* you come across a letter (17 February 1944) in which Orwell says that he has been reading Evgenii Zamyatin's *We* and that he himself has been keeping notes for "that kind of book." And in *The Collected Essays, Journalism, and Letters* you also come across a review (4 January 1946) Orwell wrote of *We,* from which it is apparent that *We* resembles *1984.* Or perhaps you learned in a preface to an edition of *1984* that Orwell was influenced by *We,* and you have decided to look into the matter. You want to know exactly how great the influence is. You borrow *We* from the library, read it, and perceive resemblances in plot, character, and theme. But it's not simply a question of listing resemblances between the two books. Your topic is: What do the resemblances add up to? After all, Orwell in the letter said he had already been working in Zamyatin's direction without even knowing Zamyatin's book, so your investigation may find, for example, that the closest resemblances are in relatively trivial details and that everything really important in *1984* was already implicit in Orwell's earlier books; or your investigation may find that Zamyatin gave a new depth to Orwell's thought; or it may find that though Orwell borrowed heavily from Zamyatin, he missed the depth of *We.* In the earliest stage of your research, then, you don't know what you will find, so you cannot yet formulate a thesis (or, at best, you can formulate only a tentative thesis). But you know that there is a topic, that it interests you, and that you are ready to begin the necessary legwork.

LOCATING MATERIAL

First Steps

First, prepare a working bibliography, that is, a list of books and articles that must be looked at. The card catalog of a library is an excellent place to begin. If your topic is Orwell and Zamyatin, you'll want at least to glance at whatever books by and about these two authors are available. When you have looked over the most promising portions of this material (in secondary sources, chapter headings and indexes will often guide you), you will have found some interesting things. But you want to get a good idea of the state of current scholarship on your topic, and you realize that you must go beyond the card catalog's listings under *Orwell, Zamyatin,* and such obviously related topics as *utopian literature.* Doubtless there are pertinent articles in journals, but you cannot start thumbing through them at random.

The easiest way to locate articles and books on literature written in a modern language—that is, on a topic other than literature of the ancient world—is to consult the *MLA International Bibliography,* which until 1969 was published as part of *PMLA (Publications of the Modern Language Associa-*

tion) and since 1969 has been published separately. This bibliography, pub-lished annually, lists scholarly studies published in a given year; you look, therefore, in the most recent issue under *Orwell* (in the section on *English Lit-erature,* the subsection on *Twentieth Century*) to see if anything is listed that sounds relevant. A look at *Zamyatin* also may turn up material. (Note that in the past few years the number of entries in the *MLA International Bibliogra-phy* has so increased that for each year from 1969 the annual bibliography consists of more than one volume. Writings on literature in English are in one volume, writings on European literature in another; so the volume that gives you information about Orwell will not be the one that gives you information about Zamyatin.)

If, by the way, you are indeed working on Orwell, when you consult the *MLA International Bibliography* for 1975 you'll find you are lucky; it lists an article in an issue of a periodical entitled *Modern Fiction Studies* that is itself a bibliography of writings on Orwell. If you consult this article, you'll see that it is a supplement to an earlier bibliography of writings on Orwell, published in *Bulletin of Bibliography* in 1974. This last item could also have been located by looking at the *MLA International Bibliography* for 1974.

Because your time is severely limited, you probably cannot read every-thing published on your two authors. At least for the moment, therefore, you will use only the last ten years of this bibliography. Presumably, any important earlier material will have been incorporated into some of the recent studies listed, and if when you come to read these recent studies you find references to an article of, say, 1958 that sounds essential, of course you will read that ar-ticle, too.

Other Bibliographic Aids

The *MLA International Bibliography* is not the only valuable guide to scholarship. The *Year's Work in English Studies,* though concerned only with English authors (hence it will have nothing on Zamyatin, a Russian, unless an article links Zamyatin with an English author), and though not nearly so com-prehensive even on English authors as the *MLA International Bibliography,* is useful partly because it is selective—presumably listing only the more signifi-cant items—and partly because it includes some evaluative comments on the books and articles it lists.

For topics in American literature, a similar annual publication, *American Literary Scholarship* (1965–   ), is valuable for its broad coverage of articles and books on major and minor writers and for its evaluative comments. Two guides are useful to scholarly and critical studies of some canonical American figures. James Woodress et al., eds., *Eight American Authors: A Review of Re-search and Criticism,* rev. ed. (New York: Norton, 1972), covering Poe,

Emerson, Hawthorne, Thoreau, Melville, Whitman, Mark Twain, and Henry James, is now dated, but it remains a good guide to early studies of these authors. Jackson R. Bryer, ed., *Sixteen Modern American Authors: A Survey of Research and Criticism* (Durham, N.C.: Duke University Press, 1974), covering such figures as Sherwood Anderson, Willa Cather, Eugene O'Neill, and Ezra Pound (living authors were excluded) is also dated, but a supplement is in preparation at the time of this writing and may now be available.

A fair number of recent guides focus on authors who until a decade ago were relatively neglected. Two examples will have to suffice. *American Women Writers: Bibliographical Essays* (Westport, Conn.: Greenwood, 1983), edited by Maurice Duke, Jackson R. Bryer, and M. Thomas Inge includes scholarship through 1981 on 24 authors, including Bradstreet, Jewett, Chopin, Stein, O'Connor, Hurston, and Plath. *Black American Writers: Bibliographical Essays* (New York: St. Martin's, 1978), edited by M. Thomas Inge, Maurice Duke, and Jackson R. Bryer, covers slave narratives, as well as such later writers as Hughes, Ellison, and Baldwin.

None of the bibliographic aids mentioned thus far covers ancient writers; there is no point, then, in looking at these aids if you are writing about the Book of Job or Greek conceptions of the tragic hero or Roman conceptions of comedy. For articles on ancient literature, as well as on literature in modern languages, consult the annual volumes of *Humanities Index,* issued since 1974; for the period from 1965 to 1974 it was entitled *Social Sciences and Humanities Index,* and before that (1907–1964) it was *International Index.* In *Humanities Index* (to use the current title) you can find listings of articles in periodicals on a wide range of topics. This breadth is bought at the cost of depth, for *Humanities Index,* though it includes the chief scholarly journals, includes neither the less well known scholarly journals nor the more popular magazines, nor does it include books.

For the more popular magazines, consult the *Readers' Guide to Periodical Literature.* If, for example, you want to do a research paper on the reception given to Sir Laurence Olivier's films of Shakespeare, the *Readers' Guide* can quickly lead you to reviews in such magazines as *Time, Newsweek,* and *Atlantic.*

Bibliographies of the sort mentioned are guides, and there are so many of them that guides to these guides have been published. Two invaluable guides to reference works (that is, to bibliographies and to such helpful compilations as handbooks of mythology, place names, and critical terms) are James L. Harner, *Literary Research Guide: A Guide to Reference Sources for the Study of Literature in English and Related Topics* (New York: MLA, 1989), and Michael J. Marcuse, *A References Guide for English Studies* (Berkeley: University of California Press, 1990).

And the guides to these guides have guides: reference librarians. If you don't know where to turn to find something, turn to the librarian.

Taking Notes

Let's assume now that you have checked some bibliographies and that you have a fair number of references you must read to have a substantial knowledge of the evidence and the common interpretations of the evidence. Most researchers find it convenient, when examining bibliographies and the card catalog, to write down each reference on a 3″ × 5″ index card—one title per card. On the card put the author's full name (last name first), the exact title of the book or of the article, and the name of the journal (with dates and pages). Titles of books and periodicals (publications issued periodically—for example, monthly or four times a year) are underlined; titles of articles and of essays in books are put within quotation marks. It's also a good idea to put the library catalog number on the card to save time if you need to get the item for a second look.

Next, start reading or scanning the materials whose titles you have collected. Some of these items will prove irrelevant or silly; others will prove valuable in themselves and also in the leads they give you to further references, which you should duly record on 3″ × 5″ cards. Notes—aside from these bibliographic notes—are best taken on 4″ × 6″ cards. Smaller cards do not provide enough space for summaries of useful materials, but 4″ × 6″ cards—rather than larger cards—will serve to remind you that you should not take notes on everything. Be selective in taking notes.

1. In taking notes, write brief *summaries* rather than paraphrases. Paraphrasing rarely has any point; generally speaking, either quote exactly (and put the passage in quotation marks, with a notation of the source, including the page numbers) or summarize, reducing a page or even an entire article or chapter of a book to a single 4″ × 6″ card. Even when you summarize, indicate your source on the card so that you can give appropriate credit in your paper. (On plagiarism, see pages 231–233.)

2. In your summary you will sometimes quote a phrase or a sentence—putting it in quotation marks—but quote sparingly. You are not doing stenography, but rather, thinking and assimilating knowledge; for the most part, then, you should digest your source rather than engorge it whole. Thinking now, while taking notes, will also help you avoid plagiarism later. If, on the other hand, you mindlessly copy material at length when taking notes, when you are writing the paper later you may be tempted to copy it yet again, perhaps without giving credit. Similarly, if you photocopy pages from articles or books and then merely underline some passages, you will probably not be thinking; you will just be underlining. But if you make a terse summary on a note card, you will be forced to think and to find your own words for the idea. Most of the direct quotations you copy should be effectively stated passages or especially crucial passages or both. In your finished paper some of these quotations will provide authority and emphasis.

3. If you quote but omit some irrelevant material within the quotation, be sure to indicate the omission by three spaced periods, as explained on page 222.

4. *Never* copy a passage, changing an occasional word under the impression that you are thereby putting it into your own words. Notes of this sort will find their way into your paper, your reader will sense a style other than your own, and suspicions of plagiarism may follow.

5. In the upper corner of each note card write a brief key—for example, "Orwell's first reading of *We*" or "Characterization" or "Thought control"— so that later you can tell at a glance what is on the card.

As you work, you'll find yourself returning again and again to your primary materials—and you'll probably find to your surprise that a good deal of the secondary material is unconvincing or even wrong, despite the fact that it is printed in a handsome book or a scholarly journal. At times, under the weight of evidence, you will have to abandon some of your earlier views, but at times you will have your own opinions reinforced, and at times you will feel that your ideas have more validity than those you are reading. One of the things we learn from research is that not everything in print is true; this discovery is one of the pleasures we get from research.

DRAFTING THE PAPER

The difficult job of writing up your findings remains, but if you have taken good notes and have put useful headings on each card, you are well on your way. Read through the cards and sort them into packets of related material. Discard all notes, however interesting, that you now see are irrelevant to your paper. Go through the cards again and again, sorting and resorting, putting together what belongs together. Probably you will find that you have to do a little additional research—somehow you aren't quite clear about this or that—but after you have done this additional research, you should be able to arrange the packets into a reasonable and consistent sequence. You now have a kind of first draft, or at least a tentative organization for your paper. Two further pieces of advice:

1. Beware of the compulsion to include every note card in your essay; that is, beware of telling the reader, "*A* says ...; *B* says ...; *C* says ..."
2. You must have a point, a thesis.

Remember: As you studied the evidence, you increasingly developed or documented or corrected a thesis. You may, for example, have become convinced that the influence of Zamyatin was limited to a few details of plot and character and that Orwell had already developed the framework and the chief attitudes that are implicit in *1984*. Similarly, now, as you write and revise your paper, you will probably still be modifying your thesis to some extent, discovering what in fact the evidence implies.

The final version of the paper, however, should be a finished piece of work, without the inconsistencies, detours, and occasional dead ends of an early draft. Your readers should feel that they are moving toward a conclusion (by means of your thoughtful evaluation of the evidence) rather than merely reading an anthology of commentary on the topic. And so we should get some such structure as: "There are three common views on ... The first two are represented by *A* and *B*; the third, and by far the most reasonable, is *C*'s view that ... *A* argues ... but ... The second view, *B*'s, is based on ... but ... Although the third view, *C*'s, is not conclusive, still ... Moreover, *C*'s point can be strengthened when we consider a piece of evidence that he does not make use of...."

Be sure, when you quote, to *write a lead-in,* such as "*X* concisely states the common view" or "*Z*, without offering any proof, asserts that ...." Let the reader know where you are going, or, to put it a little differently, let the reader know how the quotation fits into your argument.

Quotations and summaries, in short, are accompanied by judicious analyses of your own so that by the end of the paper your readers not only have read a neatly typed paper (see page 219) and have gained an idea of what previous writers have said, but also are persuaded that under your guidance they have seen the evidence, heard the arguments justly summarized, and reached a sound conclusion.

A bibliography or list of works consulted (see pages 238–245) is usually appended to a research paper so that readers may easily look further into the primary and secondary material if they wish; but if you have done your job well, readers will be content to leave the subject where you left it, grateful that you have set matters straight.

DOCUMENTATION

What to Document: Avoiding Plagiarism

Honesty requires that you acknowledge your indebtedness for material, not only when you quote directly from a work, but also when you appropriate an idea that is not common knowledge. Not to acknowledge such borrowing is plagiarism. If in doubt whether to give credit, give credit.

You ought, however, to develop a sense of what is considered **common knowledge.** Definitions in a dictionary can be considered common knowledge, so there is no need to say, "According to Webster, a novel is ..." (This is weak in three ways: It's unnecessary, it's uninteresting, and it's unclear, since "Webster" appears in the titles of several dictionaries, some good and some bad.) Similarly, the date of first publication of *The Scarlet Letter* can be considered common knowledge. Few can give it when asked, but it can be found out from innumerable sources, and no one need get the credit for providing you with the date. The idea that Hamlet delays is also a matter of common knowledge. But if you are impressed by So-and-so's argument that Claudius has been much maligned, you should give credit to So-and-so.

Suppose you happen to come across Frederick R. Karl's statement in the revised edition of *A Reader's Guide to the Contemporary English Novel* (New York: Farrar, Straus & Giroux, 1972) that George Orwell was "better as a man than as a novelist." This is an interesting and an effectively worded idea. You cannot use these words without giving credit to Karl. And you cannot retain the idea but alter the words, for example, to "Orwell was a better human being than he was a writer of fiction," presenting the idea as your own, for here you are simply lifting Karl's idea—and putting it less effectively. If you want to use Karl's point, give him credit and—since you can hardly summarize so brief a statement—use his exact words and put them within quotation marks.

What about a longer passage that strikes you favorably? Let's assume that in reading Alex Zwerdling's *Orwell and the Left* (New Haven: Yale, 1974) you find the following passage from page 105 interesting:

> *1984* might be said to have a predominantly negative goal, since it is much more concerned to fight *against* a possible future society than *for* one. Its tactics are primarily defensive. Winston Smith is much less concerned with the future than with the past—which is of course the reader's present.

You certainly *cannot* say:

```
The goal of 1984 can be said to be chiefly negative because

it is devoted more to opposing some future society than it

is to fighting for a future society. Smith is more concerned

with the past (our present) than he is with the future.
```

This passage is simply a theft of Zwerdling's property: The writer has stolen Zwerdling's automobile and put a different color paint on it. How, then, can a writer use Zwerdling's idea? (1) Give Zwerdling credit and quote directly, or (2) give Zwerdling credit and summarize his point in perhaps a third of the length, or (3) give Zwerdling credit and summarize the point but include—within quotation marks—some phrase you think is especially quotable. Thus:

1. *Direct quotation.* In a study of Orwell's politics, Alex Zwerdling says, "*1984* might be said to have a predominantly negative goal, since it is much more concerned to fight *against* a possible future society than *for* one" (105).
2. *Summary.* The goal of *1984*, Zwerdling points out, is chiefly opposi-

tion to, rather than advocacy of, a certain kind of future society (105).

3. *Summary with selected quotation.* Zwerdling points out that the goal of *1984* is "predominantly negative," opposition to, rather than advocacy of, a certain kind of future society (105).

If for some reason you do not wish to name Zwerdling in your lead-in, you will have to give his name with the parenthetical citation so that a reader can identify the source:

```
The goal of 1984, one critic points out, is "predominantly
negative" (Zwerdling 105), opposition to, rather than advo-
cacy of, a certain kind of future society.
```

But it is hard to imagine why the writer preferred to say "one critic," rather than to name Zwerdling immediately, since Zwerdling sooner or later must be identified.

How to Document: Footnotes and Internal Parenthetical Citations

Documentation tells your reader exactly what your sources are. Until recently, the standard form was the footnote, which, for example, told the reader that the source of such-and-such a quotation was a book by so-and-so. But in 1984 the Modern Language Association, which had established the footnote form used in hundreds of journals, university presses, and classrooms, substituted a new form. It is this new form—parenthetical citations within the text (rather than at the foot of the page or the end of the essay)—that we will discuss at length. Keep in mind, though, that footnotes still have their uses.

FOOTNOTES

If you are using only one source, your instructor may advise you to give the source in a footnote. (Check with your instructors to find out their preferred forms of documentation.)

Let's say that your only source is a textbook. Let's say, too, that all of your quotations will be from a single story—Kate Chopin's "The Story of an Hour"—printed in this book on pages 12–14. The simplest way to cite your source is to type the digit 1 (elevated, and *without* a period after it) after your first reference to (or quotation from) the story and then to put a footnote at the bottom of the page, explaining where the story can be found. After the last line of type on the page, triple-space, indent five spaces from the left-hand margin, raise the typewriter carriage half a line, and type the arabic number 1. Do *not* put a period after it. Then lower the carriage half a line, and type a statement (double-spaced) to the effect that all references are to this book.

Notice that although the footnote begins by being indented five spaces, if the note runs to more than one line the subsequent lines are typed flush left.

^{1}Chopin's story appears in Sylvan Barnet, ed., <u>The Harper</u>
<u>Anthology of Fiction</u> (New York: HarperCollins, 1991), 25-27.

If a book has two or three editors, give all the names but with the abbreviation "eds." instead of "ed." (*not* within quotation marks). If it has more than three editors, give the name of only the first editor, followed by "et al." (the Latin abbreviation for "and others") and "eds." See the next example.

Even if you are writing a comparison of, say, two stories in a book, you may use a note of this sort. It might run thus:

^{1}All page references, given parenthetically within the
essay, refer to stories in Sylvan Barnet et al., eds., <u>Lit-</u>
<u>erature for Composition,</u> 3rd ed. (New York: HarperCollins,
1992).

If you use such a note, do not put a footnote after each quotation that follows. Give the citations right in the body of the paper, by putting the page references in parentheses after the quotations.

INTERNAL PARENTHETICAL CITATIONS

Information on page 222 distinguishes between embedded quotations (which are short, are run right into your own sentence, and are enclosed within quotation marks) and quotations that are set off on the page (for example, three or more lines of poetry, five or more lines of typed prose that are not enclosed within quotation marks).

For an embedded quotation, put the page reference in parentheses immediately after the closing quotation mark, *without* any intervening punctuation. Then, after the parenthesis that follows the number, put the necessary punctuation (for instance, a comma or a period).

Woolf says that there was "something marvelous as well as
pathetic" about the struggling moth (90). She goes on to explain . . .

Notice that the period comes *after* the parenthetical citation. Notice, similarly, that in the next example *no* punctuation comes after the first citation—because none is needed—and a comma comes *after* (not before or within) the second citation, because a comma is needed in the sentence.

This is ironic because almost at the start of the story, in

the second paragraph, Richards with the best of motives "hastened" (63) to bring his sad message; if he had at the start been "too late" (64), Mallard would have arrived at home first.

For a quotation that is not embedded within the text but is set off (indented ten spaces), put the parenthetical citation on the last line of the quotation, two spaces *after* the period that ends the quoted sentence.

Long sentences are not necessarily hard to follow. For instance, a reader has no trouble with this sentence, from Juanita Miranda's essay:

> The Philistine's scorn when he sees David, David's reply (a mixture of scorn and pity, for David announces that he comes "in the name of the Lord"), the observation that David was eager to do battle (he "<u>ran</u> toward the army to meet the Philistine"), the explanation that David cut off Goliath's head with Goliath's own sword-- all of these details help us to see the scene, to believe in the characters, and yet of course the whole story is, on the literal level, remote from our experience. (249)

Why is the sentence easy to follow? Partly because it uses parallel constructions ("The Philistine's scorn . . ., David's reply"; "the observation that . . ., the explanation that"; "to see, . . . to believe"), and partly because Miranda does not hesitate to repeat the names of David and Goliath. In certain places if she had (as we might normally expect) substituted the pronoun <u>he,</u> the passage probably would have become muddled. For instance, we have no trouble with "David cut off Goliath's head with Goliath's own sword," but we might have been at least briefly uncertain if Miranda had written "David cut off Goliath's head with his own sword."

Notice that the indented quotation ends with a period. After the period there are two spaces and then the citation in parentheses.

Four additional points:

1. "p." "pg.," and "pp." are *not* used in citing pages.
2. If a story is very short—perhaps running for only a page or two—your instructor may tell you not to keep cite the page reference for each quotation. Simply mention in the footnote that the story appears on, say, pages 200–202.
3. If you are referring to a poem, your instructor may tell you to use parenthetical citations of line numbers rather than of page numbers. But, again, your footnote will tell the reader that the poem can be found in this book, and on what page.
4. If you are referring to a play with numbered lines, your instructor may prefer that in your parenthetical citations you give act, scene, and line, rather than page numbers. Use arabic (not roman) numerals, separating the act from the scene, and the scene from the line, by periods. Here, then, is how a reference to act three, scene two, line 118 would be given:

(3.2.118)

PARENTHETICAL CITATIONS AND LIST OF WORKS CITED

Footnotes have fallen into disfavor. Parenthetical citations are now usually clarified not by means of a footnote but by means of a list, headed Works Cited, given at the end of the essay. In this list you give alphabetically (last name first) the authors and titles that you have quoted or referred to in the essay.

Briefly, the idea is that the reader of your paper encounters an author's name and a parenthetical citation of pages. By checking the author's name in Works Cited, the reader can find the passage in the book. Suppose you are writing about Kate Chopin's "The Story of an Hour." Let's assume that you have already mentioned the author and the title of the story—that is, you have let the reader know the subject of the essay—and now you introduce a quotation from the story in a sentence such as this. (Notice the parenthetical citation of page numbers immediately after the quotation.)

True, Mrs. Mallard at first expresses grief when she hears the news, but soon (unknown to her friends) she finds joy in it. So, Richards's "sad message" (64), though sad in Richards's eyes, is in fact a happy message.

Turning to Works Cited, the reader, knowing the quoted words are by Chopin, looks for Chopin and finds the following:

Chopin, Kate. "The Story of an Hour." Literature for Composition, 3rd ed. Eds. Sylvan Barnet et al. New York: HarperCollins, 1992.

Thus the essayist is informing the reader that the quoted words ("sad message") are to be found on page 64 of this anthology.

If you have not mentioned Chopin's name in some sort of lead-in, you will have to give her name within the parentheses so that the reader will know the author of the quoted words:

```
What are we to make out of a story that ends by telling us
that the leading character has died "of joy that kills"
(Chopin 64)?
```

(Notice, by the way, that the closing quotation marks come immediately after the last word of the quotation; the citation and the final punctuation—in this case, the essayist's question mark—come *after* the closing quotation marks.)

If you are comparing Chopin's story with Gilman's "The Yellow Wallpaper," in Works Cited you will give a similar entry for Gilman—her name, the title of the story, the book in which it is reprinted, and the page numbers that the story occupies.

If you are referring to several works reprinted within one volume, instead of listing each item fully, it is acceptable in Works Cited to list each item simply by giving the author's name, the title of the work, then a period, two spaces, and the name of the anthologist, followed by the page numbers that the selection spans. Thus a reference to Chopin's "The Story of an Hour" would be followed only by: Barnet, 63–65. This form requires that the anthology itself be cited under the name of the first-listed editor, thus:

```
Barnet, Sylvan, et al., eds. Literature for Composition. 3rd
    ed. New York: HarperCollins, 1992.
```

If you are writing a research paper, you will use many sources. Within the essay itself you will mention an author's name, quote or summarize from this author, and follow the quotation or summary with a parenthetical citation of the pages. In Works Cited you will give the full title, place of publication, and other bibliographic material.

Here are a few examples, all referring to an article by Joan Templeton, "The *Doll House* Backlash: Criticism, Feminism, and Ibsen." The article appeared in *PMLA* 104 (1989): 28–40, but this information is given only in Works Cited, not within the text of the student's essay.

If in the text of your essay you mention the author's name, the citation following a quotation (or a summary of a passage) is merely a page number in parentheses, followed by a period, thus:

```
In 1989 Joan Templeton argued that many critics, unhappy
with recognizing Ibsen as a feminist, sought "to render Nora
inconsequential" (29).
```

Or:

> In 1989 Joan Templeton noted that many critics, unhappy with
> recognizing Ibsen as a feminist, have sought to make Nora
> trivial (29).

If you don't mention the name of the author in a lead-in, you will have to give
the name within the parenthetic citation:

> Many critics, attempting to argue that Ibsen was not a femi-
> nist, have tried to make Nora trivial (Templeton 29).

Notice in all of these examples that the final period comes after the parenthetic citation. *Exception:* If the quotation is longer than four lines and, therefore,
is set off by being indented ten spaces from the left margin, end the quotation
with the appropriate punctuation (period, question mark, or exclamation
mark), hit the space bar twice, and type (in parentheses) the page number. In
this case, do not put a period after the citation.

Another point: If your list of Works Cited includes more than one work
by an author, in your essay when you quote or refer to one or the other you'll
have to identify *which* work you are drawing on. You can provide the title in a
lead-in, thus:

> In "The <u>Doll House</u> Backlash: Criticism, Feminism, and
> Ibsen," Templeton says, "Nora's detractors have often been,
> from the first, her husband's defenders" (30).

Or you can provide the information in the parenthetic citation, giving a shortened version of the title—usually the first word, unless it is *A, An,* or *The,* in
which case the second word usually will do, though certain titles may require
still another word or two, as in this example:

> According to Templeton, "Nora's detractors have often been,
> from the first, her husband's defenders" ("<u>Doll House</u> Back-
> lash" 30).

FORMS OF CITATION IN WORKS CITED

In looking over the following samples of entries in Works Cited, remember:

1. The list of Works Cited is arranged alphabetically by author (last name
   first).
2. If a work is anonymous, list it under the first word of the title unless

the first word is *A, An,* or *The,* in which case list it under the second word.

3. If a work is by two authors, although the book is listed alphabetically under the first author's last name, the second author's name is given in the normal order, first name first.

4. If you list two or more works by the same author, the author's name is not repeated but is represented by three hyphens followed by a period and two spaces.

5. Each item begins flush left, but if an entry is longer than one line, subsequent lines in the entry are indented five spaces.

For details about almost every imaginable kind of citation, consult Joseph Gibaldi and Walter S. Achtert, *MLA Handbook for Writers of Research Papers,* 2nd ed. (New York: Modern Language Association, 1984). We give here, however, information concerning the most common kinds of citations.

Here are sample citations of the kinds of publications you are most likely to include in your list of Works Cited.

Entries (arranged alphabetically) begin flush with the left margin. If an entry runs more than one line, indent the subsequent line or lines five spaces from the left margin.

A book by one author:

```
Douglas, Ann. The Feminization of American Culture. New
     York: Knopf, 1977.
```

Notice that the author's last name is given first, but otherwise the name is given as on the title page. Do not substitute initials for names written out on the title page, but you may shorten the publisher's name—for example, from Little, Brown and Company to Little.

Take the title from the title page, not from the cover or the spine, but disregard unusual typography—for instance, the use of only capital letters or the use of *&* for *and*. Underline the title and subtitle with one continuous underline, but do not underline the period. The place of publication is indicated by the name of the city. If the city is not well known or if several cities have the same name (for instance, Cambridge, Massachusetts, and Cambridge, England) the name of the state is added. If the title page lists several cities, give only the first.

A book by more than one author:

```
Gilbert, Sandra, and Susan Gubar, The Madwoman in the Attic:
     The Woman Writer and the Nineteenth-Century Literary
     Imagination. New Haven: Yale UP 1979.
```

Notice that the book is listed under the last name of the first author (Gilbert) and that the second author's name is then given with first name (Susan) first. *If the book has more than three authors,* give the name of the first author only (last name first) and follow it with "et al." (Latin for "and others.")

A book in several volumes:

McQuade, Donald, et al., eds. <u>The Harper American</u>

<u>Literature</u>. 2 vols. New York: HarperCollins, 1987.

Pope, Alexander. <u>The Correspondence of Alexander Pope</u>. 5

vols. Ed. George Sherburn. Oxford: Clarendon, 1955.

Notice that the total number of volumes is given after the title, regardless of the number that you have used.

If you have used more than one volume, within your essay you will parenthetically indicate a reference to, for instance, page 30 of volume 3 thus: (3:30). If you have used only one volume of a multivolume work—let's say you used only volume 2 of McQuade's anthology—in your entry in Works Cited write, after the period following the date, Vol. 2. In your parenthetical citation within the essay you will therefore cite only the page reference (without the volume number), since the reader will (on consulting Works Cited) understand that in this example the reference is in volume 2.

If, instead of using the volumes as whole, you used only an independent work within one volume—say an essay in volume 2—in Works Cited omit the abbreviation "vol." Instead, give an arabic 2 (indicating volume 2) followed by a colon, a space, and the page numbers that encompass the selection you used:

Didion, Joan. "Some Dreamers of the Golden Dream." The Harp-

er American Literature. Ed. Donald McQuade et al. 2 vols.

New York: HarperCollins, 1987. 2:2198-2210.

Notice that this entry for Didion specifies not only that the book consists of two volumes, but also that only one selection ("Some Dreamers of the Golden Dream," occupying pages 2198–2210 in volume 2) was used. If you use this sort of citation in Works Cited, in the body of your essay a documentary reference to this work will be only to the page; the volume number will *not* be added.

A book with a separate title in a set of volumes:

Churchill, Winston. <u>The Age of Revolution</u>. Vol. 3 of <u>A His-</u>

<u>tory of the English-Speaking Peoples</u>. New York: Dodd,

1957.

Jonson, Ben. The Complete Masques. Ed. Stephen Orgel. Vol. 4

of The Yale Ben Jonson. New Haven: Yale UP, 1969.

A revised edition of a book:

Ellmann, Richard. James Joyce. Rev. ed. New York: Oxford UP,

1982.

Chaucer, Geoffrey. The Works of Geoffrey Chaucer. Ed. F. N.

Robinson. 2nd ed. Boston: Houghton, 1957.

A reprint, such as a paperback version of an older clothbound book:

Rourke, Constance. American Humor. 1931. Garden City, New

York: Doubleday, 1953.

Notice that the entry cites the original date (1931) but indicates that the writer is using the Doubleday reprint of 1953.

An edited book other than an anthology:

Keats, John. The Letters of John Keats. Ed. Hyder Edward

Rollins. 2 vols. Cambridge, Mass.: Harvard UP, 1958.

An anthology: You can list an anthology either under the editor's name or under the title.

A work in a volume of works by one author:

Sontag, Susan. "The Aesthetics of Silence." In Styles of

Radical Will. New York: Farrar, 1969. 3–34.

This entry indicates that Sontag's essay, called "The Aesthetics of Silence" appears in a book of hers entitled *Styles of Radical Will.* Notice that the page numbers of the short work are cited (not page numbers that you may happen to refer to, but the page numbers of the entire piece).

A work in an anthology, that is, in a collection of works by several authors: Begin with the author and the title of the work you are citing, not with the name of the anthologist or the title of the anthology. The entry ends with the pages occupied by the selection you are citing:

Bowen, Elizabeth. "Hand in Glove." <u>The Oxford Book of</u>
    <u>English Ghost Stories</u>. Ed. Michael Cox and R. A. Gilbert.
    Oxford: Oxford UP, 1986. 444-452.

Porter, Katherine Anne. "The Jilting of Granny Weatherall."
    <u>Literature for Composition</u>. Ed. Sylvan Barnet, et al. 3rd
    ed. New York: HarperCollins, 1992. 930-936.

Normally, you will give the title of the work you are citing (probably an essay, short story, or poem) in quotation marks. If you are referring to a book-length work (for instance, a novel or a full-length play), underline it to indicate italics. If the work is translated, after the period that follows the title, write "Trans." and give the name of the translator, followed by a period and the name of the anthology.

If the collection is a multivolume work and you are using only one volume, in Works Cited you will specify the volume, as in the example (page 240) of Didion's essay. Because the list of Works Cited specifies the volume, your parenthetical documentary reference within your essay will specify (as mentioned earlier) only the page numbers, not the volume. Thus, although Didion's essay appears on pages 2198–2210 in the second volume of a two-volume work, a parenthetical citation will refer only to the page numbers because the citation in Works Cited specifies the volume.

Remember that the pages specified in the entry in your list of Works Cited are to the *entire selection,* not simply to pages you may happen to refer to within your paper.

If you are referring to a *reprint of a scholarly article,* give details of the original publication, as in the following example:

Mack, Maynard. "The World of Hamlet." <u>Yale Review</u> 41 (1952):
    502-523. Rpt. in <u>Hamlet</u>. By William Shakespeare. Ed. Ed-
    ward Hubler. New York: New American Library, 1963.
    234-256.

Two or more works in an anthology: If you are referring to more than one work in an anthology (for example, in this book), in order to avoid repeating all the information about the anthology in each entry in Works Cited, under each author's name (in the appropriate alphabetical place) give the author and title of the work, then a period, two spaces, and the name of the anthologist, followed by the page numbers that the selection spans. Thus, a reference to Shakespeare's *Hamlet* would be followed only by

Barnet 407-512

rather than by a full citation of this book. This form requires that the anthology itself also be listed, under Barnet.

Two or more works by the same author: Notice that the works are given in alphabetical order (*Fables* precedes *Fools*) and that the author's name is not repeated but is represented by three hyphens followed by a period and two spaces. If the author is the translator or editor of a volume, the three hyphens are followed not by a period but by a comma, then a space, then the appropriate abbreviation (trans. or ed.), then (two spaces after the period) the title:

```
Frye, Northrop.  Fables of Identity: Studies in Poetic

     Mythology. New York: Harcourt, 1963.

-- .  Fools of Time: Studies in Shakespearean Tragedy. Toron-
to: U of Toronto P, 1967.
```

A translated book:

```
Gogol, Nikolai. Dead Souls. Trans. Andrew McAndrew. New

     York: New American Library, 1961.
```

If you are discussing the translation itself, as opposed to the book, list the work under the translator's name. Then put a comma, a space, and "trans." After the period following "trans." skip two spaces, then give the title of the book, a period, two spaces, and then "By" and the author's name, first name first. Continue with information about the place of publication, publisher, and date, as in any entry to a book.

An introduction, foreword, or afterword, or other editorial apparatus:

```
Fromm, Erich. Afterword. 1984. By George Orwell. New Ameri-

     can Library, 1961.
```

Usually a book with an introduction or some such comparable material is listed under the name of the author of the book rather than the name of the author of the editorial material (see the citation to Pope on page 240). But if you are referring to the editor's apparatus rather than to the work itself, use the form just given.

Words such as *preface, introduction, afterword,* and *conclusion* are capitalized in the entry but are neither enclosed within quotation marks nor underlined.

A book review: First, an example of a review that does not have a title:

```
Vendler, Helen. Rev. of Essays on Style. Ed. Roger Fowler.

    Essays in Criticism 16 (1966): 457-463.
```

If the review has a title, give the title after the period following the reviewer's name, before "Rev." If the review is unsigned, list it under the first word of the title, or the second word if the first word is *A, An,* or *The.* If an unsigned review has no title, begin the entry with "Rev. of " and alphabetize it under the title of the work being reviewed.

An encyclopedia: The first example is for a signed article, the second for an unsigned article:

```
Lang, Andrew. "Ballads." Encyclopaedia Britannica. 1910 ed.

"Metaphor." The New Encyclopaedia Britannica: Micropaedia.

    1974 ed.
```

An article in a scholarly journal: Some journals are paginated consecutively; that is, the pagination of the second issue picks up where the first issue left off. Other journals begin each issue with a new page 1. The forms of the citations in Works Cited differ slightly.

First, the citation of *a journal that uses continuous pagination:*

```
Burbick, Joan. "Emily Dickinson and the Economics of

    Desire." American Literature 58 (1986): 361-378.
```

This article appeared in volume 58, which was published in 1986. (Notice that the volume number is followed by a space, then by the year, in parentheses, then by a colon, a space, and the page numbers of the entire article.) Although each volume consists of four issues, you do *not* specify the issue number when the journal is paginated continuously.

For a journal that paginates each issue separately (a quarterly journal will have four page 1's each year), give the issue number directly after the volume number and a period, with no spaces before or after the period:

```
Spillers, Hortense J. "Martin Luther King and the Style of

    the Black Sermon." The Black Scholar 3.1 (1971), 14-27.
```

An article in a weekly, biweekly, or monthly publication:

```
McCabe, Bernard. "Taking Dickens Seriously." Commonweal 14

    May 1965.
```

Notice that the volume number and the issue number are omitted for popular weeklies or monthlies such as *Time* and *Atlantic*.

An article in a newspaper: Because newspapers usually consist of several sections, a section number may precede the page number. The example indicates that an article begins on page 1 of section 2 and is continued on a later page:

```
Wu, Jim. "Authors Praise New Forms." New York Times 8 March

    1987, Sec. 2: 3 +.
```

SAMPLE ESSAY WITH DOCUMENTATION

Some research papers are largely concerned with the relation of a work to its original context. Several examples have been mentioned already, such as Elizabethan views of Julius Caesar, Charlotte Perkins Gilman's representation of medical treatment for women, and Orwell's use (in *1984*) of Zamyatin's *We*.

Another kind of research paper is chiefly concerned with studying a critical problem, especially with deciding between a variety of interpretations of a literary work. A paper of this sort draws on existing interpretations, but it is much more than a summary of them since it evaluates them and finally offers its own conclusions. The essay reprinted below is of this kind.

```
Jean Lee

Professor McCabe

English 102, sec. B

October 18, 1991
```

```
    Do the Pink Ribbons in Hawthorne's "Young Goodman Brown"

                   Have a Meaning?

    In the first six paragraphs of "Young Goodman Brown,"

Hawthorne mentions three times that Faith, Brown's wife,

wears a cap with pink ribbons (50-51). The pink ribbons are

mentioned twice more in the story. The first of these later

references occurs when Brown is in the forest. Having recog-
```

nized Faith's voice, Brown gazes heavenward, calls to her, sees something fluttering down, seizes it, and finds that it is "a pink ribbon" (55). "My Faith is gone!" he immediately calls out. "There is no good on earth; and sin is but a name. Come devil! for to thee the world is given" (55). The next (and final) reference to the pink ribbons occurs near the end of the story. When he entered Salem village on "the next morning," Brown "spied the head of Faith, with the pink ribbons" (58), not surprising since he now sees the townspeople in their usual dress and activities.

No one can doubt that Brown's wife, named Faith, symbolizes Brown's religious faith, but many scholars have expressed some doubt about the meaning of her pink ribbons. More precisely, scholars have usually expressed doubt about someone else's interpretation of the ribbons, and then confidently offered their own. One of the first persons to comment on the pink ribbon suggested that Hawthorne himself made a mistake in giving them so much emphasis in the scene in the forest. In 1941 F. O. Matthiessen, in American Renaissance, quoted approximately a full page of the story, beginning with the paragraph that starts "Aloft in the air," and ending with the paragraph that begins "'My Faith is gone!' cried he, after one stupefied moment." Matthiessen praised the scene but offered one objection:

> As long as what Brown saw is left wholly in the
> realm of hallucination, Hawthorne's created illusion
> is compelling. . . . Only the literal insistence on
> the damaging pink ribbon obtrudes the label of a
> confining allegory and short-circuits the range of
> association. (284)

Matthiessen does not explain why he finds the ribbon more "literal" than, say, the "blue arch [of the sky] and the stars brightening in it" or the cloud that "hurried across the zenith and hid the brightening stars" (55). After all, Brown does not emerge from the forest carrying this ribbon, and the next morning compare it with the ribbons in Faith's cap. If he did, we could, like Matthiessen, complain about the author's "literal insistence on that damaging pink ribbon," but as Edward Wagenknecht has pointed out (61), the ribbon that flutters from the sky is no more real than anything else that Brown sees in the forest. If the devil can conjure up images of Brown's townspeople, surely he can also conjure up an image of a ribbon.

A few years after Matthiessen expressed reservations about the ribbon, Mark Van Doren quoted the passage about Brown seizing the ribbon after it catches on the branch of a tree, and then commented:

> Few things in fiction are more startling, or more important, than this pink ribbon. Is it there, or is it only dreamed? If it is there, what explanation can there be save the one young Brown accepts? The Devil exists, and Faith has become one of his converts. All three answers come at once, in a texture of fact and implication which Hawthorne has woven as closely as life is woven. The ribbon may not be there, but in that case this is no ordinary dream, no nightmare . . . which will be gone tomorrow. For Brown is changed. He thinks there is no good on earth, "and sin is but a name." (78)

What is especially interesting is Van Doren's clear implication that it doesn't matter whether Brown seizes a real ribbon or only dreams that he does. What matters is that for Brown it is evidence that his wife is unholy. Probably all readers will agree with Van Doren that the encounter in the forest, real or dreamed or conjured by the devil, changes Brown.

There is no such agreement, however, about the significance of the color of the ribbon. According to E. Arthur

Robinson, "Faith's pink ribbons symbolize passion" (223).
Robinson compares the pink ribbon to "crimson or purple"
symbols of "woman's physical nature" in other stories by
Hawthorne, particularly Georgiana's flaw in "The Birthmark"
and Beatrice's poisonous plant in "Rappaccini's Daughter"
(224). But the connection with Goodman Brown's faith is unclear. A pink ribbon worn by Faith, if clarified by other
details in the story, might serve to tell a reader what to
make out of this woman -- for instance, that she _really_ is
highly sexual, or that this faith _really_ is "faith in the
flesh," or some such thing -- but Robinson does not offer
these arguments, and the text does nothing to support them
with additional details. Robinson's conclusion is that Brown
comes to realize that "his father was a man like himself and
his mother a woman like Faith" (222), and that Brown glumly
accepts sensuality in his wife's nature as well as in his
own.

    Robinson was not the first to argue that the pink ribbon
implied passion. In 1957, six years before Robinson
published his essay, Roy R. Male saw the pink ribbons as one
element in "a fiery orgy of lust" (77). But given that pink
suggests, if anything, innocent little baby girls, why conclude that here it suggests "lust" or even "passion"? If one
wants to argue that Faith pretends to be sweet and innocent
but is not, one would argue that she is hypocritical, and
might even argue that the ribbons symbolize hypocrisy disguised as innocence, but there is no evidence that the ribbons symbolize sexual passion. Further, if they do symbolize
Brown's wife's sexual passion, what is their connection with
Brown? What do they tell us about Brown's religious faith?
In the forest, he takes the pink ribbon as evidence that his
wife is of the devil's party, and he therefore announces
that he has lost his faith, but if the pink color is to sug-

gest passion, Brown's loss of faith would be a loss of belief in passion -- an interpretation that makes no sense in the story.

Another school of thought argues that the pink symbolizes not lust but youthful femininity, and by extension, the weakness, superficiality, or frivolity of Brown's religious beliefs. Thomas E. Connolly argues that "the ribbons seem to be symbolic of [Brown's] initial illusion . . . that his faith will lead him to heaven. The pink ribbons on a Puritan lady's cap, signs of youth, joy, and happiness, are actually entirely out of keeping with the severity of the rest of her dress. . . ." (374). James W. Mathews offers a roughly similar view, arguing that "the insubstantiality of Brown's religious faith manifests itself in the pink ribbons of his wife's cap; their texture is aery and their color the pastel of infancy" (74).

Paul J. Hurley, though without commenting explicitly on the color of the ribbons, belongs to the same school:

> Goodman Brown . . . intends to get to heaven by clinging to Faith's skirts. . . . The ribbons, with their suggestions of the frivolous and ornamental, represent the ritualistic trappings of religious observance. Goodman Brown, it seems, has placed his faith and his hopes of salvation in the formal observances of religious worship rather than in the purity of his own heart and soul. (416)

Not all recent critics, of course, accept the view that the ribbons are a sign of the superficiality of Brown's faith. Edward Wagenknecht suggests (62) that the arguments of Mathews and Hurley would be more convincing if Brown, rather than his wife, wore a ribbon. Against Wagenknecht's view, however, one might argue that allegory works in a different way. If in this allegory Faith stands for Brown's religious faith, then what is said about Faith -- for instance what is said about her clothing -- is understood to be said about Brown himself.

It seems to be a mistake to insist that the color of the ribbons is symbolic of lust, feminine passion, or insubstantial faith. None of these interpretations is traditional and therefore immediately plausible even without additional supporting detail. And no such additional detail is offered in the story to make them plausible. For instance, none of Faith's pious (or apparently pious) neighbors objects to the ribbons, nor does Brown find the ribbons out of keeping with Puritan dress. Similarly, the alleged association of pink with superficiality is not traditional, and Hawthorne does not establish it by giving related details.

What, then, can we make of the ribbons? Looking at the unconvincing allegorical interpretations, perhaps the first thing to say is that we should not try to make too much of these ribbons. Perhaps the second thing to say is that the early references to the ribbons do not serve to characterize Faith as lustful, superficial, or whatever (and certainly not to characterize Brown's religious faith as marked by any of these traits) but do serve to identify Faith as a specific person -- the woman who wears pink ribbons in her cap. In the forest, then, when the ribbon drifts down, Brown cannot doubt that his wife is present, is a participant in the wicked assembly. (Of course Brown may be deceived; perhaps he has dreamed the episode, or perhaps he has been duped by a show conjured up by the devil, but that's another issue.) Convinced that even Faith is a worshipper of evil, Brown loses his faith not so much in God as in his fellow creatures. "Young Goodman Brown" of course has allegorical elements, but there is no reason to insist that every detail, down to the color of the ribbons, is allegorical.

Nothing is gained by insisting that the pink ribbons "mean" something. Their function is to convince Brown that his wife is in the forest, and that is enough for some ribbons to do.

Works Cited

Connolly, Thomas E. "Hawthorne's 'Young Goodman Brown': An Attack on Puritanic Calvinism." <u>American Literature</u> 28 (1956): 370-75.

Hawthorne, Nathaniel. "Young Goodman Brown." <u>The Harper Anthology of Fiction</u>. Ed. Sylvan Barnet. New York: HarperCollins, 1991. 50-59.

Hurley, Paul J. "Young Goodman Brown's 'Heart of Darkness.'" <u>American Literature</u> 37 (1966): 410-19.

Male, Roy R. <u>Hawthorne's Tragic Vision</u>. Austin, Tex.: U of Texas P, 1957.

Matthiessen, F. O. <u>American Renaissance</u>. New York: Oxford UP, 1941.

Mathews, James W. "Antinomianism in 'Young Goodman Brown.'" <u>Studies in Short Fiction</u> 3 (1965): 73-75.

Robinson, E. Arthur. "The Vision of Goodman Brown: A Source and Interpretation." <u>American Literature</u> 35 (1963): 218-25.

Van Doren, Mark. <u>Nathaniel Hawthorne</u>. New York: William Sloane, 1948.

Wagenknecht, Edward. <u>Nathaniel Hawthorne: The Man, His Tales and Romances</u>. New York: Continuum, 1989.

11

Essay

Examinations

WHAT EXAMINATIONS ARE

Chapters 4–8, on writing essays about nonfiction, fiction, drama, poetry, and film, discuss not only the job of writing essays but also the nature of the artistic forms themselves, on the assumption that writing an essay requires knowledge of the subject, as well as skill with language. Here a few words will be spent in discussing the nature of examinations; perhaps one can write better essay answers when one knows what examinations are.

An examination not only measures learning and thinking but stimulates them. Even so humble an examination as a short-answer quiz—chiefly a device to coerce students to do the assigned reading—is a sort of push designed to move students forward. Of course, internal motivation is far superior to external, but even such crude external motivation as a quiz can have a beneficial effect. Students know this; indeed, they often seek external compulsion, choosing a particular course "because I want to know something about … and I know that I won't do the reading on my own." (Teachers often teach a new course for the same reason; we want to become knowledgeable about, say, Asian-American literature, and we know that despite our lofty intentions we may not seriously confront the subject unless we are under the pressure of facing a class.)

In short, however ignoble it sounds, examinations force students to acquire learning and then to convert learning into thinking. Sometimes, it is not until preparing for the final examination that students—rereading the chief texts and classroom notes—see what the course was really about; until this late stage, the trees obscure the forest, but now, reviewing and sorting things out. a pattern emerges. The experience of reviewing and then of writing an examination, though fretful, can be highly exciting as connections are made and ideas take on life. Such discoveries about the whole subject matter of a course can almost never be made by writing critical essays on topics of one's own construction, for such topics rarely require a view of the whole. Further, we are more likely to make imaginative leaps when trying to answer questions that other people pose to us, rather than questions we pose to ourselves. (Again, every teacher knows that in the classroom questions are asked that stimulate the teacher to see things and to think thoughts that would otherwise have been neglected.) And although questions posed by others cause anxiety, when they have been confronted and responded to on an examination, the student often makes yet another discovery—a self-discovery, a sudden and satisfying awareness of powers one didn't know one had.

WRITING ESSAY ANSWERS

Let's assume that before the examination you have read the assigned material, marked the margins of your books, made summaries of the longer readings and of the classroom comments, reviewed all this material, and had a decent night's sleep. Now you are facing the examination sheet.

Here are seven obvious but important practical suggestions:

1. Take a moment to jot down, as a sort of outline or source of further inspiration, a few ideas that strike you after you have thought a little about the question. You may at the outset realize that, say, you want to make three points, and unless you jot these down—three key words will do—you may spend all the allotted time on one point.

2. Answer the question: If you are asked to compare two characters, compare them; don't just write two character sketches. Take seriously such words as *compare, summarize,* and especially *evaluate*.

3. You often can get a good start merely by turning the question into an affirmation, for example, by turning "In what ways is the poetry of Anne Sexton influenced by Robert Lowell" into "The poetry of Anne Sexton is influenced by Lowell in at least … ways."

4. Don't waste time summarizing at length what you have read unless asked to do so—but, of course, you may have to give a brief summary in order to support a point. The instructor wants to see that you can *use* your reading, not merely that you have *done* the reading.

5. Budget your time. Do not spend more than the allotted time on a question.

6. Be concrete. Illustrate your arguments with facts—the names of authors, titles, dates, characters, details of plot, and quotations if possible.

7. Leave space for last-minute additions. Either skip a page between essays, or write only on the right-hand pages so that on rereading you can add material at the appropriate place on the left-hand pages.

Beyond these general suggestions we can best talk about essay examinations by looking at the five commonest sorts of questions:

1. A passage to explicate
2. A historical question (for example, "Trace the influence of Maupassant on Kate Chopin")
3. A critical quotation to be evaluated
4. A wild question (such as "What would Virginia Woolf think of Vonnegut's *Cat's Cradle*?"; "What would Macbeth do if he were in Hamlet's place?")
5. A comparison (for example, "Compare the dramatic monologues of Browning with those of T. S. Eliot")

A few remarks on each of these types may be helpful.

1. On explication, see pages 32–38 and pages 162–166. As a short rule, look carefully at the tone (speaker's attitude toward self, subject, and audience) and at the implications of the words (their connotations and associations), and see whether a pattern of imagery is evident. For example, religious language (*adore, saint*) in a secular love poem may precisely define the nature of the lover and of the beloved. Remember, *an explication is not a paraphrase* (a putting into other words) but an attempt to show the relations of the parts by calling attention to implications. Organization of such an essay is rarely a problem, since most explications begin with the first line and go on to the last.

2. A good essay on a historical question will offer a nice combination of argument and evidence; that is, the thesis will be supported by concrete details (names, dates, perhaps, even brief quotations). A discussion of Chopin's debt to Maupassant cannot be convincing if it does not specify certain works and certain characteristics. If you are asked to relate a writer or a body of work to an earlier writer or period, list the chief characteristics of the earlier writer or period, and then show *specifically* how the material you are discussing is related to these characteristics. If you quote some relevant lines from the works, your reader will feel that you know not only titles and stock phrases but also the works themselves.

3. If you are asked to evaluate a critical quotation, read it carefully, and in your answer take account of *all* the quotation. If, for example, the quoted critic has said, "Alice Walker in her fiction always ... but in her nonfiction rarely ...," you will have to write about fiction and nonfiction; it will not be enough to talk only about Alice Walker's novels or only about her essays (unless, of course, the instructions on the examination ask you to take only as much of the quotation as you wish). Watch especially for words like *always, for the most part, never;* that is, although the passage may on the whole approach the truth, you may feel that some important qualifications are needed. This is not being picky; true thinking involves making subtle distinctions, yielding as-

sent only so far and no further. And (again) be sure to give concrete details, supporting your argument with evidence.

4. Curiously, a wild question, such as "What would Woolf think of *Cat's Cradle?*" or "What would Macbeth do in Hamlet's place?" usually produces rather tame answers: A half-dozen ideas about Woolf or Macbeth are neatly applied to Vonnegut or Hamlet, and the gross incompatibilities are thus revealed. But, as the previous paragraph suggests, it may be necessary to do more than set up bold and obvious oppositions. The interest in such a question and in the answer to it may be largely in the degree to which superficially different figures resemble each other in some important ways. Remember that the wildness of the question does not mean that all answers are equally acceptable; as usual, any good answer will be supported by concrete detail.

5. On comparisons, see pages 41–44. Because comparisons are especially difficult to write, be sure to take a few moments to jot down a sort of outline so that you know where you will be going. A comparison of Browning's and Eliot's monologues might treat three poems by each, devoting alternate paragraphs to one author; or it might first treat one author's poems and then turn to the other's; but if it adopts this second strategy, the essay may break into two parts. You can guard against this weakness by announcing at the outset that you can treat one author first, then the other; by reminding your reader during your treatment of the first author that certain points will be picked up when you get to the second author; and by briefly reminding your reader during the treatment of the second author of certain points already made in the treatment of the first.

Appendix A:
Two Stories

Young Goodman Brown
Nathaniel Hawthorne (1804–1864)

Young Goodman[1] Brown came forth, at sunset, into the street at Salem village; but put his head back, after crossing the threshold, to exchange a parting kiss with his young wife. And Faith, as the wife was aptly named, thrust her own pretty head into the street, letting the wind play with the pink ribbons of her cap while she called to Goodman Brown.

"Dearest heart," whispered she, softly and rather sadly, when her lips were close to his ear, "prithee put off your journey until sunrise and sleep in your own bed to-night. A lone woman is troubled with such dreams and such thoughts that she's afeared of herself sometimes. Pray tarry with me this night, dear husband, of all nights in the year."

"My love and my Faith," replied young Goodman Brown, "of all nights in the year, this one night must I tarry away from thee. My journey, as thou callest it, forth and back again, must needs be done 'twixt now and sunrise. What, my sweet, pretty wife, dost thou doubt me already, and we but three months married?"

"Then God bless you!" said Faith, with the pink ribbons; "and may you find all well when you come back."

"Amen!" cried Goodman Brown. "Say thy prayers, dear Faith, and go to bed at dusk, and no harm will come to thee."

So they parted; and the young man pursued his way until, being about to turn the corner by the meeting house, he looked back and saw the head of Faith still peeping after him with a melancholy air, in spite of her pink ribbons.

"Poor little Faith!" thought he, for his heart smote him. "What a wretch am I to leave her on such an errand! She talks of dreams, too. Methought as she spoke there was trouble in her face, as if a dream had warned her what work is to

[1]**Goodman**   polite term of address for a man of humble standing

be done to-night. But no, no; 'twould kill her to think it. Well, she's a blessed angel on earth; and after this one night, I'll cling to her skirts and follow her to heaven."

With this excellent resolve for the future, Goodman Brown felt himself justified in making more haste on his present evil purpose. He had taken a dreary road, darkened by all the gloomiest trees of the forest, which barely stood aside to let the narrow path creep through, and closed immediately behind. It was all as lonely as could be; and there is this peculiarity in such a solitude, that the traveller knows not who may be concealed by the innumerable trunks and the thick boughs overhead; so that with lonely footsteps he may yet be passing through an unseen multitude.

"There may be a devilish Indian behind every tree," said Goodman Brown, to himself and he glanced fearfully behind him as he added, "What if the devil himself should be at my very elbow!"

His head being turned back, he passed a crook of the road, and, looking forward again, beheld the figure of a man, in grave and decent attire, seated at the foot of an old tree. He arose at Goodman Brown's approach and walked onward side by side with him.

"You are late, Goodman Brown," said he. "The clock of the Old South was striking as I came through Boston, and that is full fifteen minutes agone."

"Faith kept me back a while," replied the young man, with a tremor in his voice, caused by the sudden appearance of his companion, though not wholly unexpected.

It was now deep dusk in the forest, and deepest in that part of it where these two were journeying. As nearly as could be discerned, the second traveller was about fifty years old, apparently in the same rank of life as Goodman Brown, and bearing a considerable resemblance to him, though perhaps more in expression than features. Still they might have been taken for father and son. And yet, though the elder person was as simply clad as the younger, and as simple in manner too, he had an indescribable air of one who knew the world, and who would not have felt abashed at the governor's dinner table, or in King William's court, were it possible that his affairs should call him thither. But the only thing about him that could be fixed upon as remarkable was his staff, which bore the likeness of a great black snake, so curiously wrought that it might almost be seen to twist and wriggle itself like a living serpent. This, of course, must have been an ocular deception, assisted by the uncertain light.

"Come, Goodman Brown," cried his fellow-traveller, "this is a dull pace for the beginning of a journey. Take my staff, if you are so soon weary."

"Friend," said the other, exchanging his slow pace for a full stop, "having kept covenant by meeting thee here, it is my purpose now to return whence I came. I have scruples touching the matter thou wot'st[2] of."

"Sayest thou so?" replied he of the serpent, smiling apart. "Let us walk on, nevertheless, reasoning as we go; and if I convince thee not thou shalt turn back. We are but a little way in the forest yet."

"Too far! too far!" exclaimed the goodman, unconsciously resuming his

---

[2]**wot'st**   knowest

walk. "My father never went into the woods on such an errand, nor his father before him. We have been a race of honest men and good Christians since the days of the martyrs; and shall I be the first of the name of Brown that ever took this path and kept—"

"Such company, thou wouldst say," observed the elder person, interpreting his pause. "Well said, Goodman Brown! I have been as well acquainted with your family as with ever a one among the Puritans; and that's no trifle to say. I helped your grandfather, the constable, when he lashed the Quaker woman so smartly through the streets of Salem; and it was I that brought your father a pitch-pine knot, kindled at my own hearth, to set fire to an Indian village, in King Philip's war.[3] They were my good friends, both; and many a pleasant walk have we had along this path, and returned merrily after midnight. I would fain be friends with you for their sake."

"If it be as thou sayest," replied Goodman Brown, "I marvel they never spoke of these matters, or, verily, I marvel not, seeing that the least rumor of the sort would have driven them from New England. We are a people of prayer, and good works to boot, and abide no such wickedness."

"Wickedness or not," said the traveller with the twisted staff, "I have a very general acquaintance here in New England. The deacons of many a church have drunk the communion wine with me; the selectmen of divers towns make me their chairman; and a majority of the Great and General Court are firm supporters of my interest. The governor and I, too—But these are state secrets."

"Can this be so!" cried Goodman Brown, with a stare of amazement at his undisturbed companion. "Howbeit, I have nothing to do with the governor and council; they have their own ways, and are no rule for a simple husbandman[4] like me. But, were I to go on with thee, how should I meet the eye of that good old man, our minister, at Salem village? Oh, his voice would make me tremble both Sabbath day and lecture day!"

Thus far the elder traveller had listened with due gravity; but now burst into a fit of irrepressible mirth, shaking himself so violently that his snake-like staff actually seemed to wriggle in sympathy.

"Ha! ha! ha!" shouted he again and again; then composing himself, "Well, go on, Goodman Brown, go on; but, prithee, don't kill me with laughing."

"Well, then, to end the matter at once," said Goodman Brown, considerably nettled, "there is my wife, Faith. It would break her dear little heart; and I'd rather break my own."

"Nay, if that be the case," answered the other, "e'en go thy ways, Goodman Brown. I would not for twenty old women like the one hobbling before us that Faith should come to any harm."

As he spoke he pointed his staff at a female figure on the path, in whom Goodman Brown recognized a very pious and exemplary dame, who had taught him his catechism in youth, and was still his moral and spiritual adviser, jointly with the minister and Deacon Gookin.

---

[3]**King Philip's war**   war waged by the Colonists (1675–76) against the Wampanoag Indian leader Metacom, known as "King Philip."

[4]**husbandman**   farmer or, more generally, any man of humble standing

"A marvel, truly, that Goody[5] Cloyse should be so far in the wilderness at night fall," said he. "But with your leave, friend, I shall take a cut through the woods until we have left this Christian woman behind. Being a stranger to you, she might ask whom I was consorting with and whither I was going."

"Be it so," said his fellow-traveller. "Betake you the woods, and let me keep the path."

Accordingly the young man turned aside, but took care to watch his companion, who advanced softly along the road until he had come within a staff's length of the old dame. She, meanwhile, was making the best of her way, with singular speed for so aged a woman, and mumbling some indistinct words—a prayer, doubtless—as she went. The traveller put forth his staff and touched her withered neck with what seemed the serpent's tail.

"The devil!" screamed the pious old lady.

"Then Goody Cloyse knows her old friend?" observed the traveller, confronting her and leaning on his writhing stick.

"Ah, forsooth, and is it your worship indeed?" cried the good dame. "Yea, truly is it, and in the very image of my old gossip, Goodman Brown, the grandfather of the silly fellow that now is. But—would your worship believe it?—my broomstick hath strangely disappeared, stolen, as I suspect, by that unhanged witch, Goody Cory, and that, too, when I was all anointed with the juice of smallage and cinquefoil and wolf's bane—"

"Mingled with fine wheat and the fat of a new-born babe," said the shape of old Goodman Brown.

"Ah, your worship knows the recipe," cried the old lady, cackling aloud. "So, as I was saying, being all ready for the meeting, and no horse to ride on, I made up my mind to foot it; for they tell me there is a nice young man to be taken into communion to-night. But now your good worship will lend me your arm, and we shall be there in a twinkling."

"That can hardly be," answered her friend. "I may not spare you my arm, Goody Cloyse; but here is my staff, if you will."

So saying, he threw it down at her feet, where, perhaps, it assumed life, being one of the rods which its owner had formerly lent to the Egyptian magi. Of this fact, however, Goodman Brown could not take cognizance. He had cast up his eyes in astonishment, and, looking down again, beheld neither Goody Cloyse nor the serpentine staff but his fellow-traveller alone, who waited for him as calmly as if nothing had happened.

"That old woman taught me my catechism," said the young man; and there was a world of meaning in this simple comment.

They continued to walk onward, while the elder traveller exhorted his companion to make good speed and persevere in the path, discoursing so aptly that his arguments seemed rather to spring up in the bosom of his auditor than to be suggested by himself. As they went, he plucked a branch of maple to serve for a walking-stick, and began to strip it of the twigs and little boughs, which were wet with evening dew. The moment his fingers touched them they became

[5]**Goody** contraction of Goodwife, a polite term of address for a married woman of humble standing

strangely withered and dried up as with a week's sunshine. Thus the pair proceeded, at a good free pace, until suddenly, in a gloomy hollow of the road, Goodman Brown sat himself down on the stump of a tree and refused to go any farther.

"Friend," said he, stubbornly, "my mind is made up. Not another step will I budge on this errand. What if a wretched old woman do choose to go to the devil when I thought she was going to heaven: is that any reason why I should quit my dear Faith and go after her?"

"You will think better of this by and by," said his acquaintance, composedly. "Sit here and rest yourself a while; and when you feel like moving again, there is my staff to help you along."

Without more words, he threw his companion the maple stick, and was as speedily out of sight as if he had vanished into the deepening gloom. The young man sat a few moments by the roadside, applauding himself greatly, and thinking with how clear a conscience he should meet the minister in his morning walk, nor shrink from the eye of good old Deacon Gookin. And what calm sleep would be his that very night, which was to have been spent so wickedly, but so purely and sweetly now, in the arms of Faith! Amidst these pleasant and praiseworthy meditations, Goodman Brown heard the tramp of horses along the road, and deemed it advisable to conceal himself within the verge of the forest, conscious of the guilty purpose that had brought him thither, though now so happily turned from it.

On came the hoof tramps and the voices of the riders, two grave old voices, conversing soberly as they drew near. These mingled sounds appeared to pass along the road, within a few yards of the young man's hiding place; but, owing doubtless to the depth of the gloom at that particular spot, neither the travellers nor their steeds were visible. Though their figures brushed the small boughs by the wayside, it could not be seen that they intercepted, even for a moment, the faint gleam from the strip of bright sky athwart which they must have passed. Goodman Brown alternately crouched and stood on tiptoe, pulling aside the branches and thrusting forth his head as far as he durst without discerning so much as a shadow. It vexed him the more, because he could have sworn, were such a thing possible, that he recognized the voices of the minister and Deacon Gookin, jogging along quietly, as they were wont to do, when bound to some ordination or ecclesiastical council. While yet within hearing, one of the riders stopped to pluck a switch.

"Of the two, reverend sir," said the voice like the deacon's, "I had rather miss an ordination dinner than to-night's meeting. They tell me that some of our community are to be here from Falmouth and beyond, and others from Connecticut and Rhode Island, besides several of the Indian powwows, who, after their fashion, know almost as much deviltry as the best of us. Moreover, there is a goodly young woman to be taken into communion."

"Mighty well, Deacon Gookin!" replied the solemn old tones of the minister. "Spur up, or we shall be late. Nothing can be done, you know, until I get on the ground."

The hoofs clattered again; and the voices, talking so strangely in the empty air, passed on through the forest, where no church had ever been gathered or solitary Christian prayed. Whither, then, could these holy men be journeying so deep into the heathen wilderness? Young Goodman Brown caught hold of a tree for support, being ready to sink down on the ground, faint and overburdened with the heavy sickness of his heart. He looked up to the sky, doubting whether there really was a heaven above him. Yet, there was the blue arch, and the stars brightening in it.

"With heaven above, and Faith below, I will yet stand firm against the devil!" cried Goodman Brown.

While he still gazed upward into the deep arch of the firmament and had lifted his hands to pray, a cloud, though no wind was stirring, hurried across the zenith and hid the brightening stars. The blue sky was still visible, except directly overhead, where this black mass of cloud was sweeping swiftly northward. Aloft in the air, as if from the depths of the cloud, came a confused and doubtful sound of voices. Once the listener fancied that he could distinguish the accents of towns-people of his own, men and women, both pious and ungodly, many of whom he had met at the communion table, and had seen others rioting at the tavern. The next moment, so indistinct were the sounds, he doubted whether he had heard aught but the murmur of the old forest, whispering without a wind. Then came a stronger swell of those familiar tones, heard daily in the sunshine at Salem village, but never until now from a cloud of night. There was one voice, of a young woman, uttering lamentations, yet with an uncertain sorrow, and entreating for some favor, which, perhaps, it would grieve her to obtain; and all the unseen multitude, both saints and sinners, seemed to encourage her onward.

"Faith!" shouted Goodman Brown, in a voice of agony and desperation; and the echoes of the forest mocked him, crying, "Faith! Faith!" as if bewildered wretches were seeking her all through the wilderness.

The cry of grief, rage, and terror was yet piercing the night, when the unhappy husband held his breath for a response. There was a scream, drowned immediately in a louder murmur of voices, fading into far-off laughter, as the dark cloud swept away, leaving the clear and silent sky above Goodman Brown. But something fluttered lightly down through the air and caught on the branch of a tree. The young man seized it, and beheld a pink ribbon.

"My Faith is gone!" cried he, after one stupefied moment. "There is no good on earth; and sin is but a name. Come, devil; for to thee is this world given."

And, maddened with despair, so that he laughed loud and long, did Goodman Brown grasp his staff and set forth again, at such a rate that he seemed to fly along the forest path, rather than to walk or run. The road grew wilder and drearier and more faintly traced, and vanished at length, leaving him in the heart of the dark wilderness, still rushing onward with the instinct that guides mortal man to evil. The whole forest was peopled with frightful sounds—the creaking of the trees, the howling of wild beasts, and the yell of Indians; while sometimes the wind tolled like a distant church bell, and sometimes gave a broad roar around the traveller, as if all Nature were laughing him to scorn. But he was himself the chief horror of the scene, and shrank not from its other horrors.

"Ha! ha! ha!" roared Goodman Brown when the wind laughed at him.

"Let us hear which will laugh loudest! Think not to frighten me with your devil-try! Come witch, come wizard, come Indian powwow, come devil himself, and here comes Goodman Brown. You may as well fear him as he fear you!"

In truth, all through the haunted forest there could be nothing more fright-ful than the figure of Goodman Brown. On he flew among the black pines, brandishing his staff with frenzied gestures, now giving vent to an inspiration of horrid blasphemy, and now shouting forth such laughter as set all the echoes of the forest laughing like demons around him. The fiend in his own shape is less hideous than when he rages in the breast of man. Thus sped the demoniac on his course, until, quivering among the trees, he saw a red light before him, as when the felled trunks and branches of a clearing have been set on fire, and throw up their lurid blaze against the sky, at the hour of midnight. He paused, in a lull of the tempest that had driven him onward, and heard the swell of what seemed a hymn, rolling solemnly from a distance with the weight of many voices He knew the tune; it was a familiar one in the choir of the village meeting-house. The verse died heavily away, and was lengthened by a chorus, not of hu-man voices, but of all the sounds of the benighted wilderness pealing in awful harmony together. Goodman Brown cried out; and his cry was lost to his own ear by its unison with the cry of the desert.

In the interval of silence he stole forward until the light glared full upon his eyes. At one extremity of an open space, hemmed in by the dark wall of the for-est, arose a rock, bearing some rude, natural resemblance either to an altar or a pulpit, and surrounded by four blazing pines, their tops aflame, their stems un-touched, like candles at an evening meeting. The mass of foliage that had over-grown the summit of the rock was all on fire, blazing high into the night and fit-fully illuminating the whole field. Each pendent twig and leafy festoon was in a blaze. As the red light arose and fell, a numerous congregation alternately shone forth, then disappeared in shadow, and again grew, as it were, out of the dark-ness, peopling the heart of the solitary woods at once.

"A grave and dark-clad company," quoth Goodman Brown.

In truth, they were such. Among them, quivering to-and-fro between gloom and splendor, appeared faces that would be seen next day at the council board of the province, and others which, Sabbath after Sabbath, looked devout-ly heavenward, and benignantly over the crowded pews, from the holiest pulpits in the land. Some affirm that the lady of the governor was there. At least there were high dames well known to her, and wives of honored husbands, and wid-ows, a great multitude, and ancient maidens, all of excellent repute, and fair young girls, who trembled lest their mothers should espy them. Either the sud-den gleams of light flashing over the obscure field bedazzled Goodman Brown, or he recognized a score of the church members of Salem village famous for their especial sanctity. Good old Deacon Gookin had arrived, and waited at the skirts of that venerable saint, his revered pastor. But, irreverently consorting with these grave, reputable, and pious people, these elders of the church, these chaste dames and dewy virgins, there were men of dissolute lives and women of spotted fame, wretches given over to all mean and filthy vice, and suspected even of hor-rid crimes. It was strange to see, that the good shrank not from the wicked, nor were the sinners abashed by the saints. Scattered also among their pale-faced enemies were the Indian priests, or powwows, who had often scared their native forest with more hideous incantations than any known to English witchcraft.

"But, where is Faith?" thought Goodman Brown; and, as hope came into his heart, he trembled.

Another verse of the hymn arose, a slow and mournful strain, such as the pious love, but joined to words which expressed all that our nature can conceive of sin, and darkly hinted at far more. Unfathomable to mere mortals is the lore of fiends. Verse after verse was sung; and still the chorus of the desert swelled between, like the deepest tone of a mighty organ; and, with the final peal of that dreadful anthem there came a sound, as if the roaring wind, the rushing streams, the howling beasts, and every other voice of the unconcerted wilderness were mingling and according with the voice of guilty man in homage to the prince of all. The four blazing pines threw up a loftier flame, and obscurely discovered shapes and visages of horror on the smoke wreaths above the impious assembly. At the same moment the fire on the rock shot redly forth and formed a glowing arch above its base, where now appeared a figure. With reverence be it spoken, the figure bore no slight similitude, both in garb and manner, to some grave divine of the New England churches.

"Bring forth the converts!" cried a voice that echoed through the field and rolled into the forest.

At the word, Goodman Brown stepped forth from the shadow of the trees and approached the congregation, with whom he felt a loathful brotherhood by the sympathy of all that was wicked in his heart. He could have well nigh sworn that the shape of his own dead father beckoned him to advance, looking downward from a smoke wreath, while a woman, with dim features of despair, threw out her hand to warn him back. Was it his mother? But he had no power to retreat one step, nor to resist, even in thought, when the minister and good old Deacon Gookin seized his arms and led him to the blazing rock. Thither came also the slender form of a veiled female, led between Goody Cloyse, that pious teacher of the catechism, and Martha Carrier, who had received the devil's promise to be queen of hell. A rampant hag was she. And there stood the proselytes beneath the canopy of fire.

"Welcome, my children," said the dark figure, "to the communion of your race. Ye have found thus young your nature and your destiny. My children, look behind you!"

They turned; and flashing forth, as it were, in a sheet of flame, the fiend worshippers were seen; the smile of welcome gleamed darkly on every visage.

"There," resumed the sable form, "are all whom ye have reverenced from youth. Ye deemed them holier than yourselves, and shrank from your own sin, contrasting it with their lives of righteousness and prayerful aspirations heavenward. Yet here are they all in my worshipping assembly. This night it shall be granted you to know their secret deeds: how hoary bearded elders of the church have whispered wanton words to the young maids of their households; how many a woman, eager for widow's weeds, has given her husband a drink at bedtime, and let him sleep his last sleep in her bosom; how beardless youths have made haste to inherit their fathers' wealth; and how fair damsels—blush not, sweet ones—have dug little graves in the garden, and bidden me, the sole guest, to an infant's funeral. By the sympathy of your human hearts for sin ye shall scent out all the places—whether in church, bed-chamber, street, field, or forest—where crime has been committed, and shall exult to behold the whole earth one stain of guilt, one mighty blood spot. Far more than this. It shall be yours to penetrate, in every bosom, the deep mystery of sin, the fountain of all wicked arts, and which inexhaustibly supplies more evil impulses than human power—than my power at its utmost—can make manifest in deeds. And now, my children, look upon each other."

They did so; and, by the blaze of the hell-kindled torches, the wretched man beheld his Faith, and the wife her husband, trembling before that unhallowed altar.

"Lo, there ye stand, my children," said the figure, in a deep and solemn tone, almost sad with its despairing awfulness, as if his once angelic nature could yet mourn for our miserable race. "Depending upon one another's hearts, ye had still hoped that virtue were not all a dream. Now are ye undeceived. Evil is the nature of mankind. Evil must be your only happiness. Welcome, again, my children, to the communion of your race."

"Welcome," repeated the fiend worshippers, in one cry of despair and triumph.

And there they stood, the only pair, as it seemed, who were yet hesitating on the verge of wickedness in this dark world. A basin was hollowed, naturally, in the rock. Did it contain water, reddened by the lurid light? or was it blood? or, perchance, a liquid flame? Herein did the shape of evil dip his hand and prepare to lay the mark of baptism upon their foreheads, that they might be partakers of the mystery of sin, more conscious of the secret guilt of others, both in deed and thought, than they could now be of their own. The husband cast one look at his pale wife, and Faith at him. What polluted wretches would the next glance show them to each other, shuddering alike at what they disclosed and what they saw!

"Faith! Faith!" cried the husband, "look up to heaven, and resist the wicked one."

Whether Faith obeyed he knew not. Hardly had he spoken when he found himself amid calm night and solitude, listening to a roar of the wind which died heavily away through the forest. He staggered against the rock, and felt it chill and damp; while a hanging twig, that had been all on fire, besprinkled his cheek with the coldest dew.

The next morning young Goodman Brown came slowly into the street of Salem village, staring around him like a bewildered man. The good old minister was taking a walk along the graveyard to get an appetite for breakfast and meditate his sermon and bestowed a blessing, as he passed, on Goodman Brown. He shrank from the venerable saint as if to avoid an anathema. Old Deacon Gookin was at domestic worship and the holy words of his prayer were heard through the open window. "What God doth the wizard pray to?" quoth Goodman Brown. Goody Cloyse, that excellent old Christian, stood in the early sunshine at her own lattice, catechizing a little girl who had brought her a pint of mornings milk. Goodman Brown snatched away the child as from the grasp of the fiend himself. Turning the corner by the meeting-house, he spied the head of

Faith, with the pink ribbons, gazing anxiously forth, and bursting into such joy at sight of him that she skipped along the street and almost kissed her husband before the whole village. But Goodman Brown looked sternly and sadly into her face, and passed on without a greeting.

Had Goodman Brown fallen asleep in the forest and only dreamed a wild dream of a witch-meeting?

Be it so, if you will; but, alas! it was a dream of evil omen for young Goodman Brown. A stern, a sad, a darkly meditative, a distrustful, if not a desperate man did he become from the night of that fearful dream. On the Sabbath day, when the congregation were singing a holy psalm, he could not listen because an anthem of sin rushed loudly upon his ear and drowned all the blessed strain. When the minister spoke from the pulpit with power and fervid eloquence, and, with his hand on the open Bible, of the sacred truths of our religion, and of saint-like lives and triumphant deaths, and of future bliss or misery unutterable, then did Goodman Brown turn pale, dreading lest the roof should thunder down upon the gray blasphemer and his hearers. Often, awakening suddenly at midnight, he shrank from the bosom of Faith; and at morning or eventide, when the family knelt down at prayer, he scowled and muttered to himself, and gazed sternly at his wife, and turned away. And when he had lived long, and was borne to his grave a hoary corpse, followed by Faith, an aged woman, and children and grandchildren, a goodly procession, besides neighbors, not a few, they carved no hopeful verse upon his tombstone, for his dying hour was gloom.

The Lottery
Shirley Jackson (1919–1965)

The morning of June 27th was clear and sunny, with the fresh warmth of a full-summer day; the flowers were blossoming profusely and the grass was richly green. The people of the village began to gather in the square, between the post office and the bank, around ten o'clock; in some towns there were so many people that the lottery took two days and had to be started on June 26th, but in this village, where there were only about three hundred people, the whole lottery took less than two hours, so it could begin at ten o'clock in the morning and still be through in time to allow the villagers to get home for noon dinner.

The children assembled first, of course. School was recently over for the summer, and the feeling of liberty sat uneasily on most of them; they tended to gather together quietly for a while before they broke into boisterous play, and their talk was still of the classroom and the teacher, of books and reprimands. Bobby Martin had already stuffed his pockets full of stones, and the other boys soon followed his example, selecting the smoothest and roundest stones; Bobby and Harry Jones and Dickie Delacroix—the villagers pronounced this name "Dellacroy"—eventually made a great pile of stones in one corner of the square and guarded it against the raids of the other boys. The girls stood aside, talking among themselves, looking over their shoulders at the boys, and the very small children rolled in the dust or clung to the hands of their older brothers or sisters.

Soon the men began to gather, surveying their own children, speaking of planting and rain, tractors and taxes. They.stood together, away from the pile of stones in the corner, and their jokes were quiet and they smiled rather than laughed. The women, wearing faded house dresses and sweaters, came shortly after their menfolk. They greeted one another and exchanged bits of gossip as they went to join their husbands. Soon the women, standing by their husbands, began to call to their children, and the children came reluctantly, having to be called four or five times. Bobby Martin ducked under his mother's grasping hand and ran, laughing, back to the pile of stones. His father spoke up sharply, and Bobby came quickly and took his place between his father and his oldest brother.

The lottery was conducted—as were the square dances, the teenage club, the Halloween program—by Mr. Summers, who had time and energy to devote to civic activities. He was a round-faced, jovial man and he ran the coal business, and people were sorry for him, because he had no children and his wife was a scold. When he arrived in the square, carrying the black wooden box, there was a murmur of conversation among the villagers and he waved and called, "Little late today, folks." The postmaster, Mr. Graves, followed him, carrying a three-legged stool, and the stool was put in the center of the square and Mr. Summers set the black box down on it. The villagers kept their distance, leaving a space between themselves and the stool, and when Mr. Summers said, "Some of you fellows want to give me a hand?" there was a hesitation before two men, Mr. Martin and his oldest son, Baxter, came forward to hold the box steady on the stool while Mr. Summers stirred up the papers inside it.

The original paraphernalia for the lottery had been lost long ago, and the black box now resting on the stool had been put into use even before Old Man Warner, the oldest man in town, was born. Mr. Summers spoke frequently to the villagers about making a new box, but no one liked to upset even as much tradition as was represented by the black box. There was a story that the present box had been made with some pieces of the box that had preceded it, the one that had been constructed when the first people settled down to make a village here. Every year, after the lottery, Mr. Summers began talking again about a new box, but every year the subject was allowed to fade off without anything's being done. The black box grew shabbier each year; by now it was no longer completely black but splintered badly along one side to show the original wood color, and in some places faded or stained.

Mr. Martin and his oldest son, Baxter, held the black box securely on the stool until Mr. Summers had stirred the papers thoroughly with his hand. Because so much of the ritual had been forgotten or discarded, Mr. Summers had been successful in having slips of paper substituted for the chips of wood that had been used for generations. Chips of wood, Mr. Summers had argued, had been all very well when the village was tiny, but now that the population was more than three hundred and likely to keep on growing, it was necessary to use something that would fit more easily into the black box. The night before the lottery, Mr. Summers and Mr. Graves made up the slips of paper and put them in the box, and it was then taken to the safe of Mr. Summers's coal company and locked up until Mr. Summers was ready to take it to the square next morning. The rest of the year, the box was put away, sometimes one place, sometimes another; it had spent one year in Mr. Graves's barn and another year underfoot in the post office, and sometimes it was set on a shelf in the Martin grocery and left there.

There was a great deal of fussing to be done before Mr. Summers declared the lottery open. There were lists to make up—of heads of families, heads of households in each family, members of each household in each family. There was the proper swearing-in of Mr. Summers by the postmaster, as the official of the lottery; at one time, some people remembered, there had been a recital of some sort, performed by the official of the lottery, a perfunctory, tuneless chant that had been rattled off duly each year; some people believed that the official of the lottery used to stand just so when he said or sang it, others believed that he was supposed to walk among the people, but years and years ago this part of the ritual had been allowed to lapse. There had been, also, a ritual salute, which the official of the lottery had had to use in addressing each person who came up to draw from the box, but this also had changed with time, until now it was felt necessary only for the official to speak to each person approaching. Mr. Summers was very good at all this; in his clean white shirt and blue jeans, with one hand resting carelessly on the black box, he seemed very proper and important as he talked interminably to Mr. Graves and the Martins.

Just as Mr. Summers finally left off talking and turned to the assembled villagers, Mrs. Hutchinson came hurriedly along the path to the square, her sweater thrown over her shoulders, and slid into place in the back of the crowd. "Clean forgot what day it was," she said to Mrs. Delacroix, who stood next to her, and they both laughed softly. "Thought my old man was out back stacking wood," Mrs. Hutchinson went on, "and then I looked out the window and the kids were gone, and then I remembered it was the twenty-seventh and came a-running." She dried her hands on her apron, and Mrs. Delacroix said, "You're in time, though. They're still talking away up there."

Mrs. Hutchinson craned her neck to see through the crowd and found her husband and children standing near the front. She tapped Mrs. Delacroix on the arm as a farewell and began to make her way through the crowd. The people separated goodhumoredly to let her through; two or three people said, in voices just loud enough to be heard across the crowd, "Here comes your Missus, Hutchinson," and "Bill, she made it after all." Mrs. Hutchinson reached her husband, and Mr. Summers, who had been waiting, said cheerfully, "Thought we were going to have to get on without you, Tessie." Mrs. Hutchinson said, grinning, "Wouldn't have me leave m'dishes in the sink, now would you, Joe?," and soft laughter ran through the crowd as the people stirred back into position after Mrs. Hutchinson's arrival.

"Well, now," Mr. Summers said soberly, "guess we better get started, get this over with, so's we can go back to work. Anybody ain't here?"

"Dunbar," several people said. "Dunbar, Dunbar."

Mr. Summers consulted his list. "Clyde Dunbar," he said "That's right. He's broke his leg, hasn't he? Who's drawing for him?"

"Me, I guess," a woman said, and Mr. Summers turned to look at her. "Wife draws for her husband," Mr. Summers said. "Don't you have a grown boy to do it for you, Janey?" Although Mr. Summers and everyone else in the village knew the answer perfectly well, it was the business of the official of the lottery to ask such questions formally. Mr. Summers waited with an expression of polite interest while Mrs. Dunbar answered.

"Horace's not but sixteen yet," Mrs. Dunbar said regretfully. "Guess I gotta fill in for the old man this year."

"Right," Mr. Summers said. He made a note on the list he was holding. Then he asked, "Watson boy drawing this year?"

A tall boy in the crowd raised his hand. "Here," he said. "I'm drawing for m'mother and me." He blinked his eyes nervously and ducked his head as several voices in the crowd said things like "Good fellow, Jack," and "Glad to see your mother's got a man to do it."

"Well," Mr. Summers said, "guess that's everyone. Old Man Warner make it?"

"Here," a voice said, and Mr. Summers nodded.

A sudden hush fell on the crowd as Mr. Summers cleared his throat and looked at the list. "All ready?" he called. "Now, I'll read the names—heads of families first—and the men come up and take a paper out of the box. Keep the paper folded in your hand without looking at it until everyone has had a turn. Everything clear?"

The people had done it so many times that they only half listened to the directions, most of them were quiet, wetting their lips, not looking around. Then Mr. Summers raised one hand high and said, "Adams." A man disengaged himself from the crowd and came forward. "Hi, Steve," Mr. Summers said, and Mr. Adams said, "Hi, Joe." They grinned at one another humorlessly and nervously. Then Mr. Adams reached into the black box and took out a folded paper. He held it firmly by one corner as he turned and went hastily back to his place in the crowd, where he stood a little apart from his family, not looking down at his hand.

"Allen," Mr. Summers said. "Anderson .... Bentham."

"Seems like there's no time at all between lotteries any more." Mrs. Delacroix said to Mrs. Graves in the back row. "Seems like we got through with the last one only last week."

"Time sure goes fast," Mrs. Graves said.

"Clark .... Delacroix."

"There goes my old man," Mrs. Delacroix said. She held her breath while her husband went forward.

"Dunbar," Mr. Summers said, and Mrs. Dunbar went steadily to the box while one of the women said, "Go on, Janey," and another said, "There she goes."

"We're next," Mrs. Graves said. She watched while Mr. Graves came around from the side of the box, greeted Mr. Summers gravely, and selected a slip of paper from the box. By now, all through the crowd there were men holding the small folded papers in their large hands, turning them over and over nervously. Mrs. Dunbar and her two sons stood together, Mrs. Dunbar holding the slip of paper.

"Harburt .... Hutchinson."

"Get up there, Bill," Mrs. Hutchinson said, and the people near her laughed.

"Jones."

"They do say," Mr. Adams said to Old Man Warner, who stood next to him, "that over in the north village they're talking of giving up the lottery."

Old Man Warner snorted, "Pack of crazy fools," he said. "Listening to the young folks, nothing's good enough for *them*. Next thing you know, they'll be wanting to go back to living in caves, nobody work any more, live *that* way for a while. Used to be a saying about 'Lottery in June, corn be heavy soon.' First thing you know, we'd all be eating stewed chickweed and acorns. There's *always* been a lottery," he added petulantly. "Bad enough to see young Joe Summers up there joking with everybody."

"Some places have already quit lotteries," Mrs. Adams said.

"Nothing but trouble in *that*," Old Man Warner said stoutly. "Pack of young fools."

"Martin." And Bobby Martin watched his father go forward. "Overdyke .... Percy."

"I wish they'd hurry," Mrs. Dunbar said to her older son. "I wish they'd hurry."

"They're almost through," her son said.

"You get ready to run tell Dad," Mrs. Dunbar said.

Mr. Summers called his own name and then stepped forward precisely and selected a slip from the box. Then he called, "Warner."

"Seventy-seventh year I been in the lottery," Old Man Warner said as he went through the crowd. "Seventy-seventh time."

"Watson." The tall boy came awkwardly through the crowd. Someone said, "Don't be nervous, Jack," and Mr. Summers said, Take your time, son."

"Zanini."

After that, there was a long pause, a breathless pause, until Mr. Summers, holding his slip of paper in the air, said, "All right, fellows." For a minute, no one moved, and then all the slips of paper were opened. Suddenly, all women began to speak at once saying, "Who is it?," "Who's got it?," "Is it the Dunbars?," "Is it the Watsons?" Then the voices began to say, "It's Hutchinson. It's Bill." "Bill Hutchinson's got it."

"Go tell your father," Mrs. Dunbar said to her older son.

People began to look around to see the Hutchinsons. Bill Hutchinson was standing quiet, staring down at the paper in his hand. Suddenly, Tessie Hutchinson shouted to Mr. Summers "You didn't give him time enough to take any paper he wanted. I saw you. It wasn't fair!"

"Be a good sport, Tessie," Mrs. Delacroix called, and Mrs. Graves said, "All of us took the same chance."

"Shut up, Tessie," Bill Hutchinson said.

"Well, everyone," Mr. Summers said, "that was done pretty fast, and now we've got to be hurrying a little more to get done in time." He consulted his next list. "Bill," he said, "you draw for the Hutchinson family. You got any other households in the Hutchinsons?"

"There's Don and Eva," Mrs. Hutchinson yelled. "Make *them* take their chance!"

"Daughters draw with their husbands' families, Tessie," Mr. Summers said gently. "You know that as well as anyone else."

"It wasn't fair," Tessie said.

"I guess not, Joe," Bill Hutchinson said regretfully. "My daughter draws with her husband's family, that's only fair. And I've got no other family except the kids."

"Then, as far as drawing for families is concerned, it's you." Mr. Summers said in explanation, "and as far as drawing for households is concerned, that's you, too. Right?"

"Right," Bill Hutchinson said.

"How many kids, Bill?" Mr. Summers asked formally.

"Three," Bill Hutchinson said. "There's Bill, Jr., and Nancy, and little Dave. And Tessie and me."

"All right, then," Mr. Summers said. "Harry, you got their tickets back?"

Mr. Graves nodded and held up the slips of paper. "Put them in the box, then," Mr. Summers directed. "Take Bill's and put it in."

"I think we ought to start over," Mrs. Hutchinson said, as quietly as she could. "I tell you it wasn't *fair*. You didn't give him time enough to choose. Ev*ery*body saw that."

Mr. Graves had selected the five slips and put them in the box, and he dropped all the papers but those onto the ground where the breeze caught them and lifted them off.

"Listen, everybody," Mrs. Hutchinson was saying to the people around her.

"Ready, Bill?" Mr. Summers asked, and Bill Hutchinson, with one quick glance around at his wife and children, nodded.

"Remember," Mr. Summers said, "take the slips and keep them folded until each person has taken one. Harry, you help little Dave." Mr. Graves took the hand of the little boy, who came willingly with him up to the box. "Take a paper out of the box, Davy," Mr. Summers said. Davy put his hand into the box and laughed. "Take just *one* paper," Mr. Summers said. "Harry, you hold it for him." Mr. Graves took the child's hand and removed the folded paper from the tight fist and held it while little Dave stood next to him and looked up at him wonderingly.

"Nancy next," Mr. Summers said. Nancy was twelve, and her school friends breathed heavily as she went forward, switching her skirt, and took a slip daintily from the box. "Bill, Jr.," Mr. Summers said, and Billy, his face red and his feet over-large, nearly knocked the box over as he got a paper out. "Tessie," Mr. Summers said. She hesitated for a minute, looking around defiantly, and then set her lips and went up to the box. She snatched a paper out and held it behind her.

"Bill," Mr. Summers said, and Bill Hutchinson reached into the box and felt around, bringing his hand out at last with the slip of paper in it.

The crowd was quiet. A girl whispered, "I hope it's not Nancy," and the sound of the whisper reached the edges of the crowd.

"It's not the way it used to be," Old Man Warner said clearly. "People ain't the way they used to be."

"All right," Mr. Summers said. "Open the papers. Harry, you open little Dave's."

Mr. Graves opened the slip of paper and there was a general sigh through the crowd as he held it up and everyone could see that it was blank. Nancy and Bill, Jr., opened theirs at the same time, and both beamed and laughed, turning around to the crowd and holding their slips of paper above their heads.

"Tessie," Mr. Summers said. There was a pause, and then Mr. Summers looked at Bill Hutchinson, and Bill unfolded his paper and showed it. It was blank.

"It's Tessie," Mr. Summers said, and his voice was hushed. "Show us her paper, Bill."

Bill Hutchinson went over to his wife and forced the slip of paper out of her hand. It had a black spot on it, the black spot Mr. Summers had made the night before with the heavy pencil in the coal-company office. Bill Hutchinson held it up, and there was a stir in the crowd.

"All right, folks," Mr. Summers said, "let's finish quickly." Although the villagers had forgotten the ritual and lost the original black box, they still remembered to use stones. The pile of stones the boys had made earlier was ready; there were stones on the ground with the blowing scraps of paper that had come out of the box. Mrs. Delacroix selected a stone so large she had to pick it up with both hands and turned to Mrs. Dunbar. "Come on," she said. "Hurry up."

Mrs. Dunbar had small stones in both hands, and she said, gasping for breath, "I can't run at all. You'll have to go ahead and I'll catch up with you."

The children had stones already, and someone gave little Davy Hutchinson a few pebbles.

Tessie Hutchinson was in the center of a cleared space by now, and she held her hands out desperately as the villagers moved in on her. "It isn't fair," she said. A stone hit her on the side of the head.

Old Man Warner was saying, "Come on, come on, everyone." Steve Adams was in the front of the crowd of villagers, with Mrs. Graves beside him.

"It isn't fair, it isn't right," Mrs. Hutchinson screamed, and then they were upon her.

Appendix B: Glossary of Literary Terms

The terms briefly defined here are for the most part more fully defined earlier in the text. Hence many of the entries below are followed by page references to the earlier discussions.

Absurd, Theater of the plays, especially those written in the 1950s and 1960s, that call attention to the incoherence of character and of action, the inability of people to communicate, and the apparent purposelessness of existence

accent stress given to a syllable (168)

act a major division of a play

action (1) the happenings in a narrative or drama, usually physical events (*B* marries *C*, *D* kills *E*), but also mental changes (*F* moves from innocence to experience); in short, the answer to the question, "What happens?" (2) less commonly, the theme or underlying idea of a work (123)

allegory a work in which concrete elements (for instance, a pilgrim, a road, a splendid city) stand for abstractions (humanity, life, salvation), usually in an unambiguous, one-to-one relationship. The literal items (the pilgrim, and so on) thus convey a meaning, which is usually moral, religious, or political. To take a nonliterary example: The Statue of Liberty holds a torch (enlightenment, showing the rest of the world the way to freedom), and at her feet are broken chains (tyranny overcome). A caution: Not all of the details in an allegorical work are meant to be interpreted. For example, the hollowness of the Statue of Liberty does not stand for the insubstantiality or emptiness of liberty.

alliteration repetition of consonant sounds, especially at the beginnings of words (*f*ree, *f*orm, *ph*antom) (171)

allusion an indirect reference; thus when Lincoln spoke of "a nation dedicated to the proposition that all men are created equal" he was making an allusion to the Declaration of Independence.

ambiguity multiplicity of meaning, often deliberate, that leaves the reader uncertain about the intended significance

anagnorisis a recognition or discovery, especially in tragedy—for example, when the hero understands the reason for his or her fall (118)

analysis an examination that usually proceeds by separating the object of study into parts (38–44)

anapest a metrical foot consisting of two unaccented syllables followed by an accented one. Example, showing three anapests: "As I came / to the edge / of the wood" (168)

anecdote a short narrative, usually reporting an amusing event in the life of an important person

antagonist a character or force that opposes (literally, "wrestles") the main character

apostrophe address to an absent figure, or to a thing as if it were present and could listen. Example: "Oh rose, thou art sick!" (154)

approximate rhyme only the final consonant-sounds are the same, as in *crown/alone* or *pail/fall*

archetype a theme, image, motive, or pattern that occurs so often in literary works it seems to be universal. Examples: a dark forest (for mental confusion), the sun (for illumination)

assonance repetition of similar vowel sounds in stressed syllables. Example: *light/bride* (171)

atmosphere the emotional tone (for instance, joy or horror) in a work, most often established by the setting (77–78)

ballad a short narrative poem, especially one that is sung or recited, often in a stanza of four lines, with 8, 6, 8, 6 syllables, with the second and fourth lines rhyming. A **popular ballad** is a narrative song that has been transmitted orally by what used to be called "the folk"; a **literary ballad** is a conscious imitation (without music) of such a work, often with complex symbolism.

blank verse unrhymed iambic pentameter, that is, unrhymed lines of ten syllables, with every second syllable stressed (173)

cacophony an unpleasant combination of sounds

caesura a strong pause within a line of verse (169–70)

catastrophe the concluding action, especially in a tragedy

catharsis Aristotle's term for the purgation or purification of the pity and terror supposedly experienced while witnessing a tragedy

character (1) a person in a literary work (Romeo); (2) the personality of such a figure (sentimental lover, or whatever). Characters (in the first sense) are some times classified as either "flat" (one-dimensional) or "round" (fully realized, complex). (68–74)

characterization the presentation of a character, whether by describing the character directly, by showing the character in action, or by presenting several characters who help define one another (68–71)

cliché an expression that through overuse has ceased to be effective. Examples: acid test, sigh of relief, the proud possessor

climax the culmination of a conflict; a turning point, often the point of greatest tension in a plot (67–68, 124)

comedy a literary work, especially a play, characterized by humor and by a happy ending (116, 119–20)

comparison and contrast to compare is strictly to note similarities, whereas to contrast is to note differences. *Compare* is now often used for both activities. (41–44)

complication an entanglement in a narrative or dramatic work that causes a conflict

conflict a struggle between a character and some obstacle—for example, another character or fate—or between internal forces, such as divided loyalties (67–68)

connotation the associations (suggestions, overtones) of a word or expression. Thus *seventy* and *three score and ten* both mean "one more than sixty-nine," but because *three score and ten* is a biblical expression, it has an association of holiness; see *denotation*.

consonance repetition of consonant sounds, especially in stressed syllables. Also called half rhyme or slant rhyme. Example: *arouse/doze* (171)

convention a pattern (for instance, the 14-line poem, or sonnet) or motif (for instance, the bumbling police officer in detective fiction) or other device occurring so often that it is taken for granted. Thus it is a convention that actors in a performance of *Julius Caesar* are understood to be speaking Latin, though in fact they are speaking English. Similarly, the soliloquy (a character alone on the stage speaks his or her thoughts aloud) is a convention, for in real life sane people do not talk aloud to themselves.

couplet a pair of lines of verse, usually rhyming (172)

crisis a high point in the conflict, which leads to the turning point (67–68)

criticism the analysis or evaluation of a literary work

dactyl a metrical foot consisting of a stressed syllable followed by two un-stressed syllables. Example: *underwear* (169)

denotation the dictionary meaning of a word. Thus *soap opera* and *daytime serial* have the same denotation, but the connotations (associations, emotion-al overtones) of *soap opera* are less favorable.

dénouement the resolution or the outcome (literally, the "unknotting") of a plot (67–68)

deus ex machina literally, "a god out of a machine"; any unexpected and ar-tificial way of resolving the plot—for example, by introducing a rich uncle, thought to be dead, who arrives on the scene and pays the debts that other-wise would overwhelm the young hero

dialogue exchange of words between characters; speech

diction the choice of vocabulary and of sentence structure. There is a differ-ence in diction between "One never knows" and "You never can tell."

didactic pertaining to teaching; having a moral purpose

dimeter a line of poetry containing two feet (169)

discovery see *anagnorisis* (118)

drama (1) a play; (2) conflict or tension, as in "The story lacks drama"

dramatic irony see *irony*

dramatic monologue a poem spoken entirely by one character but addressed to one or more other characters whose presence is strongly felt

effaced narrator the narrator reports but does not editorialize or enter into the minds of any of the characters in the story (87)

elegy a lyric poem, usually a meditation on a death

elision omission (usually of a vowel or unstressed syllable), as in *o'er* (for "over") and in "Th' inevitable hour"

end rhyme identical sounds at the ends of lines of poetry (171)

end-stopped line a line of poetry that ends with a pause because the gram-matical structure and the sense reach (at least to some degree) completion

English (or **Shakespearean**) **sonnet** a poem of fourteen lines (three qua-trains and a couplet), rhyming *ababcdcdefefgg* (172)

enjambment a line of poetry in which the grammatical and logical sense run on without pause into the next line or lines (170)

epic a long narrative, especially in verse, which usually records heroic material in an elevated style

epigram a brief, witty poem or saying

epigraph a quotation at the beginning of the work, just after the title, often giving a clue to the theme

epiphany a "showing forth," as when an action reveals a character with particular clarity

episode an incident or scene that has unity in itself but that is also a part of a larger action

epistle a letter, in prose or verse

essay a work, usually in prose and usually fairly short, that purports to be true and that treats its subject tentatively. In most literary essays the reader's interest is as much in the speaker's personality as in any argument that is offered. (57–65)

euphony literally, "good sound," a pleasant combination of sounds

explication a line-by-line unfolding of the meaning of a text (32–38, 162–66)

exposition a setting-forth of information. In fiction and drama, introductory material introducing characters and the situation; in an essay, the presentation of information, as opposed to the telling of a story or the setting forth of an argument

eye rhyme words that look as though they rhyme but do not rhyme when pronounced. Example: *come/home* (171)

fable a short story (often involving speaking animals) with an easily grasped moral

farce comedy based not on clever language or on subtleties of characters but on broadly humorous situations (for instance, a man mistakenly enters the ladies' locker room)

feminine rhyme a rhyme of two or more syllables, with the stress falling on a syllable other than the last. Examples: *fatter/batter; tenderly/slenderly* (171)

fiction an imaginative work, usually a prose narrative (novel, short story), that reports incidents that did not in fact occur. The word may include all works that invent a world, such as a lyric poem or a play.

figurative language words intended to be understood in a way that is other than literal. Thus *lemon* used literally refers to a citrus fruit, but *lemon* used figuratively refers to a defective machine, especially a defective automobile. Other examples: "He's a beast," "She's a witch," "A sea of troubles." Literally, such expressions are nonsense, but writers use them to express meanings inexpressible in literal speech. Among the commonest kinds of figures of speech are *apostrophe, metaphor,* and *simile* (see the discussions of these words in this glossary). (149–53)

flashback an interruption in a narrative that presents an earlier episode

flat character a one-dimensional character (for instance, the figure who is only and always the jealous husband, or the flirtatious wife) as opposed to a round or many-sided character

fly-on-the-wall narrator a narrator, never editorializing and never entering a character's mind, who reports only what is said and done

foil a character who makes a contrast with another, especially a minor character who helps set off a major character

foot a metrical unit, consisting of two or three syllables, with a specified arrangement of the stressed syllable or syllables. Thus the iambic foot consists of an unstressed syllable followed by a stressed syllable. (168–69)

foreshadowing suggestions of what is to come (74–77)

free verse poetry in lines of irregular length that are usually unrhymed (173–74)

genre kind or type, roughly analogous to the biological term *species*. The four chief literary genres are nonfiction, fiction, poetry, and drama, but these can be subdivided into further genres. Thus fiction obviously can be divided into the short story and the novel, and drama obviously can be divided into tragedy and comedy. These can be divided still further—for instance, tragedy into heroic tragedy and bourgeois tragedy, comedy into romantic comedy and satirical comedy.

gesture physical movement, especially in a play (129–31)

half rhyme repetition in accented syllables of the final consonant sound but without identity in the preceding vowel sound; words of similar but not identical sound. Also called near rhyme, slant rhyme, approximate rhyme, and off-rhyme. Examples: *light/bet; affirm/perform* (171)

hamartia a flaw in the tragic hero, or an error made by the tragic hero (118)

heptameter a metrical line of seven feet (169)

hero, heroine the main character (not necessarily heroic or even admirable) in a work; cf. *protagonist*

heroic couplet an end-stopped pair of rhyming lines of iambic pentameter (172)

hexameter a metrical line of six feet (169)

hubris, hybris a Greek word, usually translated as "overweening pride," "arrogance," "excessive ambition" and often said to be characteristic of tragic figures (116)

hyperbole figurative language using overstatement, as in "He died a thousand deaths" (162)

iamb, iambic a poetic foot consisting of an unaccented syllable followed by an accented one. Example: *alone* (168)

image, imagery imagery is established by language that appeals to the senses, especially sight ("deep blue sea") but also other senses ("tinkling bells," "perfumes of Arabia") (153)

innocent eye a naive narrator in whose narration the reader sees more than the narrator sees

internal rhyme rhyme within a line (171)

interpretation the exposition of meaning, chiefly by means of analysis

irony a contrast of some sort. For instance, in **verbal irony** or **Sophoclean irony** the contrast is between what is said and what is meant ("You're a great guy" meant bitterly). In **dramatic irony** the contrast is between what is intended and what is accomplished (Macbeth usurps the throne, thinking he will then be happy, but the action leads him to misery), or between what the audience knows (a murderer waits in the bedroom) and what a character says (the victim enters the bedroom, innocently saying, "I think I'll have a long sleep") (117, 162)

Italian (or **Petrarchan**) **sonnet** a poem of fourteen lines, consisting of an octave (rhyming *abbaabba*) and a sestet (usually *cdecde* or *cdccdc*) (172)

litotes a form of understatement in which an affirmation is made by means of a negation; thus "He was not underweight," meaning "He was grossly overweight"

lyric poem a short poem, often songlike, with the emphasis not on narrative but on the speaker's emotion or reverie

masculine rhyme rhyme of one-syllable words (*lies/cries*) or, if more than one syllable, words ending with accented syllables (*behold/foretold*) (171)

melodrama a narrative, usually in dramatic form, involving threatening situations but ending happily. The characters are usually stock figures (virtuous heroine, villainous landlord).

metaphor a kind of figurative language equating one thing with another: "This novel is garbage" (a book is equated with discarded and probably inedible food), "a piercing cry" (a cry is equated with a spear or other sharp instrument) (149–50)

meter a pattern of stressed and unstressed syllables (168–70)

metonymy a kind of figurative language in which a word or phrase stands not for itself but for something closely related to it: *saber-rattling* means "militaristic talk or action"

monologue a relatively long, uninterrupted speech by a character

monometer a metrical line consisting of only one foot (169)

mood the atmosphere, usually created by descriptions of the settings and characters

motif a recurrent theme within a work, or a theme common to many works

motivation grounds for a character's action (132–34)

myth (1) a traditional story reflecting primitive beliefs, especially explaining the mysteries of the natural world (why it rains, or the origin of mountains); (2) a body of belief, not necessarily false, especially as set forth by a writer. Thus one may speak of Yeats or Hardy as myth-makers, referring to the visions of reality that they set forth in their works.

narrative, narrator a narrative is a story (an anecdote, a novel); a narrator is one who tells a story (not the author, but the invented speaker of the story). On kinds of narrators, see *point of view*. (85–89)

novel a long work of prose fiction, especially one that is relatively realistic

novella a work of prose fiction longer than a short story but shorter than a novel, say about 40 to 80 pages

objective point of view the narrator reports but does not editorialize or enter into the minds of any of the characters in the story (87).

octave, octet an eight-line stanza, or the first eight lines of a sonnet, especially of an Italian sonnet (182)

octosyllabic couplet a pair of rhyming lines, each line with four iambic feet

ode a lyric exalting someone (for instance, a hero) or something (for instance, a season)

omniscient narrator a speaker who knows the thoughts of all of the characters in the narrative (86–87)

onomatopoeia words (or the use of words) that sound like what they mean. Examples: *buzz, whirr* (171)

oxymoron a compact paradox, as in "a mute cry," "a pleasing pain," "proud humility"

parable a short narrative that is at least in part allegorical and that illustrates a moral or spiritual lesson

paradox an apparent contradiction, as in Christ's words: "Whosoever will save his life shall lose it; but whosoever will lose his life for my sake, the same shall save it" (162)

paraphrase a restatement, which sets forth an idea in diction other than that of the original (45, 148–49)

parody a humorous imitation of a literary work, especially of its style

pathos pity, sadness

pentameter a line of verse containing five feet (169)

peripeteia a reversal in the action (118)

persona literally, a mask; the "I" or speaker of a work, sometimes identified with the author but usually better regarded as the voice or mouthpiece created by the author (57–58, 142–44)

personification a kind of figurative language in which an inanimate object, animal, or other nonhuman is given human traits. Examples: "the creeping tide" (the tide is imagined as having feet), "the cruel sea" (the sea is imagined as having moral qualities) (151–52)

plot the episodes in a narrative or dramatic work—that is, what happens—or the particular arrangement (sequence) of these episodes (66–68, 124–28)

poem an imaginative work in meter or in free verse, usually employing figurative language

point of view the perspective from which a story is told—for example, by a major character or a minor character, or a fly on the wall; see also *narrative, narrator* (85–89)

prosody the principles of versification (167)

protagonist the chief actor in any literary work. The term is usually preferable to *hero* and *heroine* because it can include characters—for example, villainous or weak ones—who are not aptly called heroes or heroines.

quatrain a stanza of four lines (172)

realism presentation of plausible characters (usually middle-class) in plausible (usually everyday) circumstances, as opposed, for example, to heroic characters engaged in improbable adventures. Realism in literature seeks to give the illusion of reality.

recognition see *anagnorisis* (118)

refrain a repeated phrase, line, or group of lines in a poem, especially in a ballad

resolution the dénouement or untying of the complication of the plot (67–68)

reversal a change in fortune, often an ironic twist (118)

rhetorical question a question to which no answer is expected or to which only one answer is plausible. Example: "Do you think I am unaware of your goings-on?"

rhyme similarity or identity of accented sounds in corresponding positions, as, for example, at the ends of lines: *love/dove; tender/slender* (170–71)

rhythm in poetry, a pattern of stressed and unstressed sounds; in prose, some sort of recurrence (for example, of a motif) at approximately identical intervals (166–67, 170)

rising action in a story or play, the events that lead up to the climax (67, 124–25)

rising meter a foot (for example, iambic or anapestic) ending with a stressed syllable

romance narrative fiction, usually characterized by improbable adventures and love

round character a many-sided character, one who does not always act predictably, as opposed to a "flat" or one-dimensional, unchanging character

run-on line a line of verse whose syntax and meaning require the reader to go on, without a pause, to the next line; an enjambed line (170)

sarcasm crudely mocking or contemptuous language; heavy verbal irony

satire literature that entertainingly attacks folly or vice; amusingly abusive writing (119)

scansion description of rhythm in poetry; metrical analysis (166–70)

scene (1) a unit of a play, in which the setting is unchanged and the time continuous; (2) the setting (locale, and time of the action); (3) in fiction, a dramatic passage, as opposed to a passage of description or of summary

selective omniscience a point of view in which the author enters the mind of one character and for the most part sees the other characters only from the outside (86)

sentimentality excessive emotion, especially excessive pity, treated as appropriate rather than as disproportionate

sestet a six-line stanza, or the last six lines of an Italian sonnet (172)

sestina a poem with six stanzas of six lines each, and a concluding stanza of three lines. The last word of each line in the first stanza appears as the last word of a line in each of the next five stanzas, but in a different order. In the final (three-line) stanza, each line ends with one of these six words, and each line includes in the middle of the line one of the other three words.

setting the time and place of a story, play, or poem (for instance, a Texas town in winter, about 1900) (77–78, 103, 131–32)

short story a fictional narrative, usually in prose, rarely longer than 30 pages and often much briefer

simile a kind of figurative language explicitly making a comparison, for example by using *as, like,* or a verb such as *seems* (149)

soliloquy a speech in a play, in which a character alone on the stage speaks his or her thoughts aloud

sonnet a lyric poem of 14 lines; see *English sonnet, Italian sonnet* (172)

speaker see *persona* (57–58, 142–44)

spondee a metrical foot consisting of two stressed syllables (169)

stage direction a playwright's indication to the actors or readers—for example, offering information about how an actor is to speak a line

stanza a group of lines forming a unit that is repeated in a poem (171–73)

stereotype a simplified conception, especially an oversimplification—for example, a stock character such as the heartless landlord, the kindly old teacher, the prostitute with a heart of gold. Such a character usually has only one personality trait, and this is boldly exaggerated.

stream of consciousness the presentation of a character's unrestricted flow of thought, often with free associations, and often without punctuation

stress relative emphasis on one syllable as compared with another (168)

structure the organization of a work, the relationship between the chief parts, the large-scale pattern—for instance, a rising action or complication followed by a crisis and then a resolution

style the manner of expression, evident not only in the choice of certain words (for instance, colloquial language) but in the choice of certain kinds of sentence structure, characters, settings, and themes

subplot a sequence of events often paralleling or in some way resembling the main story

summary a synopsis or condensation (44–45, 66–67)

symbol a person, object, action, or situation that, charged with meaning, suggests another thing (for example, a dark forest may suggest confusion or perhaps evil), though usually with less specificity and more ambiguity than an allegory. A symbol usually differs from a metaphor in that a symbol is expanded or repeated and works by accumulating associations. (78–85, 103, 153–55)

synecdoche a kind of figurative language in which the whole stands for a part ("the law," for a police officer), or a part ("all hands on deck," for all persons) stands for the whole (151)

tale a short narrative, usually less realistic and more romantic than a short story; a yarn

tercet a unit of three lines of verse (172)

tetrameter a verse line of four feet (169)

theme what the work is about; an underlying idea of a work; a conception of human experience suggested by the concrete details. Thus the theme of *Macbeth* often is said to be that "Vaulting ambition o'erleaps itself." (89–101, 103–04)

thesis the point or argument that a writer announces and develops. A thesis differs from a *topic* by making an assertion. "The fall of Oedipus" is a topic, but "Oedipus falls because he is impetuous" is a thesis, as is "Oedipus is impetuous, but his impetuosity has nothing to do with his fall." (18–19, 45–46)

third-person narrator the teller of a story who does not participate in the happenings (86–87)

tone the prevailing attitude (for instance, ironic, genial, objective) as perceived by the reader. Notice that a reader may feel that the tone of the persona of the work is genial while the tone of the author of the same work is ironic. (58–59)

topic a subject, such as "Hamlet's relation to Horatio." A topic becomes a thesis when a predicate is added to this subject, thus: "Hamlet's relation to Horatio helps to define Hamlet." (45–50)

tragedy a serious play showing the protagonist moving from good fortune to bad and ending in death or a deathlike state (116–119)

tragic flaw a supposed weakness (for example, arrogance) in the tragic protagonist (118)

tragicomedy a mixture of tragedy and comedy, usually a play with serious happenings that expose the characters to the threat of death but that ends happily (120–21)

transition a connection between one passage and the next

trimeter a verse line with three feet (169)

triplet a group of three lines of verse, usually rhyming (172)

trochee a metrical foot consisting of a stressed syllable followed by an unstressed syllable. Example: *garden* (168)

understatement a figure of speech in which the speaker says less than what he or she means; an ironic minimizing, as in "You've done fairly well for yourself" said to the winner of a multimillion-dollar lottery (162)

unity harmony and coherence of parts; absence of irrelevance

verse (1) a line of poetry; (2) a stanza of a poem

vers libre free verse; unrhymed poetry (173–74)

villanelle a poem with five stanzas of three lines rhyming *aba*, and a concluding stanza of four lines rhyming *abaa*. The first and third lines of the first stanza rhyme. The entire first line is repeated as the third line of the second and fourth stanzas; the entire third line is repeated as the third line of the third and fifth stanzas. These two lines form the final two lines of the last (four-line) stanza.

voice see *persona, style,* and *tone* (58, 142–44)

Indexes

INDEX OF AUTHORS, TITLES, AND FIRST LINES OF POEMS

INDEX OF TERMS

Symbols Commonly Used in Marking Papers

All instructors have their own techniques for commenting on essays, but many make substantial use of the following symbols. When instructors use a symbol, they assume that the student will carefully read the marked passage and will see the error or will check the appropriate reference.

agr	faulty agreement between subject and verb
awk (k)	awkward
cap	use a capital letter
cf	comma fault
choppy	too many short sentences; subordinate; see pp. 210–211
diction	inappropriate word; see p. 204
emph	emphasis is obscured
frag	fragmentary sentence
id	unidiomatic expression
ital	underline to indicate italics; see p. 223
k	awkward
l	logic; this does not follow
lc	use lower case, not capitals
mm	misplaced modifier
¶	new paragraph
pass	weak use of the passive; see p. 209
ref	reference of pronoun vague or misleading
rep	awkward repetition; see pp. 207–208
sp	misspelling
sub	subordinate; see pp. 210–211